TABLE OF CONTENTS

Unless otherwise indicated, all Scripture quotations are taken from the King James Version of the Bible.

The Wisdom Commentary, Volume 2 · ISBN 1-56394-284-4/B-220

Copyright © 2003 by **MIKE MURDOCK**

All publishing rights belong exclusively to Wisdom International

Published by The Wisdom Center

4051 Denton Hwy. · Ft. Worth, TX 76117 · 1-888-WISDOM 1 (1-888-947-3661)

Website: **thewisdomcenter.tv**

Printed in the United States of America.

The Evidence
Of God's Presence
Far Outweighs
The Proof Of His Absence.

-MIKE MURDOCK

1

ANGELS

Angels Exist.

Scriptures clearly reveal their *purpose, abilities and limitations.*

The angelic creation of Heaven is divided into categories called thrones, dominions, principalities and powers. These words evidently represent different ranks or graduations of angels with their own responsibilities.

Thrones appear to be angels created to sit on thrones and to rule.

Dominions refer to those who exercise rule under God.

Principalities refer to those who govern.

Powers refer to those who exercise some particular assigned authority.

God has a system of governing the universe.

His Sovereignty rules over all things, but God as an administrator delegates authority (pages 78-79 in *Secrets of Successful Marriages* by Dr. Matthew N.O. Sadiku, Covenant Publishers).

For example, in Daniel 12:1, Michael is referred to as the angel who stands for Israel.

In Daniel 10:13, reference is made to the prince of the kingdom of Persia.

Daniel 10:20 refers to the prince of Greece.

God obviously has assigned a throne, a "Prime Minister," who exercises authority over each nation. Thus, a hierarchical, administrative authority is vested in angels.

41 Facts About Angels

1. Angels Have Personalities, Having Bodies Not Limited In Time Or Space. "Yea, whiles I was speaking in prayer, even the man Gabriel, whom I had seen in the vision at the beginning, being caused to fly swiftly, touched me about the time of the evening oblation" (Daniel 9:21).

2. Angels Voluntarily Worship God. "Praise ye Him, all His angels: praise ye Him, all His hosts" (Psalm 148:2).

3.   Angels Possess The Capacity Of Knowledge. "But of that day and hour knoweth no man, no, not the angels of heaven, but My Father only" (Matthew 24:36).

4.   Angels Were Created To Live And Exist In The Sphere Of The Heavenlies. "But of that day and that hour knoweth no man, no, not the angels which are in heaven, neither the Son, but the Father" (Mark 13:32).

5.   Angels Supervise The Life Of All Men As Ministering Spirits. "Are they not all ministering spirits, sent forth to minister for them who shall be heirs of salvation?" (Hebrews 1:14).

When man was created to live on earth, angels were to execute and administer God's will on earth.   That is why we call them ministering spirits, supervising or overseeing the lives of people.

6.   When Lucifer Rebelled Against God, He Was Successful In Leading Away From Him A Third Of The Angelic Creation. "And his tail drew the third part of the stars of heaven, and did cast them to the earth: and the dragon stood before the woman which was ready to be delivered, for to devour her child as soon as it was born" (Revelation 12:4).

Satan brought that group of fallen angels, called demons, into a kingdom like God's system. A child of God is surrounded every moment by this host of fallen angels as well as by that of ministering angels. Having once chosen to obey satan, these demons obey him perfectly and completely. They persist in executing satan's will for you. And satan's will for you is to defeat the will of God for you at every moment of your life.

7.   Both Holy And Fallen Angels Exist. *Fallen* angels are usually referred to as "demons," though the term is not in Scripture.

8.   Some Angels Carry Small Books. John, the revelator, saw this happen. "And I saw another mighty angel come down from heaven, clothed with a cloud: and a rainbow was upon his head, and his face was as it were the sun, and his feet as pillars of fire: And he had in his hand a little book open: and he set his right foot upon the sea, and his left foot on the earth," (Revelation 10:1,2).

9.   Angels Fly. "And I saw another angel fly in the midst of heaven, having the everlasting gospel to preach unto them that dwell on the earth, and to every nation, and kindred, and tongue, and people, Saying with a loud voice, Fear God, and give glory to Him; for the hour of His judgement is come: and worship Him that made heaven, and earth, and the sea, and the fountains of waters" (Revelation 14:6,7).

10. Angels Can Talk And Communicate. They are conversationalists. "And the third angel followed them, saying with a loud voice, If any man worship the beast and his image, and receive his mark in his forehead, or in his hand," (Revelation 14:9).

11. Angels Praise And Worship God Aloud. Adoration comes natural to them. "And suddenly there was with the angel a multitude of the heavenly host praising God, and saying, Glory to God in the highest, and on earth peace, good will toward men" (Luke 2:13,14).

12. Angels Refuse To Be Worshiped. They know their place. "And I John saw these things, and heard them. And when I had heard and seen, I fell down to worship before the feet of the angel which shewed me these things. Then saith he unto me, See thou do it not: for I am thy fellowservant, and of thy brethren the prophets, and of them which keep the sayings of this book: worship God" (Revelation 22:8,9).

13. Angels Urge Men To Worship God Also. Angels know the benefits and rewards of praise.

They minister to people.

They want us to succeed. It is a desire of their heart to see us become bonded with God. That is their ministry and calling and Assignment. "And I John saw these things, and heard them. And when I had heard and seen, I fell down to worship before the feet of the angel which shewed me these things. Then saith he unto me, See thou not: for I am thy fellowservant, and of thy brethren the prophets, and of them which keep the sayings of this book: worship God" (Revelation 22:8,9).

14. Angels Consider Themselves Servants, Not God. "And I John saw these things, and heard them. And when I had heard and seen, I fell down to worship before the feet of the angel which shewed me these things. Then saith he unto me, See thou not: for I am thy fellow-servant, and of thy brethren the prophets, and of them which keep the sayings of this book: worship God" (Revelation 22:8,9).

15. It Is Possible To See An Angel Face To Face. "And when Gideon perceived that he was an angel of the Lord, Gideon said, Alas, O Lord God! for because I have seen an angel of the Lord face to face" (Judges 6:22). (Also, see Exodus 33:20.)

16. Angels Are Often Used To Bring Good News. "And the angel of the Lord appeared unto the woman, and said unto her, Behold now, thou art barren, and bearest not: but thou shalt conceive, and bear a son" (Judges 13:3). (Refers to Manoah and his wife...and their son, Samson.)

17. Angels Often Give Specific Instructions. "Now therefore beware, I pray thee, and drink not wine nor strong drink, and eat not any unclean thing: For, lo, thou shalt conceive, and bear a son, and no razor shall come on his head: for the child shall be a Nazarite unto God from the womb: and he shall begin to deliver Israel out of the hand of the Philistines" (Judges 13:4-6).

18. Angels Foresee And Can Prophetically Know Ahead Of Time Things That Will Be Happening. (See Judges 13:4,5.)

19. Angels Do Not Always Give Their Name. "But I asked him not whence he was, neither told he me his name:" (Judges 13:6).

20. God Will Sometimes Send An Angel Upon The Request From A Sincere Man Of God. "Then Manoah intreated the Lord, and said, O my Lord, let the man of God which thou didst send come again unto us, and teach us what we shall do unto the child that shall be born. And God hearkened to the voice of Manoah; and the angel of God came again unto the woman as she sat in the field: but Manoah her husband was not with her" (Judges 13:8,9).

Exception... "For Manoah knew not that he was an angel of the Lord" (Judges 13:16-19). Eventually, Manoah knew... "that he was an angel of the Lord" (Judges 3:21).

21. Angels Sometimes Bring Bad News. "And there followed another angel, saying, Babylon is fallen, is fallen, that great city, because she made all nations drink of the wine of the wrath of her fornication" (Revelation 14:8).

22. Angels Warn. "And the third angel followed them, saying with a loud voice, If any man worship the beast and his image, and receive his mark in his forehead, or in his hand, The same shall drink of the wine of the wrath of God, which is poured out without mixture into the cup of his indignation; and he shall be tormented with fire and brimstone in the presence of the holy angels, and in the presence of the Lamb: And the smoke of their torment ascendeth up for ever and ever: and they have no rest day nor night, who worshiped the beast and his image, and whosoever receiveth the mark of his name" (Revelation 14:9-11).

There were three angels that came and visited with Abraham...one of them was the Lord...they warned of what they were going to do to Sodom and Gomorrah. "And the Lord appeared unto him in the plains of Mamre: and he sat in the tent door in the heat of the day; And he lift up his eyes and looked, and, lo, three men stood by him: and when he saw them, he ran to meet them from the tent door, and bowed himself toward the ground," (Genesis 18:1,2).

23. Some Angels Do Not Stay With You But Have Other Assignments. *Ministering* angels *remain* (read Hebrews 1:14). These are sometimes called "guardian" angels.

Messenger angels *depart.* "And Mary said, Behold the handmaid of the Lord; be it unto me according to thy word. And the angel departed from her" (Luke 1:38,39).

24. Angels Excel In Strength. "Bless the Lord, ye His angels, that excel in strength," (Psalm 103:20).

25. Angels Know The Future Events In Each Member Of Your Family. That is why Gabriel told Mary about her cousin's pregnancy. "And, behold, thy cousin Elizabeth, she hath also conceived a son in her old age: and this is the sixth month with her, who was called barren" (Luke 1:36).

26. Angels Know The Plans Of God Before You Do. That is why He brought the plan to Zacharias, to show him the future son he would have—John the Baptist (see Luke 1).

He showed Mary, the mother of Jesus, the plan ahead of time (see Luke 1).

27. Angels Know Where You Are At All Times. Zacharias, a certain priest, was praying in the temple. "According to the custom of the priest's office, his lot was to burn incense when he went into the temple of the Lord. And the whole multitude of the people were praying without at the time of incense. And there appeared unto him an angel of the Lord standing on the right side of the altar of incense" (Luke 1:9-11).

Gabriel knew exactly where Mary was. Later, Gabriel, that same angel went to Nazareth. "And in the sixth month the angel Gabriel was sent from God unto a city of Galilee, named Nazareth, To a virgin espoused to a man whose name was Joseph, of the house of David; and the virgin's name was Mary" (Luke 1:26,27).

28. The Presence Of Angels Sometimes Creates Instant Discomfort And Unease. It did to Zacharias. "And there appeared unto him an angel of the Lord standing on the right side of the alter of incense. And when Zacharias saw him, he was troubled, and fear fell upon him" (Luke 1:11,12).

29. Angels Know When You Do Not Believe In Them. That is why he answered Zacharias who was doubtful. "I am Gabriel, that stand in the presence of God; and am sent to speak unto thee, and to shew thee these glad tidings. And, behold, thou shalt be dumb, and not able to speak, until the day that these things shall be performed, because thou believest not my words, which shall be fulfilled in their season" (Luke 1:19,20).

30. Angels Know The Future Of Your Children. Zacharias experienced this as the angel discussed his future son, John the Baptist. "And thou shalt have joy and gladness; and many shall rejoice at his birth. For he shall be great in the sight of the Lord, and shall drink neither wine nor strong drink; and he shall be filled with the Holy Ghost, even from his mother's womb. And many of the children of Israel shall he turn to the Lord their God" (Luke 1:14-16).

Think about this...angels know the very nature, personality and the Assignment of your children...before you do.

31. Angels Can Appear To You When Others Around Never See Them Or Know About Them. It happened to Zacharias. After the angel talked with him, he came out of the temple. But, nobody knew that an angel had visited him. "And the people waited for Zacharias, and marvelled that he tarried so long in the temple. And when he came out, he could not speak unto them: and they perceived that he had seen a vision in the temple: for he beckoned unto them, and remained speechless" (Luke 1:21,22).

In the preceding verses, the angel had told him that he would be unable to speak because of his doubts.

32. Angels Know Those Who Are Highly Favored Of God. Everyone does not receive the same favor from God.

Angels know the difference. "And the angel came in unto her, [Mary] and said, Hail, thou that are highly favoured, the Lord is with thee: blessed art thou among women" (Luke 1:28).

33. Angels Know The Names Of Each Member Of Your Family. "But the angel said unto him, Fear not, Zacharias: for thy prayer is heard; and thy wife Elizabeth shall bear thee a son, and thou shalt call his name John" (Luke 1:13).

This should encourage you...you are not the *only* one interceding for your children and family!

Angels are aware of your spouse. Their troubles. Their pain. The events in their life.

34. Angels Will Discuss Their Own Assignment With You. "And the angel answering said unto him, I am Gabriel, that stand in the presence of God; and am sent to speak unto thee, and to shew thee these glad tidings" (Luke 1:19).

35. Angels Know The Happiest Events You Are About To

Experience. "But the angel said unto him, Fear not, Zacharias: for thy prayer is heard; and thy wife Elizabeth shall bear thee a son, and thou shalt call his name John. And thou shalt have joy and gladness; and many shall rejoice at his birth" (Luke 1:13,14).

36. Angels Are Often Sent To Bring Good News Of A Coming Event In Our Lives. "And the angel answering said unto him, "I am Gabriel, that stand in the presence of God; and am sent to speak unto thee" (Luke 1:19).

37. Angels Know When Our Prayers Are Answered. It happened in the life of Zacharias. "But the angel said unto him, Fear not, Zacharias: for thy prayer is heard; and thy wife Elizabeth shall bear thee a son, and thou shalt call his name John" (Luke 1:13).

38. Angels Are Sent To Talk To Us. "And the angel answering said unto him, "I am Gabriel, that stand in the presence of God; and am sent to speak unto thee" (Luke 1:19).

39. Angels Will Often Reveal Themselves And Their Names To You. It happened to Zacharias, the priest. The angel spoke to him, "And the angel answering said unto him, I am Gabriel, that stand in the presence of God; I am sent to speak unto thee, and to shew thee these glad tidings" (Luke 1:19).

40. Angels Often Give Specific Instructions. "Now therefore beware, I pray thee, and drink not wine nor strong drink, and eat not any unclean thing: For, lo, thou shalt conceive, and bear a son; and no razor shall come on his head: for the child shall be a Nazarite unto God from the womb: and he shall begin to deliver Israel out of the hand of the Philistines" (Judges 13:4,5).

41. The Angels Know How God Does His Work. "Then said Mary unto the angel, How shall this be, seeing I know not a man? And the angel answered and said unto her, The Holy Ghost shall come upon thee, and the power of the Highest shall overshadow thee: therefore also that holy thing which shall be born to thee shall be called the Son of God" (Luke 1:34,35).

RECOMMENDED BOOKS AND TAPES:
B-26 The God Book (160 pages/$10)
B-27 The Jesus Book (164 pages/$10)

Anger Can Be
The Birthplace
For Solutions.

-MIKE MURDOCK

ANGER

Anger Is Important To Understand, Harness And Master.

10 Facts You Should Know About Anger

1. Anger Is A Clue To Your Assignment. When Moses saw an Egyptian beating an Israelite, anger rose up within him. That anger was a *clue*. It was a *signal*. The situation that infuriated him was the one God had ordained him to change, correct and alter.

2. Anger Is The Birthplace Of Change. Situations only change when anger is born. You will not solve a problem, consciously or unconsciously, until you experience a holy and righteous anger rising up within you.

You will not change a situation until it becomes intolerable.

For many years in the South, African-Americans were intimidated...forced to sit in the back of the bus. They might still be doing that today had it not been for a courageous woman named Rosa Parks. This work-weary black lady took her place in a crowded bus in Montgomery, Alabama. When the bus filled, she refused to stand for a white man to have her seat. It was the catalyst for dramatic, appropriate and long-needed change in America. That kind of courage deserves honor and respect.

3. Whatever You Can Tolerate, You Cannot Change. Whatever you refuse to accept, whatever makes you mad enough to take action, is a clue to your Assignment.

MADD, Mothers Against Drunk Driving, was started by a mother who saw her child killed on the street by a drunken driver. Her anger birthed a response.

4. You Must Despise The Present Before The Future Will Listen To You. If you can adapt to your present, you will never enter your future. Only those who cannot tolerate the present are qualified to enter their future.

It has happened in my own life. When I was a teenager, I felt a great attraction to the courtroom. I wanted to be an attorney. I sat for hours in those courtrooms in my little hometown of Lake Charles,

Louisiana. I took notes by the hour on cases that came up. I still have a hatred of injustice.

I can become angry about it right now while I am writing you this chapter, just thinking about people who have not been represented properly. I read law books continually and still continually read books dealing with the legal system. Watching the process of law and observing the manipulation that occurs in the courtroom still infuriates me. I believe this *anger is a clue to the anointing on my life.*

Because so many are uninformed, something comes alive in me. A desire to teach is overwhelming. I speak at seminars throughout the world. Sometimes I almost miss my airplane schedule because I become so obsessed with teaching, that to walk out of the seminar becomes extremely difficult.

Unproductive employees are a source of great agitation to me. I believe it is a clue to a mantle on my life. It is important to me that I unlock the mystery of achievement through Wisdom Keys and the books that I write.

Listen carefully to ministers who teach about prosperity. *They hate poverty.* They despise lack. It grieves them deeply to see families wounded, destroyed and devastated because of poverty. Their messages are full of fury and sound almost angry! Why? Destroying poverty is a calling *within* them.

Have you ever listened to ministers who have an anointing for deliverance? They become angry toward demonic spirits that possess family members.

Listen to a soul-winning evangelist. Do you hear his passion? He is moved with compassion when he sees the unsaved and those who are uncommitted to Christ.

Many things are wrong in this country. But, they will never be changed until *someone is angry enough* about it to step forward and take charge.

For instance, abortion has subtly become accepted, although it is a truly devastating blight on the moral landscape of this country. It appears that no true and articulate spokesperson has yet emerged who is capable of turning the tide, although I thank God for those who are making significant efforts to do so!

5. The Persuaded Are Persuasive. Often I have asked God to give us someone with a burning desire who can *successfully* plead the case of the unborn child. I have asked God to provide a militant intellectual, passionate zealot who will link the Word of God with the gift of life in my generation—someone passionate and on fire.

That someone could be you!

I am not talking about the issue of bombing abortion clinics or murdering those who kill unborn children.

I am speaking of *an anointing,* a mantle, a calling—when someone *rises* up to complete his Assignment in this generation: to challenge, correct and conquer the Seeds of Rebellion that have grown up around us.

6. Anger Reveals An Anointing. "And it shall come to pass in that day, that his burden shall be taken away from off thy shoulder, and His yoke from off thy neck, and the yoke shall be destroyed because of the anointing" (Isaiah 10:27). The anointing is the *burden-removing, yoke-destroying power of God in your life.*

So, *pay attention to whatever angers you.* Something inside you rises up strongly against it. Why? *Your anger qualifies you to be an enemy of that problem.* God is preparing *you* to *solve* it.

7. Focused Anger Can Birth Miracles, Victories And Change. Anger merely requires proper focus. Develop it. You must see your anger as an instruction from God to stay in The Secret Place to *find the solution for the problem,* obtain the weapons to destroy the enemy and *develop a daily agenda* designed by the Holy Spirit...*to create change.*

8. Uncontrolled Anger Destroys And Ruins. Millions have died prematurely because of uncontrolled anger. Our prison system is full of good people with an unresolved weakness—the inability to control their fury.

Anger is *energy.*

Anger is *power.*

Anger *moves hell.*

Anger can *master a situation.*

Unfocused, anger destroys and ruins.

Focused properly, it creates miraculous change.

9. Angry People Can Dramatically Change Their Generation. *An Angry Man Is An Awakened Man.* An angry man changes the minds of others.

10. Focused Fury Is Often The Key To Miraculous Change.

Remember These 3 Wisdom Keys

1. You Cannot Correct What You Are Unwilling To Confront.

2. What You Permit Will Always Continue.

3. Behavior Permitted Is Behavior Perpetuated.

People See
What You Are
Before They Hear
Who You Are.

-MIKE MURDOCK

∞ 3 ∞

APPEARANCE

People See What You Are Before They Hear Who You Are.
First Impressions May Become Lasting Impressions.
Your clothing and personal appearance affect others toward you.

I learned this many years ago. Sometimes, when I would first awaken, I would not be in the "mood" to dress up nice. So, I would put on some old casual clothes laying across the chair. Throughout the day, I *would continue to feel* the identical way I had felt when I first woke up—rather sloppy. The clothes I had put on *reinforced my early morning mood and attitude.*

6 Facts You Should Remember About Your Personal Appearance

1. **Your Appearance Influences Your Own Emotions.** I have learned a lot since those early days. Sometimes, when I am really feeling in a "don't care mood," I proceed to put on a nice suit, clean shirt and an attractive tie. Within minutes, my energy and mood *adapt* to my new appearance. I begin to feel and become the way I am dressed.

2. **Your Appearance Sends A Message To Others.** The Proverbs 31 Woman dressed to communicate her dignity. "She maketh herself coverings of tapestry; her clothing is silk and purple" (Proverbs 31:22).

3. **Your Appearance Educates Others In How You Desire To Be Approached.** That is why the prostitute dressed to seduce a man. "And, behold, there met him a woman with the attire of an harlot, and subtil of heart" (Proverbs 7:10).

4. **Your Appearance Influences What Others Feel Toward You.** That is why Joseph shaved his beard and changed his raiment when he came into the court of Pharaoh. Egyptians hated beards. Joseph packaged himself for where he was going instead of where he had been.

5. **Your Appearance Can Decide Your Acceptance Or Rejection.** Some years ago, Elvis Presley did a concert in

Indianapolis, Indiana. One of my close friends, a deputy sheriff in Indianapolis, was in charge of security backstage. He noticed that a man was walking around dressed in an old windbreaker jacket. He was shuffling around as if he were some bum off the street. As my friend prepared to evict him from the building, someone stopped and said, "That man is Colonel Parker, the manager of Elvis Presley." He was shocked and stunned. He had misjudged the man because of his *appearance.* That is why Joseph *changed* his outward appearance to create a climate of acceptance (read Genesis 41:14).

6. Your Appearance Can Influence The Decisions And Plans Of Those Who See You. Naomi mentored Ruth about her dress and appearance. When she approached Boaz, she made herself *desirable* for the man she desired (read Ruth 4:1).

Dress to create the feeling you need for the job you face.

Dress The Way You Want To Feel, Instead Of How You Are Presently Feeling.

That is One of the Secrets of Career Success.

RECOMMENDED BOOKS AND TAPES:
B-44 31 Secrets For Career Success (115 pages/$10)
B-09 Four Forces That Guarantee Career Success (32 pages/$3)

4

ATMOSPHERE

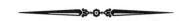

Atmosphere Matters.

Invest whatever is necessary to create the atmosphere that motivates you.

Your chosen focus requires a unique climate.

Your surroundings are so important. Your atmosphere must receive your attention. It will not happen automatically. You must control the atmosphere around your life or it will control you.

16 Keys In Creating The Environment You Need

1. Your Climate Influences The Decisions You Make. When you are in a high fashion clothing store, the music is often quiet, classical or dignified. When you go into a store where the younger generation makes purchases, the music is fast, upbeat and energizing. The merchants have created an environment that influences you to buy.

2. Your Surroundings Contain Colors That Affect You Emotionally. Many years ago, I read where a certain shade of pink was used in prisons to reduce violence and fights. Some say that body-builders can lose one third of their ability if they look at a pink wall while working out. Colors affect us. Colors affect our strength, our enthusiasm and the decisions we make.

3. Everyone Needs Something Different Around Them. You must discern what environment and atmosphere bring out the best in you.

When I need energy and must move quickly from project to project, I love to listen to praise music that is *energizing* and exciting. When I want to ponder and reflect, I love to listen to slower, more worshipful music. I know the value of *protecting the climate* around myself.

4. Nobody Else Can Create Your Atmosphere For You. You must discern it and pursue it for yourself. Others are focused on their own problems, not yours.

5. Nobody Else Really Cares About Your Specific Needs Like You Do. So, do not wait and hope someone emerges who will take an aggressive part in making it happen for you.

6. Nobody Else Is Responsible For Providing You With The Climate You Desire. It is *your* life, *your* needs and *your* decisions.

7. You Cannot Perform Your Very Best Until Everything Around You Is In Place. Yes, you may achieve and be productive to a degree. But, you can multiply the results of your life when the things *around* you strengthen and motivate you.

8. What You See Controls What You Desire. When you see a billboard advertising hamburgers, you suddenly receive a desire for hamburgers. That is why you must put around yourself *pictures* and images of the things you want.

9. What You Are Viewing Daily Affects What You Desire To Do. When children see the playground at McDonald's, they are suddenly inspired to stop everything and "go play."

10. Keep Around You Photographs Of Things You Want In Your Future. It may be a boat you want to buy, a home you want to live in or a picture of yourself 20 pounds lighter. These images are influencing *the direction* your decisions will take you.

11. Your Environment Is Worth Any Investment In Music And Equipment. Buy a stereo or whatever it takes—get the *best* possible.

Every morning, I listen to the Scriptures on cassette tape. That is the first thing I do each day. Yes, they cost. The cassette recorder costs. But, my future and my emotions are worth any investment.

I purchase candles that smell the best, strongest and last the longest. Placing them around my room helps provide the most incredible atmosphere of reflection, warmth and caring. I need that. My heart requires it. If I do not do it, it will not be done. So, because it is my life that is so vital to me, I invest *whatever is necessary*.

A few days ago, I spent over $100 on several CDs. Yet, when I purchased them, I really was not just purchasing some music on compact discs. *I was purchasing an atmosphere.*

You see, this morning, after listening to the Bible on tape, I turned the CD player on. On the six CDs were birds, a sparkling, flowing fountain and peaceful music. Within seconds, I felt like I was under the trees alone and quiet, tasting the richness of God's nature around me. Yet, I was in my *bedroom!* I did not have to spend $2,000 to take a vacation to Honolulu. I simply needed an investment in my atmosphere—the appropriate CDs.

12. Your Investment In Interior Decorating Can Increase Your Productivity Significantly. A new rug, a picture on the wall, a vase with a rose, every small thing can increase the warmth and caring of your environment.

13. The Effort And Experimentation To Discover What You Really Need Around You Is Worth Any Investment Of Your Time And Energy. That is all right, too. It is wonderful to explore variations of climates and environments. An interior decorator, the suggestions of a friend or your own personal visits to different stores can help you discover the atmosphere you prefer to work in, play around or simply relax and rest in. Each atmosphere produces a different emotion.

14. Do Not Wait On Others To Initiate Changes In Your Environment. Make any investment necessary to create the kind of environment that inspires you toward excellence and the improvement of your life.

15. Your Atmosphere Can Often Determine Your Productivity. Many businesses have discovered an increase in unity and employee morale when they played music quietly throughout their offices.

16. What You See Affects The Decisions You Are Making. It does not cost you a fortune to create a favorable atmosphere. Just think, look around and ask questions. Explore a little. Experiment.

Invest Whatever Is Necessary To Create The Atmosphere You Want To Surround You.

It is One of the Secrets of Champions.

RECOMMENDED BOOKS AND TAPES:
B-99   Secrets Of The Richest Man Who Ever Lived (180 pages/$10)
TS-25 Secrets Of The Richest Man Who Ever Lived (6 tapes/$30)

Your Attitude Determines The Season You Enter.

-MIKE MURDOCK

⇚ 5 ⇛

ATTITUDE

Your Attitude Can Determine Your Success.

Everyone discusses Attitude. You will hear a lot of statements such as, "You need to keep a good Attitude."

"You need a check-up from the neck up."

"Your Attitude will determine your altitude." These are more than just catchy phrases. They reveal an invisible awareness of the importance of your *mood birthed by your chosen focus.*

Most people with wrong Attitudes do not even realize they possess them. They use angry words, sarcasm or cynicism to create a desired response from others. They use their Attitude to *rule* and reign over those under their authority.

Children learn to use wrong Attitudes as weapons quite early in their life. Stomping their feet and screaming, a two year old can make a mother drop everything she is doing to respond and console an angry little baby boy. The game works. So, eventually in their lives, they begin to develop the opinion that their Attitude of anger can produce a desired result.

Behavior Permitted Becomes Behavior Repeated. So, each of us often develop our Attitudes from childhood, right or wrong.

50 Important Facts And Keys You Should Know About Attitude

1. Your Attitude Is The Behavior And Mood Created By Something You Have Chosen To Focus Upon. It is a viewpoint, a state of mind toward something.

2. Your Attitude Is More Powerful Than Your Gifts And Talents. You see, Attitude is the powerful force that attracts others toward you or moves them away from you. Many gifted and talented people never taste the rewards of their skills because their Attitude makes them undesirable to be near.

3. Your Attitude Is The Force That Determines Whether You Multiply Or Decrease, Grow Or Die, Attract Or Repel The Company Of Other Successful People.

4. The Scriptures Instruct You To Correct Your Own Attitude. The Apostle Paul wrote to the church at Ephesus, "Let all bitterness, and wrath, and anger, and clamour, and evil speaking, be put away from you, with all malice: And be ye kind one to another, tenderhearted, forgiving one another, even as God for Christ's sake hath forgiven you" (Ephesians 4:31,32).

5. The Scriptures Command You To Walk In Love Toward Others. "Be ye therefore followers of God, as dear children; And walk in love, as Christ also hath loved us, and hath given Himself for us an offering and a sacrifice to God for a sweetsmelling savour" (Ephesians 5:1,2).

6. The Right Attitude Is The Behavior And Conduct Produced And Desired By The Holy Spirit For You On Any Given Occasion. You see, the Apostle Paul instructs in his letter to be kind, tenderhearted and forgiving one another (see Ephesians 4:32). Why? God has forgiven us.

7. You Are Responsible For Changing Your Own Attitude. That is why the Apostle Paul instructs us, under the inspiration of the Holy Spirit, to initiate changes (see Ephesians 4:28-31).

8. Your Attitude Is The Power Tool Used By God To Reconstruct The Circumstances Around You. It minimizes the effect of negative things. It enables you to pleasure the Holy Spirit, keeping Him present to defeat your enemy.

9. Your Attitude Can Be An Effective Weapon For Victory. Regardless of what satan throws at you, an Attitude of thanksgiving and praise will attract angels and demoralize demons assigned to abort your dreams and goals.

10. When You Change Your Attitude, You Will Change The World Around You. That is why the Apostle Paul said that he had learned to be content and happy, regardless of the state or situation around him. His Attitude of *rejoicing* made the difference.

11. Any Wrong Attitude Is Often Communicated Through Your Posture, And Even By The Way You Walk. Have you ever watched people at the mall? Of course you have! You can sense instantly whether they are brisk, alive and vibrant or whether they are demoralized, discouraged and disappointed with life. Their Attitude is easily evidenced by *their body posture.* That mood was created by something they have chosen to think about, *meditate* upon and build their life around.

12. What You Magnify In Your Mind Is Controlling Your Attitude. If you meditate upon your own mistakes, you will become very discouraged and self-critical. Eventually, that turns to an abnormal criticism of others as well. When a husband focuses on the mistakes of his wife, his Attitude will become sarcastic and cynical.

13. Your Attitude Is Attracting Or Repelling The Right People Into Your Life. Ruth was a servant. Her humble Attitude got the attention of Boaz. He instructed his servants to make it easier for her life. You see, when you observe thankful and gracious people, something within you wants to be in their presence. So, your Attitude is determining what is coming *toward* you and what moves away from you.

14. Any Wrong Attitude Is A Magnet For Others Of Like Rebellion And Anger. Watch a group of young gang members swagger down the street. Each of them is angry at the same thing—authority. They are drawn to each other like moths to the light. Any wrong Attitude is a current attracting *the wrong people* in your life. This compounds the consequences of your rebellion.

15. Your Attitude Can Decide The Entrance Or Exit Of A Miracle In Your Life. One thief went to hell, hanging next to Jesus on the cross. The other went to Heaven. The difference? *Attitude.* The woman who had hemorrhaged for 12 years with an issue of blood said in her heart, "If I can touch the hem of His garment, I know I'll be made whole" (read Matthew 9:21). Her attitude of *expectancy* brought the healing river of Jesus through her body. She was healed.

16. An Attitude Of Persistence Can Reverse The Circumstances Of Your Life In A Moment. It happened to the blind man. He heard Jesus was coming. He cried out for mercy. They told him to be quiet. He refused. His incredible determination to receive what Jesus was capable of doing in his life created the miracle!

17. Your Attitude Is Affecting Every Relationship In Your Life. It determines whether good relationships grow or wither, shrivel and die like a flower in the desert heat.

18. Your Attitude Is Determining Whether Your Boss Wants To Give You A Raise Or Terminate You. You see, you are either making his goals come to pass or moving them away from him... through your Attitude.

19. Your Attitude Is Determining Whether Your Mate Is Anxious To Come Home From Work Or Work Overtime. What pictures are you planting in the mind of your mate?

20. Your Attitude Toward Your Own Life Is Deciding Your Own Success Or Failure. If you choose to focus on your weaknesses only, you will develop a negative and self-critical spirit. It will devastate your life. I have seen people with gorgeous homes become obsessed with hating their large ears or the size of their nose—and become despisers of their own life.

21. Your Cheerful Attitude Can Create A Personal

Magnetism, Causing Others To Desire To Minister To You.

22. Your Attitude Is Controlling The Flow Of Favor Toward Your Life. It is increasing it or decreasing it.

23. Your Attitude Toward God Is Determining The Experiences You Have With Him. The Apostle Paul was a happy man. Why? He constantly thanked God for every specific blessing. "I thank my God upon every remembrance of you," (Philippians 1:3).

Thankful people stay excited. Thankful people are contagious with their joy. Thankful people avoid strife.

24. Remembering The Goodness Of God Keeps Your Attitude Corrected. It did for Paul. "And be ye kind one to another, tenderhearted, forgiving one another, even as God for Christ's sake hath forgiven you" (Ephesians 4:32). When you remember how good God has been to you, it greatly influences your mood and conduct.

25. Remembering Acts Of Kindness From Others Can Enable You To Maintain A Great Attitude Of Success And Joy. Paul said, "I thank my God upon every remembrance of you," (Philippians 1:3). He was remembering good things, right things and truthful things about those who loved him. He replayed moments in his mind when they had helped him and come to his aid in times of trouble. He was thankful to God—knowing that every good thing came from God.

26. Recognizing The Source Of Everything You Have Received Will Produce Even More Blessings. "For the Lord God is a sun and shield: the Lord will give grace and glory: no good thing will He withhold from them that walk uprightly" (Psalm 84:11). Stop for just a moment. Look at what you have.

27. Correcting Your Focus Is The First Step Toward Correcting A Wrong Attitude. If you look inside you, you will become depressed. If you look around, you will become critical. If you look back, you will develop a heart of regrets. But, when you look up, you will become joyful and excited about God. You cannot really correct your Attitude until you correct your focus. You have to be looking at the right things for the right things to grow within you.

28. What You Look At The Longest Will Become The Strongest Within You. Thought and talk magnify your moods. If you look at the weaknesses of others, that will become the obsession in every conversation. If you look at the good qualities in those you love— you will become strong in your expression of love toward them.

29. Your Attitude Will Always Improve When You Invest Time In The Secret Place, The Place Of Prayer. It will birth an Attitude adjustment. The Secret Place is the incubator for change. You must pursue the presence of the One Who has given you everything you have.

30. People With Wrong Attitudes Are Using Their Memories Incorrectly. They are retrieving photographs of past failures, disappointments and heartaches. They are linking them up and creating an inner portrait on the walls of their imagination.

31. The Apostle Paul Kept A Good Attitude Because He Recognized That Any Suffering Would Produce An Invisible Reward. He knew that if he suffered for Christ, he would eventually reign with Christ. His suffering was for a purpose. "We are troubled on every side, yet not distressed; we are perplexed, but not in despair; Persecuted, but not forsaken; cast down, but not destroyed; Always bearing about in the body the dying of the Lord Jesus, that the life also of Jesus might be made manifest in our body" (2 Corinthians 4:8-10).

32. Expect Your Own Difficult Experiences To Be An Uncommon Blessing To Others. The Apostle Paul did. "But I would ye should understand, brethren, that the things which happened unto me have fallen out rather unto the furtherance of the gospel; So that my bonds in Christ are manifest in all the palace, and in all the other places; And many of the brethren in the Lord, waxing confident by my bonds, are much more bold to speak the word without fear" (Philippians 1:12-14). He kept a good Attitude because he saw the *rewards of the sacrifice* he was making. The gospel was being preached. People were being changed. He saw the benefits of his bondage.

33. You Will Never Change Your Attitude Until You See The Ultimate Reward For Changing It. This was the secret of Joseph. "And Joseph said unto them, Fear not: for am I in the place of God? But as for you, ye thought evil against me; but God meant it unto good," (Genesis 50:19,20).

34. Your Countenance Often Reveals Your Attitude To Others. Ecclesiastes 8:1 declares, "A man's wisdom maketh his face to shine, and boldness of his face shall be changed."

35. You Cannot Change Your Attitude Until You Change What You Know. That is why the Wisdom of God is so important. Study champions. Study their secrets. Absorb the Word of God until you begin saying what God is saying.

36. Your Attitude Is Your Greatest Asset Or Your Greatest Burden To Your Life Today. It is what is keeping you progressing and multiplying, or the terrible tyrant holding you back from your promotion.

37. Your Right Attitude Is Having A Spiritual Impact On Others For Good. That is why Paul wrote, "I sent him therefore the more carefully, that, when ye see him again, ye may rejoice, and that I may be the less sorrowful" (Philippians 2:28). So, you can be a carrier of the presence of the Holy Spirit. You can minister His joy to others...through your Attitude.

38. Recognize When Other People Are Depositing A Wrong Attitude Into Your Own Spirit. I noticed one day that in the presence of certain people, I instantly began to replay every bad event in my past. It took me months to catch on. Then, I noticed that their conversations always revolved around past injustices from others. As I listened to them, I shared my own past injustices. Suddenly, it was like a little conference of "Past Painful People In My Life." Their appetite and thirst for offenses was fueling that desire in me. It was my own mistake.

39. Your Children Are Often Mirrors Of Your Own Attitude. That is why the Word of God teaches fathers not to anger their children unjustly. What does that mean? My mother scolded me fiercely one day for disciplining a child a little too hard. I began to realize that I was fueling something in that child...with my own Attitude.

40. Mothers Can Correct A Wrong Attitude In A Child By Honoring, Respecting And Publicly Praising The Labors Of A Father. For example, when you discuss the good qualities of your husband to your children, their Attitude changes toward him. When you discuss his flaws, their Attitude of Respect dies.

41. When You Focus On Worthy Qualities In Others, They Will Respond By Looking For Those Qualities In You. You are often a mirror that affects how others react to you.

42. Wrong Attitudes Can Often Result In Murder. Many are in prison today because they killed someone in a moment of anger. A lifetime of incarceration because of one uncontrolled moment. Wrong focus creates wrong Attitude.

43. You Must Recognize People Near You Who Have A Wrong Focus. You must guard the words they are speaking into your life. The *words* they are speaking are creating what *you* are feeling. "Death and life are in the power of the tongue: and they that love it shall eat the fruit thereof" (Proverbs 18:21). James teaches, "If any man offend not in word, the same is a perfect man, and able also to bridle the whole body" (James 3:2).

44. Move Away From Unhappy People Who Persist In Linking Themselves To Your Life. They will set unrealistic goals and belittle any dream you are birthing. The unthankful are always the unhappy.

45. Eliminate Unrealistic Goal-Setting That Is Birthing A Bad Attitude In You. When you set wrong deadlines or unrealistic goals, you will become bitter and angry. Faultfinding comes easy. You must set goals that are closer and easier to achieve.

46. Wrong Attitudes Are Often Created By A Sense Of Unworthiness. When you feel ineffective, useless, unnecessary, or overweight, it becomes easier to poison the climate around you.

47. Wrong Focus Creates Wrong Attitudes. Acknowledge the tragic consequences of wrong focus. Ahab focused on the vineyard of Nabal and birthed the terrible cancer of jealousy. It cost him the throne.

48. Wrong Attitude Creates A Loss Of Friends, Job Opportunities And Incredible Moments Of Enthusiasm. The Scriptures instruct us about the tragic end of those who refuse to correct their Attitude. King Saul would not correct his Attitude and lost the throne to David. The envious Attitude of Ahab inspired his wife Jezebel to kill Naboth. It produced years of sorrow and heartache.

Nebuchadnezzar became lifted up in pride. God turned him into the field as a wild beast for several years because of it.

49. If You Refuse To Correct Your Attitude, God Can Use A Tragedy To Turn You Around. God has a thousand ways to correct us. Nebuchadnezzar discovered it. Haman discovered it. God can get your attention through tragedy if you refuse to be attracted to His miracles. If you ignore His words, He will command His wrath toward your life. "Behold therefore the goodness and severity of God:" (Romans 11:22).

50. Great Achievers Have Learned To Use Their Memory To Sculpture A Victorious Attitude. David knew how to use his memory wisely. When he faced Goliath, he said, "I remember killing a lion and a bear. I defeated them. So, I can defeat you also, Goliath" (see 1 Samuel 17:34-37). He simply *replayed* victories of previous battles in his mind.

4 Important Keys That Can Correct Your Wrong Attitude

1. **Meditate On The Word Of God Daily.** "Thy word have I hid in mine heart, that I might not sin against Thee" (Psalm 119:11). Jesus instructed, "These things have I spoken unto you, that My joy might remain in you, and that your joy might be full" (John 15:11).

2. **Surround Your Home And Life With Godly Music That Honors The Holy Spirit And Attracts His Presence.** You see, music will affect your focus. He instructed us to come into His presence with singing. "Enter into His gates with thanksgiving, and into His courts with praise: be thankful unto Him, and bless His name" (Psalm 100:4).

3. Pursue Only Goals And Dreams Approved By The Holy Spirit. That will make realistic schedules possible. Ecclesiastes 3:1 makes it clear, "To every thing there is a season, and a time to every purpose under the heaven:" "A wise man's heart discerneth both time and judgment. Because to every purpose there is time and judgment, therefore the misery of man is great upon him" (Ecclesiastes 8:5,6).

4. Insist On Keeping Your Daily Appointment With The Holy Spirit In The Secret Place Where You Meet With Him Daily. "He that dwelleth in the secret place of the most High shall abide under the shadow of the Almighty" (Psalm 91:1). When you stay in His presence, your thoughts will change dramatically. I believe one of the most important sayings of Scripture in the entire Bible is Philippians 4:8,9, "Finally, brethren, whatsoever things are true, whatsoever things are honest, whatsoever things are just, whatsoever things are pure, whatsoever things are lovely, whatsoever things are of good report; if there be any virtue, and if there be any praise, think on these things. Those things, which ye have both learned, and received, and heard, and seen in Me, do: and the God of peace shall be with you."

When you change your Attitude, you will change your world, your joy and even your finances!

Our Prayer Together...

"Holy Spirit, thank You today for revealing my need of You. Enable me to change my focus. Correct the course of my thoughts! I am thankful today! I am thankful for Your Word, Your miracles and the incredible friends You have put around my life. Today I walk in joy. I will only speak those things that bring others joy and victory. In Jesus' name, Amen."

RECOMMENDED BOOKS AND TAPES:
B-31 The Seeds Of Wisdom Topical Bible (367 pages/$10)

CHURCH

Thank God For The House Of God.

Spiritual mentorship is necessary for survival. The house of God is where the Seeds of righteousness are sown. The presence of God creates memories of peace, joy and strength that cannot occur anywhere else on earth. "Not forsaking the assembling of ourselves together, as the manner of some is; but exhorting one another: and so much the more, as ye see the day approaching" (Hebrews 10:25).

Church attendance is more important than anybody knows. I have a lot of people tell me, "I can serve God at home." No, you cannot. Have you got a better idea than God? "Neglect not the assembling of yourselves and more so as you see the day approaching."

Years ago, I asked H.C. Noah, "Why do you bring so many preachers through your church?"

"They are different," he said. "Our brethren keep us balanced. We have got to be in the presence of others to balance us and keep us complete."

Ezra 7:27 says, "Blessed be the Lord God of our fathers, which hath put such a thing as this in the king's heart, to beautify the house of the Lord which is in Jerusalem:" God is interested in His house, His presence, His people.

11 Facts About Church

1. The Church Needs To Be In Agreement With What You Feel Is Important. Do not go to a church you do not believe in. You will be a deadweight there. You will be dead wood there. You will be a discouragement instead of an encouragement. For instance, I left a major church in this town. A major church. I still love the pastor. He is still a friend. He is highly thought of in this city. He lived right behind me. When I went over there, I would spend hours with him.

Finally, however, I had to leave his church. I will tell you why. First, he made fun of Richard Roberts. Now, later on they became friends, had him in, because Richard draws a crowd. But he made fun of Richard Roberts. And I called him by name and I said, "That's his style. That's his style of reacting to God. That has nothing to do with doctrine or error. That is the way he responds to the impressions of God."

Then, he made fun of Bob Tilton. He called him a huckster and prosperity preacher. He said, "Well Mike, I just don't believe that it's the right reason to give to get a result. You should give out of obedience, not because of receiving something from it." So, I had a meal with him. Took him to Elijah in 1 Kings 17. I based everything on Scripture, and when you come to me, you had better know your Word...because I do. And so I said, "Now, I want you to notice that the widow did not cooperate with the prophet when he asked her for a meal. So, he painted a photograph for her supply. He said, 'The barrel of meal shall not waste, neither shall the cruse of oil fail until the day that the Lord...and then she went and did according to the saying of Elijah.' Because he painted a portrait of result, Harvest, supply.

Proverbs 3 says, 'Honour the Lord with thy substance.' Why? 'That your barns be filled with plenty.' 'Open the windows of heaven and pour you out a blessing you don't have room enough to receive' (read Malachi 3). That was the purpose of sowing...to get a Harvest." He said, "I never saw that before." But, that is why I had to leave that church, because I could not sit there and be proud of what I believed, and what they believed. Find a church that believes in what you believe. Personality may be a little different, but they need to believe what you believe...it is vital and important.

2. The Church That You Attend Should Believe In Missions. The greatest commandment of all as far as evangelism, "Go ye into all the world, and preach the gospel" (Mark 16:15).

3. Jesus Habitually Entered The Synagogue On The Sabbath Day. "And He came to Nazareth, where He had been brought up: and, as His custom was, he went into the synagogue on the sabbath day, and stood up for to read" (Luke 4:16).

4. Champions Of Old Have Loved The House Of God. "For a day in Thy courts is better than a thousand. I had rather be a doorkeeper in the house of my God, than to dwell in the tents of wickedness" (Psalm 84:10).

5. My Love For The House Of God Brings The Blessing Of God Upon My Life. "Blessed are they that dwell in Thy house: they will be still praising Thee" (Psalm 84:4).

6. The Church Is Where You Will Find The Mercy Of God. *David knew this.* "But as for me, I will come into Thy house in the multitude of Thy mercy: and in Thy fear will I worship toward Thy holy temple" (Psalm 5:7).

7. When You Go To Church, You Obey His Commandment To Come Into His Presence. "Give unto the Lord, O ye kindreds of the people, give unto the Lord glory and strength. Give unto the Lord the glory due unto His name: bring an offering, and come into His courts" (Psalm 96:7,8).

8. It Is Where You Learn The Difference Between Those Things Which Are Holy And Those Things Which Are Unholy. "And they shall teach My people the difference between the holy and the profane, and cause them to discern between the unclean and the clean" (Ezekiel 44:23; also see Malachi 2:7).

Holiness must be *taught*.

It is not always instinctive and immediate. It is a *process* in knowledge.

9. You Need To Know What God Is Speaking To His People. The psalmist said, "I will hear what God the Lord will speak: for He will speak peace unto His people, and to His saints...." (Psalm 85:8).

10. The Presence Of God Will Increase The Years Of Your Fruitfulness In Giving To Others. "Those that be planted in the house of the Lord shall flourish in the courts of our God. They shall still bring forth fruit in old age; they shall be fat and flourishing; To shew that the Lord is upright: He is my rock, and there is no unrighteousness in Him" (Psalm 92:13-15).

11. Attending Church Will Protect You From Spiritual Isolation. It is vital that you be under the covering of a man of God in your community. Submission to an effective and knowledgeable pastor and a thriving church home is a protection against this deadly weapon. "Not forsaking the assembling of ourselves together...but exhorting one another:" (Hebrews 10:25).

It is a dangerous day in your life when the house of God ceases to be important to you.

Those Who Unlock
Your Compassion
Are Those To Whom
You Have Been Assigned.

-MIKE MURDOCK

≈ 7 ≈

COMPASSION

Compassion Has Kept The World A Livable Place.

17 Facts About Compassion

1. Everyone Is Hurting Somewhere. They may not always show it and it is not always because of deception. Neither are they trying to cover up something private. Our wounds are simply private.

The things that make us cry often embarrass us. When a wife has received a harsh look from her husband, the pain goes too deep to discuss. When the husband hears the acid words from the love of his life, he comes apart *inside*. Yet, he cannot afford to show it. Neither can she. Nobody wants to appear weak. So, every effort is made to shield ourselves, protect ourselves from the prying and often critical opinions of others.

2. Nobody Really Senses How Much You Hurt. I remind myself of this continuously. Sometimes, if someone seems a little arrogant and aggressive, I will tend to confront them on that turf. I do not mind confrontation, since I think I am right most of the time! But, they are thinking *they* are right also!

Here is the problem.

You do not *really* know what is going on in another person's mind, therefore, it is important to continuously remind yourself that *others hurt, too.*

3. Those Around You Have Painful Experiences That They Are Not Discussing With You Or Anyone Else. *Their decisions* about everything are being made to *avoid the continuance* of that pain, thus repeating their failures. So, they will not make decisions totally based on what you are saying, your conversations. They are making decisions to move away from pain.

4. Every Decision You Make Is To Move Away From Anticipated Pain. Every decision is presumed to be an escape to pleasure, away from pain.

When I remind myself of this, I am more gentle with people. More understanding. This unlocks my compassion and I become less critical and harsh. Far more patient than I would normally be. You see, I want people to be patient with me too.

Continuously remind yourself that others are going *through trials you cannot see.*

They are crying tears of pain you have never felt.

They are feeling isolated and rejected in ways you cannot imagine.

Do not become *another* burden to them.

5. Focus On Becoming A Burden Bearer. When you telephone someone, ask yourself, "Am I calling to *add* to their burden *or to remove it?*"

Maturity is the ability and willingness to bear the burdens of others.

Many years ago, I was in Fullerton, California. The church was full of people. But, the service seemed very uptight and tense. Something was wrong. I almost became belligerent and told the people something every young evangelist normally tells the people.

"If you don't like what I'm preaching, stay home. The door swings both ways. I don't have to be here myself. I can leave town if I want to. I'm going to preach this gospel...no matter what you say. I'd rather preach under a tree by myself, than compromise this gospel." (Blah. Blah. Blah.)

But, Someone restrained me. (The Holy Spirit!)

After church, I discovered the reason for the terrible deathly atmosphere of the service. One of the main board members of the church had suddenly dropped dead that afternoon. Yet, his entire family had chosen to come sit in the service that night rather than go to the funeral home. They were so desperate for God to speak a word of comfort and strength to them, they came to the crusade.

Had I said what I felt—I would have doubled their pain and heartache.

6. Someone Close To You Is Always Going Through Something You Have Not Discerned. Listen to the Holy Spirit. Become intuitive. *Nothing Is Ever As It First Appears.*

Why did I remain composed and focused during the service, even though the church atmosphere was like death? I remembered *reading* a statement by a great preacher. He said every young preacher *"should always remember that on every pew sits at least one broken heart. Heal it."*

You will meet many people today. Many need kind words desperately. Many need compassion poured out upon them today.

Everyone hurts somewhere inside.

So, wrap your words with healing oil. You are their healer, sent by God.

7. You May Be The Only Compassionate Healer That Ever Crosses Someone's Path During Their Lifetime. When you concentrate on the needs of others, God will focus on *your* needs. "Knowing that whatsoever good thing any man doeth, the same shall he receive of the Lord, whether he be bond or free" (Ephesians 6:8).

8. Uncommon Compassion Must Come From The Holy Spirit. *Ask the Holy Spirit for special compassion for those to whom you are assigned.* Sometimes it is lost during the struggle. He will restore it to you. "Brethren, if a man be overtaken in a fault, ye which are spiritual, restore such an one in the spirit of meekness; considering thyself, lest thou also be tempted. Bear ye one another's burdens, and so fulfil the law of Christ" (Galatians 6:1,2).

9. Your Compassion Affects The Destiny Of Thousands. "Keep yourselves in the love of God, looking for the mercy of our Lord Jesus Christ unto eternal life. And of some have compassion, making a difference: And others save with fear, pulling them out of the fire;" (Jude 1:21-23).

10. Compassion Is The Intense Desire To Heal The Hurting. Someone has said, "Compassion is the irresistible urge to rid a problem for someone."

11. Jesus Had Compassion Toward Those Who Were Spiritually Confused, Wasted And Bewildered. "And Jesus, when He came out, saw much people, and was moved with compassion toward them, because they were as sheep not having a shepherd: and He began to teach them many things" (Mark 6:34).

"And when the Pharisees saw it, they said unto His disciples, Why eateth your Master with publicans and sinners? But when Jesus heard that, He said unto them, They that be whole need not a physician, but they that are sick. But go ye and learn what that meaneth, I will have mercy, and not sacrifice: for I am not come to call the righteous, but sinners to repentance" (Matthew 9:11-13).

12. Jesus Had Great Compassion Toward The Sick. "And Jesus, moved with compassion, put forth His hand, and touched him, and saith unto him, I will; be thou clean. And as soon as He had spoken, immediately the leprosy departed from him, and he was cleansed" (Mark 1:41,42).

"And Jesus stood still, and called them, and said, What will ye that I shall do unto you? They say unto Him, Lord, that our eyes may be opened. So Jesus had compassion on them, and touched their eyes: and immediately their eyes received sight, and they followed Him" (Matthew 20:32-34).

13. Compassion Can Preserve Lives. It did for Moses when he was just a baby. "And the daughter of Pharaoh came down to wash herself at the river; and her maidens walked along by the river's side; and when she saw the ark among the flags, she sent her maid to fetch it. And when she had opened it, she saw the child: and, behold, the babe wept. And she had compassion on him, and said, This is one of the Hebrew's children" (Exodus 2:5,6).

14. Compassion Always Moves You Toward Someone Hurting. "But I say unto you, That in this place is one greater than the temple. But if ye had known what this meaneth, I will have mercy, and not sacrifice, ye would not have condemned the guiltless. For the Son of man is Lord even of the sabbath day. And when he was departed thence, he went into their synagogue: " (Matthew 12:6-9).

15. Those Who Unlock Your Compassion Are Those To Whom You Have Been Assigned. Whose pain matters to you? Whose pain do you feel? Whose tears affect you? Whose sorrows keep you awake at night? This kind of compassion restores. It repairs. It revitalizes the life of those nearest you.

You are the golden answer to their dilemma.

16. Caring Qualifies You As An Instrument Of Healing. What makes you cry is a clue to a problem God has anointed you to change, conquer and heal. Look at Nehemiah. His heart was broken about the walls of Jerusalem being broken down. He could not sleep at night. He could not rest. He wept long hours.

He was stirred with everything within him to write letters, connect with officials and even change his personal life to rebuild the walls.

Examine Ezra. His heart was broken over the temple in the city of Jerusalem. He could not rest. He wept and sobbed. He read Scriptures to the people. He knew that *the presence of God was the only remedy for wounded people.* He recognized that places mattered and that God would honor and reward those who sanctified a worship center in the city. *Those feelings* were signposts to his Assignment.

17. Where You Hurt The Most Is A Clue To What You May Heal The Best. "But by the grace of God I am what I am: and His grace which was bestowed upon me was not in vain; but I laboured more abundantly than they all: yet not I, but the grace of God which was with me" (1 Corinthians 15:10).

"For out of much affliction and anguish of heart I wrote unto you with many tears; not that ye should be grieved, but that ye might know the love which I have more abundantly unto you" (2 Corinthians 2:4).

Remind Yourself Continuously That Others Near You Are Hurting Inside.

≈ 8 ≈

CONVERSATION

Make Your Words Count.
Use every conversation as a practice moment for improving your speech.

8 Facts You Should Remember In Every Conversation

1.   Avoid Trivializing Conversation. Pronounce your words clearly. Enunciate every single phrase to the best of your ability. Each conversation you enter is a practice session for excellence. It is too late to walk on excellence when you walk onto a public platform. "For by thy words thou shalt be justified, and by thy words thou shalt be condemned" (Matthew 12:37).

2.   Never Speak When Another Person Is Talking. It takes away from the value of your own words. If someone interrupts you while you are speaking, do not insist on being heard. Rather, say nothing. Permit them to speak. Then, dominate your turf.

3.   Qualify Others Before Speaking The Secrets Of Your Heart. Withhold your opinion until someone who values it shows up. "A word fitly spoken is like apples of gold in pictures of silver" (Proverbs 25:11).

4.   Speak Loud Enough For Others To Hear Clearly What You Are Saying. Do not mumble.

5.   Never Assume Others Have Understood What You Have Said. Sometimes, people are thinking about many other things while you are talking. Their mind is *not* on your words. They can be nodding in total agreement with your words, while their thoughts are a thousand miles away.

6.   Encourage Others To Speak Clearly. When others mutter or mumble, speak aloud, and say, "I did not understand. Please repeat your words."

7.   Always Be Where You Are. Many years ago, I was helped by the marvelous insight of a close friend. She was a famous celebrity on the West Coast. Millions knew her. Her scrapbooks were thick and piled high regarding her fame. Hundreds of photographers had photographed her. I noticed that when people talked to her, she looked straight into their eyes. She gave full attention. Her schedule could be full, but she always *abandoned herself to the moment* when conversing with others.

She explained it simply. "Mike, I am always wherever I am." She refused to let her mind be in a different place than her body.

Here is how it helped her:

When she conversed with someone, she gave total focus on every word they spoke. Consequently, her *reactions* were accurate for that moment. Her perception was pure. Her instincts were *incredible.* Her audience always received *the best* of what she possessed in that moment. Afterwards, it was unnecessary for her to replay the conversation to see if she had forgotten to *say* the right things, *remember* the right information or have *any* regrets. They had received the best that she had. The moment ended. It was over. *Now, her future could receive her undivided attention.* She was always where she was.

8. **Always Invest The Necessary Time In Searching For The Right Word, Even In The Midst Of A Conversation.** *Right* words are worth the time involved in finding them. *Wrong* words are devastating enough to avoid.

9 Facts About Words You Should Remember

1. **Good Men Study Their Words Before They Speak Them.** "The heart of the righteous studieth to answer:" (Proverbs 15:28).

2. **The Purpose Of Words Is To Educate, Enthuse And Enlarge Those Around You.** "The lips of the wise disperse knowledge:" (Proverbs 15:7).

3. **Words Influence And Affect The Accumulation Of Your Wealth.** "A man's belly shall be satisfied with the fruit of his mouth; and with the increase of his lips shall he be filled" (Proverbs 18:20). This is almost never mentioned in prosperity teaching today. Yet using the wrong words can get you fired or prevent you from getting promoted.

I remember a time once when I was going to give someone a raise. But, then I brought them in and heard the words they were speaking. Complaining, blaming...faultfinding words can stop a boss from promoting you.

4. **Right Words Feed And Sustain Those Around You.** "The

lips of the righteous feed many: but fools die for want of wisdom" (Proverbs 10:21).

5. The Wise Avoid "Self-Praise." "Let another man praise thee, and not thine own mouth; a stranger, and not thine own lips" (Proverbs 27:2).

6. Lying Words Can Poison The Attitude Of A Boss Toward An Employee. "If a ruler hearken to lies, all his servants are wicked" (Proverbs 29:12).

Use every conversation as a practice moment.

7. Right Words Bring Health And Healing. "The tongue of the wise is health" (Proverbs 12:18).

Making your words count in every conversation will increase your communication skills dramatically.

8. The Words You Allow Others To Speak Into You Are Deciding The Wisdom You Contain. "Hear counsel, and receive instruction, that thou mayest be wise in thy latter end" (Proverbs 19:20). Solomon knew that words were the difference between his present season and his future season.

9. Right Words Can Get You Out Of Any Difficulty And Trouble. "The mouth of the upright shall deliver them" (Proverbs 12:6).

RECOMMENDED BOOKS AND TAPES:
B-55 Twenty Keys To A Happier Marriage (32 pages/$5)
B-99 Secrets Of The Richest Man Who Ever Lived (180 pages/$10)
TS-25 Secrets Of The Richest Man Who Ever Lived (6 tapes/$30)

Crisis Always Occurs
At
The Curve Of Change.

-MIKE MURDOCK

CRISIS

Crisis Never Surprises God.

Actually if anybody is ever really doing anything in the kingdom of God, crises are to be expected occasionally.

Peter believed this: "Beloved, think it not strange concerning the fiery trial which is to try you, as though some strange thing happened unto you: But rejoice, inasmuch as ye are partakers of Christ's sufferings; that, when His glory shall be revealed, ye may be glad also with exceeding joy" (1 Peter 4:12,13).

20 Important Facts To Remember During Crisis

1. Every Champion In Scripture Seemed To Move Continuously From One Crisis To Another. "But in all things approving ourselves as the ministers of God, in much patience, in afflictions, in necessities, in distresses, In stripes, in imprisonment, in tumults, in labours, in watchings, in fastings;" (2 Corinthians 6:4,5).

2. Paul Experienced Highs And Lows In Favor And Disfavor. "By honour and dishonour, by evil report and good report: as deceivers, and yet true; As unknown, and yet well known; as dying, and, behold, we live; as chastened, and not killed; As sorrowful, yet always rejoicing; as poor, yet making many rich; as having nothing, and yet possessing all things" (2 Corinthians 6:8-10).

3. Jesus Experienced Numerous Crises. It finally seemed to end at the crucifixion. Yet, even at His crucifixion, He was jeered and taunted by His enemies. Even His resurrection has been doubted by thousands (see Matthew 27:40-43).

4. Crisis Is Always The Hinge On The Door Of Promotion. Every champion has had difficult circumstances to overcome.

► Daniel was thrown into the lions' den.
► Daniel's three friends, Shadrach, Meshach and Abednego, were thrown into the fiery furnace.
► Job lost his children, possessions and good health.
► Elijah's brook dried up.
► The widow of Zarephath came to her last meal during the

famine and almost starved.

▶ Joseph experienced hatred by his brothers, false accusation against his character, then was forgotten in prison for two years after he interpreted the dream of the butler.

▶ Isaac had one foolish son, Esau, and a deceptive, manipulative son name Jacob.

A visit to a teaching workshop would benefit us. Picture this scenario. Pause for a moment and revisit the workshop where a world-renowned missionary evangelist is speaking. The place is crammed with young preachers who are excited about the revelation imparted through this man. When you walk through the door, you are looking for a tall, good-looking and powerfully built man with exquisite stature and dynamic magnetism. You ask for him, but they point to a squinty-eyed, short, bowlegged man speaking from the platform. The man is Paul.

Listen to him:

"Are they ministers of Christ? (I speak as a fool) I am more; in labours more abundant, in stripes above measure, in prisons more frequent, in deaths oft. Of the Jews five times received I forty stripes save one. Thrice was I beaten with rods, once was I stoned, thrice I suffered shipwreck, a night and a day I have been in the deep; In journeyings often, in perils of waters, in perils of robbers, in perils by mine own countrymen, in perils by the heathen, in perils in the city, in perils in the wilderness, in perils in the sea, in perils among false brethren; In weariness and painfulness, in watchings often, in hunger and thirst, in fastings often, in cold and nakedness. Beside those things that are without, that which cometh upon me daily, the care of all the churches. Who is weak, and I am not weak? who is offended, and I burn not?" (2 Corinthians 11:23-29).

Paul is not complaining in this passage. He is exultant!

"If I must needs glory, I will glory of the things which concern mine infirmities" (2 Corinthians 11:30).

5. Paul Knew That A Crisis Attracted The Power And Strength Of God. He continues: "And He said unto me, My grace is sufficient for thee: for My strength is made perfect in weakness. Most gladly therefore will I rather glory in my infirmities, that the power of Christ may rest upon me. Therefore I take pleasure in infirmities, in reproaches, in necessities, in persecutions, in distresses for Christ's sake: for when I am weak, then am I strong" (2 Corinthians 12:9,10).

6. Paul Embraced His Seasons Of Crises. "If we suffer, we shall also reign with Him" (2 Timothy 2:12).

"...if so be that we suffer with Him, that we may be also glorified together. For I reckon that the sufferings of this present time are not worthy to be compared with the glory which shall be revealed in us" (Romans 8:17,18).

7. Paul Anticipated Recognition And Reward For Surviving In His Crises. His voice was filled with energy, excitement and joy:

"I have fought a good fight, I have finished my course, I have kept the faith: Henceforth there is laid up for me a crown of righteousness, which the Lord, the righteous judge, shall give me at that day: and not to me only, but unto all them also that love His appearing" (2 Timothy 4:7,8).

8. Paul Remembered When His Difficult Days Were Caused By Ignorance Instead Of Working With God To Birth His Promotion. "For we ourselves also were sometimes foolish, disobedient, deceived, serving divers lusts and pleasures, living in malice and envy, hateful, and hating one another. But after that the kindness and love of God our Saviour toward man appeared, Not by works of righteousness which we have done, but according to His mercy He saved us, by the washing of regeneration, and renewing of the Holy Ghost; Which He shed on us abundantly through Jesus Christ our Saviour; That being justified by His grace, we should be made heirs according to the hope of eternal life" (Titus 3:3-7).

9. Paul Encouraged Us To Look Beyond The Present Crisis. "Looking for that blessed hope, and the glorious appearing of the great God and our Saviour Jesus Christ" (Titus 2:13).

10. The Apostle Peter Also Understood What Was On The Other Side Of Suffering And Crisis. "But rejoice, inasmuch as ye are partakers of Christ's sufferings; that, when His glory shall be revealed, ye may be glad also with exceeding joy. If ye be reproached for the name of Christ, happy are ye; for the spirit of glory and of God resteth upon you: on their part He is evil spoken of, but on your part He is glorified" (1 Peter 4:13,14).

11. James Saw The Crown Of Life That Lay Beyond Crisis. "Blessed is the man that endureth temptation: for when he is tried, he shall receive the crown of life, which the Lord hath promised to them that love Him" (James 1:12).

12. James Understood That Crisis Produces Patience. "Knowing this, that the trying of your faith worketh patience" (James 1:3).

13. James Knew That Patience Could Produce Every Miracle And Desired Provision You Could Ever Want. "But let patience have her perfect work, that ye may be perfect and entire, wanting nothing" (James 1:4).

14. Be Encouraged In Knowing That You Will Have A

Divine Companion Through Every Crisis. "...Fear not: for I have redeemed thee, I have called thee by thy name; thou art Mine. When thou passest through the waters, I will be with thee; and through the rivers, they shall not overflow thee: when thou walkest through the fire, thou shalt not be burned; neither shall the flame kindle upon thee" (Isaiah 43:1,2).

15. Your Crisis Will Pass. "For His anger endureth but a moment; in His favour is life: weeping may endure for a night, but joy cometh in the morning" (Psalm 30:5).

16. Learn To Picture The Rewards Beyond Crisis. "Now no chastening for the present seemeth to be joyous, but grievous: nevertheless afterward it yieldeth the peaceable fruit of righteousness unto them which are exercised thereby. Wherefore lift up the hands which hang down, and the feeble knees; And make straight paths for your feet, lest that which is lame be turned out of the way; but let it rather be healed" (Hebrews 12:11-13).

17. Never Discuss The Problems Of Your Crisis With Someone Incapable Of Solving Them. "A fool uttereth all his mind: but a wise man keepeth it in till afterwards" (Proverbs 29:11).

18. You Will Learn More In Crisis Than You Will Ever Learn In Any Victory. "Though He were a Son, yet learned He obedience by the things which He suffered;" (Hebrews 5:8).

19. Crisis Is The Season In Which God Has An Opportunity To Reveal His Love And Supernatural Power In Your Life. "And He said unto me, My grace is sufficient for thee: for My strength is made perfect in weakness. Most gladly therefore will I rather glory in my infirmities, that the power of Christ may rest upon me. Therefore I take pleasure in infirmities, in reproaches, in necessities, in persecutions, in distresses for Christ's sake: for when I am weak, then am I strong" (2 Corinthians 12:9,10).

20. In Every Crisis, Increasing Your Time Spent In The Secret Place, Your Prayer Closet, Will Bring Protection. "For in the time of trouble He shall hide me in His pavilion: in the secret of His tabernacle shall He hide me; He shall set me up upon a rock. And now shall mine head be lifted up above mine enemies round about me: therefore will I offer in His tabernacle sacrifices of joy; I will sing, yea, I will sing praises unto the Lord" (Psalm 27:5,6).

Crisis is always an exit from your present...it is your passage to promotion.

❧ 10 ❧

DELEGATION

Know Your Limitations.

It is more productive to set ten men to work rather than for you to do the work of ten men. *Delegation is simply giving others necessary instructions and motivation to complete a particular task.* This takes time and patience, but it is a long-term benefit.

Jesus commanded the multitudes. He instructed His disciples to have the people sit down. He distributed the loaves and fishes to His disciples for distribution (see Matthew 14:19).

Jesus sent His disciples to get a donkey (see Matthew 21:2).

Jesus gave instructions to a blind man to complete his healing (see John 9:6,7).

Jesus sent His disciples into cities to prepare for special meals (see Mark 14:12-15).

The early church leaders understood the importance of delegating.

"And in those days, when the number of the disciples was multiplied, there arose a murmuring of the Grecians against the Hebrews, because their widows were neglected in the daily ministration. Then the twelve called the multitude of the disciples unto them, and said, It is not reason that we should leave the word of God, and serve tables. Wherefore, brethren, look ye out among you seven men of honest report, full of the Holy Ghost and wisdom, whom we may appoint over this business. But we will give ourselves continually to prayer, and to the ministry of the word" (Acts 6:1-4).

9 Important Facts About Networking With Others

1. **Make A Checklist Of Their Specific Responsibilities.**
2. **Carefully Instruct Concerning Expectations Of Them.**
3. **Always Provide The Information And Authority Necessary For Others To Complete Those Tasks.**
4. **Set A Specific Deadline To Finish The Task.**
5. **Clearly Show Others How They Will Be Rewarded For Their Effort.** Take time to motivate and educate those you work with

so they know exactly what you expect. Take the time to delegate.

6. Do Not Delegate A Task Impossible To Do. You would not give your four year-old child car keys and tell him to take the car in for an oil change...it is impossible.

It would be impossible because of...

The IQ you are dealing with.

The level of desire and passion lacking in another.

Time constraints.

Knowledge and know how are uncommon skills and gifts.

7. Verify Any Delegation You Do. Dictate it and make copies of what you said. Verbal does not count at all.

Why? See 36 Keys out of the School of Ministry booklet.

8. Confirm That The Delegation Has Been Understood And Interpreted Accurately. Have them repeat it back to you.

When you send notes and memorandums...review them line by line.

9. Recognize That Delegation Is The Master Key To Uncommon Achievements. Uncommon Achievers have learned to delegate effectively.

Delegate Anything Another Can Do.

This is One of the Secrets of Champions.

RECOMMENDED BOOKS AND TAPES:

B-91   The Leadership Secrets Of Jesus (197 pages/$10)

B-99   Secrets Of The Richest Man Who Ever Lived (180 pages/$10)

TS-25   Secrets Of The Richest Man Who Ever Lived (6 tapes/$30)

B-137   Seeds Of Wisdom On Productivity (32 pages/$5)

~ 11 ~
DESIRE

Desire Is The Dominant Seed For Change.

You see, men rarely reach for what they need; but they will *always* reach for what they really *want.*

If you truly desire miracles and blessings in your life, you must be willing to reach for them. I have always said, "The grapes of blessing are never placed within your mouth; they are simply placed within your reach."

God *respects* a reacher.

God *rewards* a reacher.

I do not quite agree with the time worn adage, "Necessity is the mother of invention." Rather, I believe that *desire* is what gives *birth* to *miracles.*

6 Facts About Desire

1. Your Desires Are Always More Motivating Than Your Needs. It was *desire* that inspired the Wright brothers to fly. It was *desire* that motivated Thomas Edison to persist through 10,000 experiments that failed before perfecting the incandescent light bulb.

The persistence of Henry Ford is legendary. A popular story tells of his desire to create an engine with all eight cylinders cast in one block.

Every engineer who worked for him insisted it was impossible. However, Ford instructed them to pursue his project anyway and remain on the job until they succeeded.

Six months later, nothing had changed. One year later, those same engineers shook their heads dejectedly.

"It's just impossible, Mr. Ford," they said.

But Henry Ford possessed the *determination* and *desire* to succeed. He pressed them to continue. And suddenly it happened. The secret was discovered. The famous V-8 engine became a reality. Ford's unwavering *desire* revolutionized the automobile industry.

How intense is your craving for your *dreams* to happen?

Do you hate being poor? You must despise where you are before you will ever be where you want to be.

2. The Proof Of Desire Is Pursuit. I have always enjoyed listening to saxophone music. For many years I told my friends, "Oh, I would love to play the saxophone. I would give anything to learn how to play."

After talking this way for some years, one day something inside me seemed to say, "Why don't you take lessons?"

"I don't want to take lessons," I argued.

"Then shut up and stop telling everyone you want to play the saxophone," was the inner response.

What you are willing to invest your time and money toward reveals what you really want.

The *real proof* of your desire is what you are willing to *pursue.*

What do you love *talking* about? What *books* excite you? What receives your *time* and *attention?* What *dominates* your thoughts?

What you think about the most is what you have chosen to master you. Your joy, children or mate—or yes, your *Dream-Seed.*

3. The Scriptures Help Us To Understand The Power Of Desire. "Delight thyself also in the Lord; and He shall give thee the desires of thine heart" (Psalm 37:4).

"What things soever ye desire, when ye pray, believe that ye receive them, and ye shall have them" (Mark 11:24).

4. The Proof Of Passion Is The Willingness To Reach. You must possess more than a need for your miracle. You must possess true *desire;* desire enough to *reach.*

A funny thing happened several years ago with a friend of mine. As we walked down the street together, he was expressing his annoyance at preachers who were "always talking about money."

"But money is important," I reasoned with him. "Don't you think about money?"

"I never think about money!" he retorted.

I smiled and thought to myself, *he's either a fool or a liar!*

As we approached a curb, my friend suddenly spied a penny lying on the pavement. Like a deep sea diver, he dove for the coin.

I nearly burst out laughing. I was glad it was not a quarter. I might have lost him into the pavement.

5. You Will Always Reach For What You Really Desire. Whether you admit it or not. Unfortunately, many of us are like my friend. *We often dive for the pennies of life instead of reaching for the* *high quality principles that God has intended for us to live by.*

"Let the Lord be magnified, which hath pleasure in the prosperity of His servant" (Psalm 35:27).

Your desire will always make you go the *extra* mile, *push* a little harder, *reach* a little higher.

Look at the fascinating picture in Mark 5.

A certain woman had been afflicted with an issue of blood for 12 years. She had spent all her money on physicians, and her condition had merely gotten worse.

But she carried a Seed of desire within her. She wanted to be healed. She believed that if she could touch the garment of Jesus, she would be made whole.

The woman probably was in great pain.

Undoubtedly, the thronging crowd made it nearly impossible for her to reach Jesus. But she made it. She touched Him! *(When you want something badly enough, you will somehow find a way to get it.)*

"And straightway the fountain of her blood was dried up; and she felt in her body that she was healed of that plague" (Mark 5:29).

Her *need* (or sickness) had to bow to her *desire* (the miracle of her healing). Her desire became the *master* of her *need*. She forced need to whimper at the feet of desire. Desire won, and healing came.

Friend, please believe me today.

You *can* defeat sickness. You *can* conquer poverty. And it all begins with that intense burning *desire* within you.

6. You Must Learn How To Fuel The Fire Of Your Desire. God has planted within you the desire for good things.

God planted the desire for a son deep within Abraham, but Abraham had to use his faith to make it happen. Desires are like people. They are born, they grow and they can die.

3 Major Ways You Can Feed The Desire For Your Dreams

1. Visualization—Sustaining The Mental Photograph Of What You Want To Receive From God. In Mark 5, the woman carried a dream in her heart and mind of her healing. "If I may touch but His clothes," she said, "I shall be made whole." *She ignored the distraction of the crowd and reached for the dream within her—and received her miracle.*

You will never accomplish a great dream without a burning desire for it. You must *feed* that desire *daily.* You do this by continually visualizing the *rewards* and *pleasures* of its attainment.

Yes, visualization will fuel the fires of your desire for your dream.

2. Associations—Wholesome Relationships That Create A Momentum Toward Your Dream. It is exceedingly important to have the right kind of friends. Many people have lost motivation for the *dream* because they associated with faithless and foolish people.

"He that walketh with wise men shall be wise: but a companion of fools shall be destroyed" (Proverbs 13:20).

Do not expose your 16x20 Dream-Seed to 5x7 mentalities around you. Disregard unkind words of critics. Do not dignify their slander by repeating it. Criticism is usually the death gargle of a nonachiever anyway.

Dare to reach for the companionship of great thinkers. *Invest* in their books. *Listen* to their teaching cassettes. *Absorb* their spirit and victorious attitudes that have driven them to great achievement.

3. Concentration—Focus On The Completion Of One Worthwhile Goal At A Time. One of the most important things I have ever learned is *to give total attention to one thing at a time.* Many people allow their creativity to scatter their attention. Their abilities become lost through misfocus.

Your creativity is a gift. Do not let it become your enemy. Harness it. It is better to *complete* one worthwhile goal than to begin ten others.

Everyone will clamor for your attention.

And, as harsh as it may seem, you must learn to dismiss from your presence those people who distract you from a God-inspired goal. Remember, your *dream* deserves your *undivided* attention.

RECOMMENDED BOOKS AND TAPES:
B-136PB   The Wisdom Commentary, Vol. 1 (256 pages/$20)
B-114   The Law Of Recognition (248 pages/$10)

⊱ **12** ⊰

DISLOYALTY

Disloyalty Is Cancerous And Deadly.

10 Facts You Should Remember About Disloyalty

1. Disloyalty Is A Decision Made To Cause The Failure Of Another. Disloyalty is an invisible, silent and often unnoticed decision by someone close to you to destroy your dream and participate in your downfall. This individual is the worst kind of enemy you will ever have in your life.

Counterspies almost always receive life sentences. Why? Because courts do not deal lightly with someone who is a silent, invisible destroyer of the nation in which they live. A spy from another country will get off with a lighter sentence than a citizen whose disloyalty has caused the death of many.

Treason is not merely a character *flaw*. It is the *absence* of character—a purposeful decision to use the information someone has to destroy his own nation.

2. The Scriptures Reveal The Eventual Judgment On Those Who Are Disloyal. Solomon had watched his father, King David, make the mistake of his lifetime—*the tolerance of disloyalty*. I would encourage you to read this unforgettable story from 1 Kings 2. Solomon watched the tragedy unfold before his eyes on a daily basis.

3. Disloyalty Ignores The Greatness In Another. Absalom was the handsome son of David. He envied the splendor, popularity and prosperity of his father. So, he would stand and personally greet the people outside the palace each day. Like tiny *drops of poison,* his words fell into the ears of the citizens of Israel. He sowed uncertainty, doubt and discord by insinuating that David was too busy to really listen to their concerns or care about their difficulties and tears. He made himself available to them and literally stole the hearts of the people David had led for so many years. One of the most vile acts became his habit—he slept with his fathers' concubines.

Absalom did not have a character *flaw*.

Absalom had no character.

He flaunted his sin. He sneered at the greatness of his father.

4. Unconfronted Disloyalty Will Destroy You. David did not confront the disloyalty of Absalom. As David permitted him to continue to live and exist, Solomon watched this charade parade before him. He saw the kingdom come apart because of David's tolerance of wrong people close to him. When General Joab defied David's instructions by killing Absalom, disrespect for David was obvious.

5. The Greater Your Wisdom, The Quicker You Discern Disloyalty. In some ways, Solomon was wiser than his father, David. He reigned in peace for many years, primarily because he dealt swiftly and decisively with disloyalty. David permitted disloyalty to linger and his entire reign was one of warfare.

The story recorded in 1 Kings 2 is quite detailed. Solomon's brother Adonijah desired the throne, but after one special act of mercy and grace, Solomon saw the slimy hand of envy and jealously attempt to choke and destroy the kingdom. When Adonijah expressed his desire to Bathsheba, Solomon's mother, to take the concubine of David for himself, it was too much. Solomon saw the truth about his own brother. Solomon confronted the problem decisively. He killed Adonijah, and his peaceful reign continued.

Successful people are envied. They are also hated. Does that surprise you? These uncommon achievers are often despised by those who want to "climb the ladder to the top."

6. Every Uncommon Achiever Experiences Disheartening Disloyalty. Donald Trump says, "One of the problems when you become successful is that jealously and envy inevitably follow. There are people—I call them life's losers who get their sense of accomplishment and achievement from trying to stop others."

7. You Will Always Have Flawed People In Your Life. Every person has some degree of damage, personal pain and incompetence. Those who work around you may make some mistakes in decision-making and judgment. These mistakes are often the result of misinterpretation of data or trusting the wrong people. So, you will have a multitude of *opportunities* to show mercy and graciousness. Kindness is always a good Seed, when it is planted in the *proper* soil.

8. Uncommon People Recognize The Devastating Results Of Tolerating Disloyalty Close To Them. You see, when you tolerate untruthful, critical and cunning betrayers, *it endangers the progress of the truthful, the caring and the faithful around you.*

9. Disloyalty Confronted Purges Your Environment.
Several years ago, I made a decision. I travel a great deal and depend on certain supervisors to solve any problems that arise in the office. Though I was rarely around, I kept hearing reports of disloyalty, disunity and unhappiness. I could not understand it. Though I spent little time at the office, those I worked with on a daily basis seemed quite happy toward me. There was no ill will at all. Yet, the reports persisted. Then I began to hear that some of my most loyal and faithful associates were considering working in other places. This stunned me. Their dissatisfaction had never been discussed with me personally.

So, I began to analyze and interview each person. I discovered six people who were continuously poisoning the others toward me. I was shocked. You see, these six people were the ones to whom I had given the largest bonuses and the best gifts. They were the ones I tried the most to please. Yet they envied the wonderful things that happened to me. They were jealous, envious and competitive. They sowed their critical spirit into precious and wonderful people who were never around me. The Seeds began to grow.

I terminated all six in one afternoon.

I wondered what would happen. I knew the workload would increase for the others, and I had no idea who I would hire to replace them. I only understood one thing—*strife cannot be tolerated.* Ever.

It destroys too many good people.

What happened was remarkable. I walked into my office the next day and it felt like Heaven on earth. Those whose countenances had been clouded with uncertainty and fear were happy and joyous. The cloud had lifted. The rainbow had come. Disloyal people are wrong people.

10. When Wrong People Leave Your Life, Wrong Things Stop Happening. One of the biggest mistakes of my entire life has been to tolerate wrong people too long. Disloyalty is not like a common cold. You cannot take two aspirins and go to bed. Disloyalty is more like a cancer racing throughout your body.

3 Characteristics Of Disloyal People

▶ Disloyal people do not want you changed. They want you *removed.*

▶ Disloyal people do not believe they are wrong. They believe *you* are wrong.

▶ Disloyal people do not pursue a *solution* to the problem.

They believe *you* are their problem.

No amount of money can turn a disloyal employee into a loyal one. It is not a money issue. It is a *character* issue.

6 Keys In Dealing With Disloyalty

1. **Never Lie To Yourself About A Disloyal Person.** Be honest and face it with your heart.

2. **Make Certain That Every Alleged Fact Can Be Proven Beyond A Shadow Of A Doubt.** Gossip is not fact. There are good people whose names have been stained because someone pointed a finger at them. Do not receive every report as truth.

3. **Give The Accused A Forum To Be Heard.** Bring in everyone involved. Recently, one of my staff members made a statement to another staff member. I immediately called every person involved into my office. It is usually unwise to listen to an accusation against someone not present. Be sure to have the accused in your presence when the accusation is made.

4. **Ask Sincere And Appropriate Questions Of Those You Feel Might Be Disloyal.** Compare their answers with their actions. *Stop reading lips and start reading footprints.*

5. **Discuss With The Person The Reasons Why He Or She Is Being Fired.** Be honest and open, and make it as fair and equitable as possible.

6. **Make Certain The Terminated Person's Departure Is Conducted With Gentleness, Dignity And Legal Protocol.** You can be sued easily if you fail to handle a termination properly. Always consult with your lawyer. Make certain that every penny you owe that person is paid in full. If severance pay is appropriate, it is better to make the sacrifice now than end up with years of ill will sown in your direction.

Solomon refused to tolerate disloyalty in any way. This is one of the Golden Secrets that helped him become *The Richest Man Who Ever Lived.*

✑ **13** ✑

DISTRACTIONS

The Only Reason Men Fail Is Broken Focus.
Focus is anything that consumes your time, energy, finances and attention.

While traveling around the world for more than thirty years and speaking more than 12,000 times, I have listened to the details of personal battles and conflicts of many hurting people. Satan's main goal is to simply distract your focus off your Assignment. When he does this, he has mastered you. When he breaks your focus off your Assignment, he has brought pain to the heart of God, Who is his only true enemy.

Jesus encouraged His disciples to keep their focus on the kingdom of God. He assured them that their financial provisions and everything they needed would be produced through absolute *focus upon Him.* "But seek ye first the kingdom of God, and His righteousness; and all these things shall be added unto you" (Matthew 6:33).

14 Wisdom Keys To Avoid Distractions And Protect Your Focus

1. **Focus Determines Mastery.** *Anything that has the ability to keep your attention has mastered you.* Any significant progress toward the completion of your Assignment will require your every thought, your every cent, every hour of your life.

2. **Your Focus Determines Your Energy.** Think for a moment. Let us say you are sleepy, laid back on your pillows. The television is on. Suddenly, the telephone rings. Someone in your family has just had a crisis. They are being rushed to the hospital. Do you go back to sleep easily? Of course not. Your focus has changed. Suddenly, you have leaped to your feet. You put on your clothes, jump in your car, and head to the hospital. *Focus* determines your *energy.*

3. **What You Look At The Longest Becomes The Strongest In Your Life.** The Apostle Paul focused on his future. "Brethren, I count not myself to have apprehended: but this one thing I do,

forgetting those things which are behind, and reaching forth unto those things which are before, I press toward the mark for the prize of the high calling of God in Christ Jesus" (Philippians 3:13,14).

4. Broken Focus Creates Insecurity And Instability In Everything Around You. "A double minded man is unstable in all his ways" (James 1:8).

5. Only Focused Faith Can Produce Miracles From The Hand Of God. "But let him ask in faith, nothing wavering. For he that wavereth is like a wave of the sea driven with the wind and tossed. For let not that man think that he shall receive anything of the Lord" (James 1:6,7).

6. Sight Affects Desire. What you keep looking upon, you eventually pursue. "Mine eye affecteth mine heart" (Lamentations 3:51). Joshua, the remarkable leader of the Israelites, wrote this instruction from God. "Only be thou strong and very courageous, that thou mayest observe to do according to all the law, which Moses My servant commanded thee: turn not from it to the right hand or to the left, that thou mayest prosper whithersoever thou goest. This book of the law shall not depart out of thy mouth; but thou shalt meditate therein day and night, that thou mayest observe to do according to all that is written therein: for then thou shalt make thy way prosperous, and then thou shalt have good success" (Joshua 1:7,8).

7. Focusing On The Word Of God Daily Is Necessary To Complete Your Assignment Properly. God instructed the people of Israel to teach, train and mentor their children on His words. Listen to this incredible instruction: "Therefore shall ye lay up these My words in your heart and in your soul, and bind them for a sign upon your hand, that they may be as frontlets between your eyes. And ye shall teach them your children, speaking of them when thou sittest in thine house, and when thou walkest by the way, when thou liest down, and when thou risest up. And thou shalt write them upon the door posts of thine house, and upon thy gates:" (Deuteronomy 11:18-20).

8. Focusing, Hearing And Speaking The Word Of God Continually Makes You Invincible. "There shall no man be able to stand before you: for the Lord your God shall lay the fear of you and the dread of you upon all the land that ye shall tread upon, as He hath said unto you" (Deuteronomy 11:25). This is one of the reasons I keep cassettes of the Word of God in every room of my home. The first thing I do daily is turn on my tape player and listen to Scriptures being read. It washes my mind, purges my heart and harnesses my focus.

9. Focus Has Reward. "That your days may be multiplied, and the days of your children, in the land which the Lord sware unto your fathers to give them, as the days of heaven upon the earth. For if ye shall diligently keep all these commandments which I command you, to do them, to love the Lord your God, to walk in all His ways, and to cleave unto Him; Then will the Lord drive out all these nations from before you, and ye shall possess greater nations and mightier than yourselves. Every place whereon the soles of your feet shall tread shall be yours" (Deuteronomy 11:21-24).

10. What You Keep Seeing Determines Your Focus. "I will set no wicked thing before mine eyes: I hate the work of them that turn aside; it shall not cleave to me" (Psalm 101:3).

11. Your Enemy Is Anyone Who Breaks Your Focus From A God-Given Assignment. "Do thy diligence to come shortly unto me: For Demas hath forsaken me, having loved this present world, and is departed unto Thessalonica; Crescens to Galatia, Titus unto Dalmatia" (2 Timothy 4:9,10).

12. Your Friend Is Anyone Who Helps Keep You Focused On The Instructions Of God For Your Life. "For to me to live is Christ, and to die is gain" (Philemon 1:21).

13. Guard Your Personal Schedule. *Your daily agenda is your life.* You cannot save time. You cannot collect it. You cannot place it in a special bank vault. You are only permitted to spend it...wisely or foolishly. *You must do something with time.* You will invest it or you will waste it. Everyone has a hidden agenda. Those around you will be reaching to pull you "off course." You must be careful to *protect your list of priorities.*

Jesus did. There is a fascinating story in the Bible about it.

Lazarus, a close friend of Jesus, became sick. Mary and Martha, his two sisters, sent word to Jesus to come. However, "When He had heard therefore he was sick, He abode two days still in the same place where He was." Mary was upset, "Lord, if Thou hast been here, my brother had not died" (see John 11:11-44).

But Jesus had deliberately delayed His coming. He kept His own schedule. He protected His agenda. He did not allow the emergencies of others to get Him off track. *He guarded His list of priorities.*

14. Avoid Unnecessary Confrontations. It is exhausting. It is unproductive. Quarreling and arguing are a waste of time. Millions of dollars have been lost in negotiations because of an argumentative spirit. Warfare is costly, and nobody really wins.

Jesus knew the emptiness of anger. "And all they in the synagogue, when they heard these things, were filled with wrath, And rose up, and thrust Him out of the city, and led Him unto the brow of the hill whereon their city was built, that they might cast Him down headlong. But He, passing through the midst of them went His way," (Luke 4:28-30).

Jesus went His way. He did not oppose them. He did not fight them. *He had other plans.* He was about His Father's business. He focused on His own goals. "And came down to Capernaum, a city of Galilee, and taught them on the sabbath days" (Luke 4:31).

He did not withdraw into depression. He did not enter into an unnecessary dialogue with them. He did not cower in a corner of His parent's home. *He proceeded toward His mission and purpose.*

Champions fight to protect their focus.

❧ 14 ❧

EXPECTATION

You Can Only Do What You Know.

Thousands have been taught that it is wrong to expect something in return when you give something to God. They feel that this is proof of greed.

"When I give to God, I expect nothing in return" is the prideful claim of many who have been taught this terrible error.

Do you expect a salary from your boss at the end of a work week? Of course, you do. Is this greed? Hardly.

Did you expect forgiveness when you confessed your sins to Christ? Of course, you did. Is this greed? Hardly.

Stripping expectation from your Seed is theft of the *only pleasure God knows.*

24 Facts About The Law Of Expectation

1. **God's Greatest Need Is To Be Believed.** His Greatest Pain Is To Be Doubted. "But without faith it is impossible to please Him: for he that cometh to God must believe that He is, and that He is a rewarder of them that diligently seek Him" (Hebrews 11:6). Motive means *reason for doing something.* When someone on trial is accused of a murder, they try to find the motive or reason why a person would do such a horrible thing.

2. **God Expected You To Be Motivated By Supply, The Promise Of Provision.** "Give and it shall be given unto you, good measure, pressed down and shaken together, and running over, shall men give into your bosom" (Luke 6:38). (This is much more than a principle of mercy and forgiveness. This is a Principle of Supply.)

3. **God Offers Overflow As A Reason You Should Sow Seed.** Seeds of forgiveness or whatever you need. "Honour the Lord with thy substance, and with the firstfruits of all thine increase: So shall thy barns be filled with plenty, and thy presses shall burst out with new wine" (Proverbs 3:9,10). Notice that He paints the picture of *overflowing barns* to motivate us (give us a reason) for honouring Him.

4. **God Promised Benefits To Those Who Might Be Fearful**

About Tithing To Ignite Our Expectation. "Bring ye all the tithes into the storehouse, that there may be meat in Mine house, and prove Me now herewith, saith the Lord of hosts, if I will not open you the windows of heaven, and pour you out a blessing, that there shall not be room enough to receive it" (Malachi 3:10).

Read Deuteronomy 28:1-14. Here in Scripture God creates a list of the specific blessings that will occur *if you obey Him.* Why does He give you these portraits of prosperity? *To inspire you and give you a reason for obedience.*

Peter needed this kind of encouragement just like you and I do today. He felt such emptiness as he related to Christ that he and the others had "given up everything."

5. Jesus Promised A One Hundredfold Return On Our Seed-Sowing. "Then Peter began to say unto Him, Lo, we have left all, and have followed Thee. And Jesus answered and said, Verily I say unto you, There is no man that hath left house, or brethren, or sisters, or father, or mother, or wife, or children, or lands, for My sake, and the gospel's, But he shall receive an hundredfold now in this time, houses, and brethren, and sisters, and mother, and children, and lands, with persecutions; and in the world to come eternal life" (Mark 10:28-30).

Many people think it is evil to sow for a Harvest. *That is the reason to sow.*

Giving is the cure for greed, not hoarding.

When you sow to get a Harvest, you have just mastered greed.

Greed *hoards.*

Man *withholds.*

Satan *steals.*

6. The Nature Of God Alone Is The Giving Nature. When you give you have just revealed the nature of God inside you.

The only pleasure God receives is through *acts of faith.* His only need is to be believed. His greatest need is to be believed. "God is not a man, that He should lie;" (Numbers 23:19).

If an unbeliever runs to a pastor after church and says, "I want to give my heart to Christ, pastor." The pastor prays. Suppose the unbeliever then says, "Will you pray that God will give me peace and forgiveness for my confession?"

Imagine a pastor who would reply with indignation—"Of course not! That's greedy. You want something back for giving your heart to Christ?" You would be shocked if your pastor said this.

Your Father offers supply for Seed; forgiveness for confession; order for chaos.

When Jesus talked to the woman at the well of Samaria, He promised her water that she would never thirst again. Was that *wrong* to offer her something if she pursued Him? Of course not. That was the purpose of the portrait of water—to motivate her and give her a reason for *obeying Him.*

One day, my dear friend Dwight Thompson, the powerful evangelist, told me a story about the papaya. Somebody counted 470 papaya seeds in a single papaya. Also, I've been told that one papaya seed would produce a plant containing ten papayas. Now, if each of the ten contained 470 seeds, there would be 4,700 papaya seeds in one plant.

Now, just suppose you replant those 4,700 seeds to create 4,700 more plants. Do you know how much 5,000 plants containing 5,000 seeds would be? *Twenty five million seeds...on the second planting alone.*

And we are having trouble really believing in the hundredfold return. Why?

7. You Must Unlearn And Overcome The Poisonous And Traitorous Teaching That It Is Wrong To Expect Anything In Return.

8. Expectation Is The Powerful Current That Makes The Seed Work For You. "But without faith it is impossible to please Him: for he that cometh to God must believe that He is, and that He is a rewarder of them that diligently seek Him" (Hebrews 11:6).

9. Expect Protection As He Promised. "And I will rebuke the devourer for your sakes, and he shall not destroy the fruits of your ground; neither shall your vine cast her fruit before the time in the field, saith the Lord of hosts" (Malachi 3:11).

10. Expect Favor From A Boaz Close To You. "Give, and it shall be given unto you; good measure, pressed down, and shaken together, and running over, shall men give into your bosom. For with the same measure that ye mete withal it shall be measured to you again" (Luke 6:38).

11. Expect Financial Ideas And Wisdom From God As A Harvest. "But thou shalt remember the Lord thy God: for it is He that giveth thee power to get wealth," (Deuteronomy 8:18).

12. Expect Your Enemies To Fragment And Be Confused And Flee Before You. "The Lord shall cause thine enemies that rise up against thee to be smitten before thy face: they shall come out against thee one way, and flee before thee seven ways" (Deuteronomy 28:7).

13. Expect God To Bless You For Every Act Of Obedience. "And it shall come to pass, if thou shalt hearken diligently unto the voice of the Lord thy God, to observe and to do all His commandments which I command thee this day, that the Lord thy God will set thee on high above all nations of the earth: And all these blessings shall come on thee, and overtake thee, if thou shalt hearken unto the voice of the Lord thy God" (Deuteronomy 28:1,2).

A businessman approached me. "I don't really believe Jesus meant what He said about the hundredfold. We've misunderstood that."

"So, you intend to teach Jesus how to talk when you get to Heaven?" I laughed.

If He will do it for a papaya...He will do it for you and me. We are His children, not merely fruit on a tree!

I believe one of the major reasons people do not experience a supernatural abundant Harvest in finances is because they really do not expect Jesus to do what He said He would do.

14. Low Expectations Affect God. When you sow with *Expectation,* your Seed will stand before God as a testimony of your faith and confidence.

▶ Sow *expecting* God to respond favorably to every act of confidence in Him.

▶ Sow from *every* paycheck.

▶ Sow *expectantly, generously and faithfully.*

When you start looking and expecting God to fulfill His promise, the Harvest you have needed so long will come more quickly and bountifully than you have ever dreamed.

Millions are not experiencing increase because nobody has yet told them about the Principle of Seed-Faith and to expect a Harvest.

15. The Unlearned Are Simply The Untaught. Teachers are necessary. You would not have the ability to even read this book, but a teacher entered your life. You sat at their feet. You learned the alphabet. Hour after hour you sat through boring, agitating and often frustrating moments. But, it opened the Golden Door To Life.

16. You Can Only Know Something You Have Been Taught. That is why God calls mentors, ministers of the gospel and parents to impart knowledge. "And He gave some, apostles; and some, prophets; and some, evangelists; and some, pastors and teachers; For the perfecting of the saints, for the work of the ministry, for the edifying of the body of Christ: That we henceforth be no more children, tossed to and fro, and carried about with every wind of doctrine" (Ephesians 4:11,12,14).

Everyone understands sowing. Sowing is planting a Seed in soil for a desired Harvest and return.

17. Seed-Faith Is Sowing A Specific Seed In Faith That It Will Grow A Harvest Throughout Your Life. It is deciding what kind of Harvest you want to grow and sowing a Seed to make it happen.

18. Seed-Faith Is Letting Go Of Something You Have Been Given To Create Something Else You Have Been Promised.

19. Seed-Faith Is Using Something You Have To Create Something Else You Want. *Those who become infuriated over sowing toward prosperity are angry that a minister promised a hundredfold return from God for their Seed.* They hate the teaching that you can "give something you have and get something back in return from God."

20. Your Greatest Battle Is Expectation Over Your Harvest. Let's analyze this. Are they angry because they believe God *cannot* give a Harvest? Most people believe God can do anything.

Do these individuals believe that God *should not* produce a Harvest from our Seed? I don't think so. Every television reporter searches for impoverished ghetto areas to stir up the consciousness of America toward the poor. Thousands even get angry at God for not doing something for them. Most every human believes God should prosper him.

Do they believe that God *will not* really prosper people who sow into His work?

There is a lot of controversy over this.

Here is one of the greatest discoveries of my life. The anger people experience over sowing Seed into the work of God to get a Harvest is because they believe it is wrong to expect something back from God.

The hated word is *expectation.*

"When I give to God, I expect nothing in return!" droned one religious leader recently. "I give because I love Him. I give because of obedience. It is greedy to expect something in return." Yet, this same religious leader expects a paycheck every single week of his life—in return for his spiritual leadership.

It is only expecting *money* back from God that produces the point of contention.

Is it wrong to give your heart to God and expect forgiveness, mercy and a home in Heaven. Oh no! That's all right to expect an eternal home in return. Is it wrong to bring your sick body to God and expect Divine healing in return? Few disagree with that.

It is only money that bothers them. Money given to God and His work.

Why is it wrong to expect God to give a hundredfold return? This is not even logical. Think of the hundreds of doctrines taught in Scriptures. The doctrine of the blood, the Holy Spirit, angels and demons. Think of the horrifying consequences of sin, rebellion and witchcraft. If there should be rebellion in something taught in Scripture, why have we chosen to hate the Principle of Prosperity? It is against every part of our logic to hate something that brings blessing, provision and the ability to bless others.

This is a satanic thing. Oh, my friend, if you could see satan for who he really is, you would despise him with every ounce of your being. He is slimy, slick and deceptive. He truly is a serpent.

Why isn't there great anger and hatred over the preaching on hell? If I were going to refuse truth, it would be the belief in a hell. You see, it is not even natural to be anti-money.

Suppose you and I were shopping. As we walked through the mall, I saw a man huddled in the corner.

"Oh, there's a man who needs help. He looks hungry. His clothes look tattered. Let's do something good for him." You and I walk over to him.

"Sir, are you all right?"

"No," he mutters. "I have not eaten in four days. I am unemployed. I am homeless. Can you help me in any way?"

You and I rejoice. Here is our chance to bless this man. "Here, sir. Here is $20. Please buy yourself a good meal at the cafeteria."

Now suppose this happened. He takes the $20 bill. He tears it in pieces. He looks up at us angrily, "Why are you trying to give me a $20 bill?"

You would call this insanity. I would agree. I would say, "Here's a very sick man. He threw away something that could change his pain into pleasure. I handed him an answer, a solution, some money. He acts like it is a trap, a trick, poison."

Yet, the Great Provider of this universe hands us the Principle of Prosperity that will rewrite our financial future, and we erupt with anger at the thought that we could sow a Seed and reap a Harvest!

This is insanity! It is not insanity of the mind, it is insanity of the will, the *chosen* path of rebellion.

Are we against money? Of course not. When we find a quarter on the pavement, we tell every friend on the telephone that day. When we discover a $20 bill forgotten in the pocket of our old clothes in the corner of our closet, we shout! It brings fresh motivation into us. Maybe it doesn't take a lot to excite us these days—just the unexpected.

The entire warfare over the Seed-Faith message and the principles of prosperity is over this—*expectation of a financial Harvest from God.*

Now, here is the most incredible truth:

21. Expectation Is The Only Pleasure Man Can Generate In The Heart Of God. You see, faith is confidence in God. Expectation is the evidence of your faith. God said that it is impossible to pleasure Him *unless you expect something from Him.* "But without faith it is impossible to please Him: for he that cometh to God must believe that He is, and that He is a rewarder of them that diligently seek Him" (Hebrews 11:6).

You cannot even be saved unless you *expect Him* to receive you.

You cannot be healed unless you *expect Him* to heal you.

You cannot be changed unless you *expect Him* to change you.

His only pleasure is to be believed.

His only *pain* is to be *doubted*.

I'll say it again, the essence of the entire Bible is Numbers 23:19: "God is not a man, that He should lie; neither the son of man, that He should repent: hath He said, and shall He not do it? or hath He spoken, and shall He not make it good?"

God is not a man.

Man lies. *God does not.*

Think about this! God is not pleasured by streets of gold or clouds of angels. He is only happy when somebody is expecting Him to do what He said. What is *believing? Expecting God to do something He said.*

This huge controversy is not even about you or your home. Your poverty is not the goal of satan. You are not the real enemy to him.

God is the real enemy of satan.

Satan knows what pleasures God—for a human to trust Him, believe Him, depend on Him. Satan remembers the presence of God. He is a former employee.

He is an angel who refused to believe God and is tasting the eternal consequences.

The goal of satan is to rob God of every moment of pleasure received from humans.

How can he rob God? *When he stops your expectation of a miracle, he has paralyzed and stopped the only pleasure God experiences.* Every time you expect a miracle, you create a river of pleasure through the heart of God. Every time you doubt, you create waves of pain. God has feelings, too.

That is what is behind the *anti-prosperity cult* on earth.

They are not anti-money.

They are not against you having money.

They are against you expecting any money from God.

Oh, my precious friend, listen to my heart today. Why would men waste time, precious expensive television time, smearing, sneering and destroying other men of God who are praying for people to get out of poverty? This world is impoverished. Somebody said that forty percent of bankruptcies involve born-again Christians. This world is experiencing the financial crush every day. You would think that everyone would praise, advise and encourage any man of God who wanted to see you blessed, pay your bills and send your children through college. Why are we not thanking God aloud and often for the wonderful teaching that our Jehovah is a miracle God of provision?

It is not the teaching that you can have money that is bothering them.

It is the teaching that *God will supply you a Harvest when you release your Seed to Him.*

When you involve "the expectation of a return" with an offering, you arouse every devil in hell who despises their former boss, Who is pleasured by your expectation.

They hate the God you love.

They are obsessed with *depriving Him of every possible moment of pleasure* you are creating in the heart of God.

Your Father simply wants to *be believed.* That is all. He just wants to be believed. In fact, He promised that if you would just put Him above everything else in your life, He would keep providing anything you needed *for the rest of your life* (see Matthew 6:33). *He wants to be believed.* He invited you to prove His Word to you (see Malachi 3:9-11).

Here is the argument of the anti-prosperity cult. "What about greed? That is materialism. When you offer some money back for giving to God, that is satanic. That is ungodly! That is poisonous and deceptive to offer something back when you give to God."

Then, why did God offer us something back in return for Seed if that is greed? Do you feel that it is greedy to work for a salary? You are getting something in return!

God anticipated greed. He knew our need and desire for increase could be deceptive, distorted and easily used to manipulate us. So, He built in a "corrective."

He put something in the system of increase that would completely paralyze any problem with greed—GIVING.

It is impossible for you to give to God and stay greedy.

That is why He established the tithing system of returning ten percent back to Him.

That is why He promised Peter a hundredfold return for giving up everything to follow Christ (see Mark 10:28-30).

Every person who sows his Harvest has just conquered greed.

Greed *hoards.*

God *gives.*

It is impossible to give your way to greed.

Inside of each of us is an invisible command to become more, to multiply and increase. The *first commandment* ever given by God in the first book of Genesis, was to multiply and replenish and *become more.*

God is a God of increase. It is normal to become more, desire more and produce more. Remember the story regarding the man with one talent? He was punished eternally. Why? He did not do anything with his gifts and skills to increase his life. In fact, what he had was given to another person who had multiplied, used his gifts and become productive.

God is not cruel. He is not a liar and deceptive. If He gives you a desire for increase and prosperity, *He will place something inside you that can correct the problem it produces.* Giving.

All the preaching against greed and materialism is *only necessary for non-tithers and non-givers.*

Any discussion with the giver about being greedy is totally unnecessary. His Seed is proof that he has conquered it. His Seed is the corrective to potential greed.

What You Can Walk Away From Is Something You Have Mastered. What You Cannot Walk Away From Is Something That Has Mastered You.

Weeping will not correct greed.

Screaming will not correct it.

Confession will not stop greed.

Sowing is the only known cure for greed.

Obedience. Just returning the tithe. Just replanting the Seed He put in your hand.

The entire warfare and controversy over prosperity is to stop God from feelings of pleasure and feeling good about creating humans. You are not the target. This whole controversy does not revolve around you and your family. This whole controversy is between satan and God. You are only caught in the crossfire.

My Seed is the only proof I am expecting something in return. The only evidence that a farmer is looking for a Harvest is when you see him sowing his Seed. Your Seed is the proof you are expecting.

Your words are not the proof. You can talk about many things and still not really be expecting a Harvest.

Now, expectation is only possible when a Seed has been planted.

While you are withholding from God, it is impossible for your faith to work and expectations to occur. So, when God speaks to your heart to sow a Seed, you cannot even begin to expect a Harvest until you have obeyed His instruction. Your obedience in sowing immediately possesses you to be able *to expect.*

Now, your sowing does not create expectation. It makes it *possible* for you to expect.

You see, many people sow but they have not been taught the

principle of Seed-Faith—that you should expect something in return. So millions give to churches and never see a huge return on their Seed. They give to pay the bills of the church. They give because of guilt over withholding after all the blessings they have experienced. They give because a pastor meets with them privately and insists on them making "a donation to the cause." They give for many reasons.

Few sow their Seed to produce a Harvest.

Few sow with *expectation of a real return* from God.

How do you know that most do not expect a return? *They become angry over sowing.* If you believed something was coming back to you a hundred times—you would be more excited in that moment than any other time of your life.

Example: Have you ever received a sweepstakes letter in the mail that you have "won a million dollars?" Of course, you have. Now, when you are young and inexperienced, you get very excited. You tear the envelope open. You can just imagine yourself with a yacht, a beautiful Rolls Royce and a vacation in Spain. What is happening? *Expectation excites you,* energizes you, and creates a flurry of enthusiasm around you.

Expectation.

After you tear the envelope open, you suddenly realize there was part of the letter you could not see when it was closed. The part that says, "You *could* be one of those who wins a million dollars." After you open the letter, you realize that they did not promise that you won it. But, you *may have been* one of the winners. The expectation wanes and dies and withers.

You make a telephone call and realize that you were not really one of the winners. Expectations dies. Disappointment sets in.

Any disappointment you are experiencing today reveals your lack of expectation of a Harvest.

So, watch and sense the atmosphere that fills a church when an offering is being received. If there is expectation of a Harvest, *joy will fill that house.*

If expectation is present, joy is present.

Joy is the proof of expectation.

Depression and disappointment are evidences that fear is present. The fear of loss.

Expectation is an impossibility until you sow a Seed.

You can have a need and *still not expect an answer.*

You can have a great dream and *still not expect it to come to pass.*

Expectation is produced by *obedience.*

Obedience is the proof of faith.

Faith is confidence in God.

Peter declared that he had given up everything to follow Christ. What was the reaction of Jesus? Well, He did not commend him for discipleship. He did not commend him for his willingness to suffer. He did not brag on him for being a martyr. Jesus looked at him and promised that he would get everything back that he gave up, *one hundred times over* (see Mark 10:28-30).

22. Jesus Constantly Promoted Expectation. When the woman at the well of Samaria listened to Him, He promised her water that she would never thirst again. When the weary came to Him, He said, "I will give you rest." When the sinful approached Him with humility and confession, He promised them that they were forgiven.

Jesus always responded to those with great expectation. When the blind man cried out and was instructed to be silent by the crowds, Jesus reacted. Many were blind. One had great expectations of Jesus.

Jesus healed him.

23. Impossible Things Happen To Those Who Expect Them To Happen. "For verily I say unto you, That whosoever shall say unto this mountain, Be thou removed, and be thou cast into the sea; and shall not doubt in his heart, but shall believe that those things which he saith shall come to pass; he shall have whatsoever he saith" (Mark 11:23).

▶ *Anything good is going to find you.*

▶ Anything from God is going to *search you out.*

▶ Anything excellent is going to become *obvious* to you.

That is the principle of Seed-Faith.

24. You Have Something Given To You By God That Has A Future. Discover your Seed and wrap your faith around it with great expectation.

RECOMMENDED BOOKS AND TAPES:

B-06   Creating Tomorrow Through Seed-Faith (32 pages/$5)

B-82   31 Reasons People Do Not Receive Their Financial Harvest (253 pages/$12)

TS-38 31 Reasons People Do Not Receive Their Financial Harvest (6 tapes/$30)

VI-17 31 Reasons People Do Not Receive Their Financial Harvest (Video/$25)

Your Success Is Determined
By The Problems
You Solve For Others.

-*MIKE MURDOCK*

⚘ 15 ⚘

FAILURE

⟸⟸▸-O-◂⟸⟸

The Crisis Of Failure You Face Today Could Be Gone Next Month.
It is *your* decision.
Crisis Always Occurs At The Curve Of Change.
You see, *you* have the *power to change*...to make *new* decisions...to set in motion the lifestyle of a *champion*. You do not have to fail in life. You *can* succeed. *It depends entirely on you.* Yes...*you!*

You do not have to be a prisoner of your circumstances.

You can become a *creator* of your circumstances.

I am thrilled to share these powerful Wisdom Keys from the World's Greatest Book...the Holy Scriptures, "Which are able to make thee wise unto salvation through faith which is in Christ Jesus" (2 Timothy 3:15).

You can have the *heart* of a Champion.

You can have the *mind* of an Overcomer.

You can have the *spirit* of a Conqueror.

There is only One Way to inner happiness and success. It begins with a personal relationship with Jesus Christ, and obedience to the Life Principles He taught. "We are more than conquerors through Him that loved us" (Romans 8:37).

13 Facts About A Successful Life

1. Success Is A Choice. It is not necessarily a life of fame, popularity and public acceptance. Television and novels often depict the lifestyle of famous people as one of continuous pleasure...power... perfection. Tragically, the opposite is often true.

Fame can be burdensome, demanding and even cruel. This is easily proven by the alcoholism, drug addiction and even suicides often found among those in the limelight.

2. A Successful Life Is Much More Than The Accumulation Of Earthly Possessions And Wealth. Many biographies record the deep depression and insecurities of some of the wealthiest people in the world. Even King Solomon, in his backslidden state, cried out, "Therefore I hated life;" (Ecclesiastes 2:17).

3. A Successful Life Is Simply A Happy Life. It is a climate of enthusiasm emanating from you. You have *purpose.* You make *progress.* You know *direction.* You are *decisive.*

4. Success Is Satisfying Movement Toward Worthwhile Goals That God Has Scheduled For Your Life. *The Smallest Step In The Right Direction Always Creates Joy.* Remember, your happiness will always begin with movement toward that which is right.

5. Happiness Is Discovering Ingredients That Create A Successful Day, Then, Duplicating It Regularly. Any day that brings you closer to a God-given dream and goal is a successful day.

Let's face it. Something drives you to *dominate* the world around you...to *solve* your problems...to *master* your circumstances.

6. God Purposefully Planted This Drive For Mastery And Success Within You. God said, "Let us make man in Our image, after Our likeness: and let them have dominion over the fish of the sea...the fowl of the air...the cattle...all the earth, and over every creeping thing that creepeth upon the earth" (Genesis 1:26).

Note this: "Let them have dominion over the fish." God transferred the responsibility of decision-making to you and me. To dominate means to make the decision that controls another.

7. When You Are Born Into The Family Of God, His Seed For Success Is Planted Within You. "Whereby are given unto us exceeding great and precious promises: that by these ye might be partakers of the divine nature, having escaped the corruption that is in the world through lust" (2 Peter 1:4).

8. A Successful Life Is Often Expensive. It will cost you something to become a Champion. Time. Energy. Focus. *A Productive Life Is Not An Accident.* It will require effort, risk taking, reaching for relationships that might reject you, patient absorption of new information and ideas.

9. You May Even Have To Walk Away From Comfortable Circumstances And People To Achieve The Success You Want. *What You Are Willing To Walk Away From Determines What God Will Bring To You.*

10. A Successful Life Often Involves Seasons Of Pain. Your new revelations from God may expose errors in your childhood teaching. Your early teachers may have passed on to you their distortions, prejudices and doubts. Any discovery of personal error may almost tear your very heart out.

11. You Will Never Change What You Believe Until Your Belief System Cannot Produce Something You Want.

12. It Is Very Painful To Make Major Changes In Your Belief System. This is the critical place where many people fail. They refuse to acknowledge and pursue the *benefits* of change. They adapt to lack. *They forfeit their dreams to temporarily appease their fears and doubts.*

Most people fail to pursue their dreams and goals hoping to reduce their confrontations, struggles and opposition. They choose to sit as spectators in the Grandstand of Life, rather than risk the Arena of Conflict to wear the Crown of Victory.

13. You Must Take Time To Review The Benefits Of Success. "Bless the Lord, O my soul, and forget not all His benefits: Who forgiveth all thine iniquities; Who healeth all thy diseases; Who redeemeth thy life from destruction; Who crowneth thee with lovingkindness and tender mercies; Who satisfieth thy mouth with good things; so that thy youth is renewed like the eagle's" (Psalm 103:2-5).

Failure Has A Price, Too

Shockingly, most people eventually discover that it is more costly to lose than to win.

You see, failure has a price, too. What is the price of losing?

▶ *Loss Of Self-Confidence;*

▶ *Inferiority;*

▶ *Self-Directed Anger;*

▶ *Fear Of The Future;*

▶ *Low Self-Esteem That Can Even Affect Your Physical Health;*

▶ *Paralysis Of Your Creative Ideas;*

▶ *Depression;*

▶ *Self-Destructive And Suicidal Thoughts;*

▶ *Loss Of Favor With Friends;*

▶ *And Worst Of All, You Miss God's Will And Plan For Your Life.*

This is Why Success Is Worth The Price.

9 Facts About Failure

1. Your Future Was Created Before Your Failure. Failure is not fatal unless you stop.

2. Honestly Face The Reason For The Failure. Look for the starting point of the failure, not the end. You will not kill a snake by cutting off the end of its tail. Your last failure is your greatest teacher.

3. Do Not Ignore A Failure. Do not maximize it, but do not ignore it. Recognize that failure is a mentor, a teacher. Confess your failure to God.

4. Uncommon Mentors Reduce Your Failures. Failures are opportunities to change. All failures were preceded with warning signs. Look at every failure long enough to learn from it. Become an expert on recovery.

5. God Uses Failure To Reveal His Love, His Patience And His Mercy To You.

6. Failures Are Steps To Learning. Thomas Edison, said, "I don't have a failure. I've found 5,000 things that wouldn't work." Henry Ford was sneered at. Oral Roberts was laughed at.

7. Do Not Discuss Your Failure With Everybody. Never discuss a failure with someone incapable of receiving it...healing it...solving it.

8. Failure Does Not Always Occur Because Of What You Do, But Because Of Something You Failed To Do.

9. Failure Must Be Confronted And Conquered With Spiritual Weaponry. It is normal to experience doubts regarding your efforts to live a pure, holy and victorious life for God.

Why Is Your Success Worth Pursuing?

Note the rewards of a successful life mentioned in these verses:
▶ Forgiveness (see Acts 26:18)
▶ Physical Healing For Your Body (see Exodus 15:26)
▶ Protection From Your Enemies (see Isaiah 54:17)
▶ Promotion And Recognition (see Psalm 75:6,7)
▶ Financial Provision (see Philippians 4:19)
▶ Youthful Energy (see Philippians 4:13)

You Need Supernatural Power

Your personal success will never be achieved through man-made, self-help programs that ignore God and obedience to His Laws.

God Must Become The Center Of Your Life. "Not that we are sufficient of ourselves to think any thing as of ourselves; but our sufficiency is of God;" (2 Corinthians 3:5). Paul said, "I can do all things through Christ which strengtheneth me" (Philippians 4:13).

The Holy Spirit And Your Success

The early disciples were weak, unstable and powerless...*until the Holy Spirit took control of their lives.* "But ye shall receive power, after that the Holy Ghost is come upon you:" (Acts 1:8).

▶ *He Became Their Teacher.*

▶ *He Revealed The Nature Of God And His Purposes.*

▶ *He Imparted His Power For Them To Heal The Sick, Raise The Dead And Cast Out Evil Spirits* (see Matthew 10:8).

"And these signs shall follow them that believe; In My name shall they cast out devils; they shall speak with new tongues; They shall take up serpents; and if they drink any deadly thing, it shall not hurt them; they shall lay hands on the sick, and they shall recover" (Mark 16:17,18).

It was the Holy Spirit and His revelations that transformed these early disciples from weaklings into Champions.

4 Steps To Take After Times Of Failure

1. Reconstruct A More Accurate Picture Of God. He is not a harsh dictator wanting to smash earthlings at the slightest sign of error. Rather, He is a God of Miracles...Love...Compassion...and Healing. "Yea, I have loved thee with an everlasting love..with lovingkindness have I drawn thee" (Jeremiah 31:3). God is "not willing that any should perish, but that all should come to repentance" (read 2 Peter 3:9).

▶ *He Is Your Companion.* "For He hath said, I will never leave thee, nor forsake thee" (Hebrews 13:5).

▶ *He Is Your Father.* "For ye have not received the spirit of bondage again to fear; but ye have received the spirit of adoption, whereby we cry, Abba, Father" (Romans 8:15).

▶ *He Is Your Protector.* "What time I am afraid, I will trust in Thee" (Psalm 56:3).

▶ *He Is Your Healer.* "I am the Lord that healeth thee" (Exodus 15:26).

▶ *He Is Your Provider.* "But my God shall supply all your need according to His riches in glory by Christ Jesus" (Philippians 4:19).

▶ *He Is Your Teacher.* "I will instruct thee and teach thee in the way which thou shalt go: I will guide thee with Mine eye" (Psalm 32:8).

► *He Is Your Giver Of Gifts.* "Every good gift and every perfect gift is from above, and cometh down from the Father of lights, with Whom is no variableness, neither shadow of turning" (James 1:17).

Will He *Always* Love You? Will He *Always* Forgive You? Will He *Always* Heal You? Will He *Always* Restore You?

Absolutely. Yes! "For I am the Lord, I change not;" (Malachi 3:6). "Jesus Christ the same yesterday, and to day, and for ever" (Hebrews 13:8).

Will He Show Favor, Mercy And Forgiveness To You Personally? Yes! "God is no respecter of persons:" (Acts 10:34). "Him that cometh to me I will in no wise cast out" (John 6:37).

Call on God. Respect His invitation to a relationship.

It has been said that your opinion of your earthly father often influences your opinion of your Heavenly Father. So if your parents were not loving and caring, you might need an extra touch from God to get a more accurate understanding of the depth of His love and interest in your life and happiness.

This explains most of our difficulty with our faith. If you misunderstand and misinterpret God, it may be difficult for you to believe His Word.

Faith is simply confidence in His integrity.

2. Recognize The Limited Capabilities Of Your Enemy, Satan. "Submit yourselves therefore to God. Resist the devil, and he will flee from you" (James 4:7).

Satan fears you and the authority that you have over him through Christ. You are a joint-heir with Christ. Therefore, all things have been placed under your feet or control...including satan! "And hath put all things under his feet" (Ephesians 1:22).

3 Things Satan Cannot Do

1. **He Cannot Stop God From Loving You.**
2. **He Cannot Stop God From Hearing You.**
3. **He Cannot Stop God From Responding To You.**

Command satan to take his hands off your life...to stop harassing your children who have been dedicated to the Lord...to get off your property and out of your life! "Greater is He that is in you, than he that is in the world" (1 John 4:4).

3. Reach Out To Someone Close To You Who Is Hurting.

This is the Miracle Key in defeating depression, loneliness and emptiness in your life.

A successful company studies how to meet the *needs of its customers.*

Successful parents focus on the *needs of their children.*

An employee who gets promoted is the one who studies the *needs of his boss.* "Let no man seek his own, but every man another's wealth" (1 Corinthians 10:24).

Your Contribution To Others Is The Same Measuring Cup God Uses To Make Contributions To Your Own Life. So it is with a successful, winning, happy life. "Look not every man on his own things, but every man also on the things of others" (Philippians 2:4). "Knowing that whatsoever good thing any man doeth, the same shall he receive of the Lord," (Ephesians 6:8).

Find a damaged heart.

Discern a confused mind.

Feel a broken life close to you.

Pour the healing oil of Jesus on those wounds.

It will open Heaven's Windows of Blessing on your own life.

This is *The Greatest Law On Earth,* The Law Of Seed-Faith. It is *Sowing What You Have Received From God Into Someone Else In Need.*

4. Respect Yourself As A Chosen Vessel Of Healing. The Israelites who left Egypt under Moses never entered Canaan, the land of abundance. You see, they had been peasants and slaves under Egyptian bondage. And they could never shake that *slaveship mentality* even though they had left Egypt!

They *thought* like slaves.

They *talked* like slaves.

They *behaved* like slaves.

They fretted. They fumed. They doubted their capability to overcome giants in the Great Land of Promise, Canaan. They even labeled themselves as "Grasshoppers" when they saw the giants!

Joshua and Caleb were different.

They respected their Creator.

They respected *themselves.*

They saw themselves as victors, overcomers and conquerors. "Let us go up at once, and possess it; for we are well able to overcome it" (Numbers 13:30).

They were not complainers.

They were not murmurers.

They were not doubters.

They possessed "another spirit" (see Numbers 14:24).

Winners never magnify their personal weaknesses. They know their God will use any flaw to reveal His power and grace.

"My grace is sufficient for thee: for My strength is made perfect in weakness" (2 Corinthians 12:9).

▶ *Respect The New Nature God Has Given You As His Special Child.* "If any man be in Christ, he is a new creature: old things are passed away...all things are...new" (2 Corinthians 5:17).

▶ *Cherish God's Authority And Association With You.* Doing this unleashes His *power* and *might* over your enemy, satan. "Through God we shall do valiantly: for He it is that shall tread down our enemies" (Psalm 108:13).

God has already given you the power to succeed in life. You are already a Champion. Yes, you will go through crisis...but it is up to you to use this time of crisis as a stepping stone to success.

Go for it!

❧ 16 ❧

FAITH

Faith Is The Key To Everything You Want To Experience.

19 Facts About Faith

1. Faith Always Stimulates Incredible Favor From God And His Angels. Yes, faith is the magnet that attracts God toward you. You do not have to drive a Rolls Royce to impress Him. Nor is it necessary to be a Harvard graduate.

2. God Is Impressed When You Use The Faith He Has Already Given You. "God hath dealt to every man the measure of faith" (Romans 12:3).

"But without faith it is impossible to please Him: for he that cometh to God must believe that He is, that He is a rewarder of them that diligently seek Him" (Hebrews 11:6).

3. Every Miracle You Receive Can Be Traced To A Seed Of Faith. Faith is what drives ordinary men to accomplish the *extraordinary*.

Faith is what turns common men into *uncommon achievers*.

They possess different personalities and talents. *But they learned to use their faith.* They focused their believing toward their *Dream-Seed*.

4. Faith Is The Real Difference Between Champions And Losers.

Faith is the magic ingredient of every miracle.

Faith can cause your blind eyes to *see*.

Faith can cause your deaf ears to *hear* again.

Faith can cause your lame legs to receive *strength*.

Faith can make your barren womb *productive*.

Faith can *heal* your scarred and empty marriage.

Faith can *restore confidence* into your broken heart.

Faith can *break the chains* of your cocaine habit or any drug addiction.

Faith can *change you* from an alcoholic into a great achiever again.

Faith can *transform* you from a weakling into the Champion God intended you to be.

5. You Do Not Have To Understand Faith To Use It Effectively. Few people can really explain faith. It is like electricity or the wind. You cannot hold it in your hand. You cannot seal it in a jar at your house, or package it like a box of corn flakes.

6. Faith Is A Substance. God used it to create the universe.

"Through faith we understand that the worlds were framed by the Word of God, so that things which are seen were not made of things which do appear" (Hebrews 11:3). *Your Faith Is An Invisible Substance.* Like the wind or electricity, you may not see it with your natural eye, but its presence and force is proven by its results in your life. "Now faith is the substance of things hoped for, the evidence of things not seen" (Hebrews 11:1).

7. Faith Is The Ability To Believe. Remember, it is the invisible confidence within you that something exists other than what you presently see.

8. The Proof Of Your Faith Is Revealed In Your Pursuit Of The Unseen.

9. Faith Is A Seed Planted In The Soil Of Your Spirit. God planted it there at your birth. It is invisible to the natural eye, like minerals in the water. Yet, earth is very tangible in the realm of the spirit.

It may be *dead* or *dormant—or alive* and *growing.*

10. Faith That Is Inactive Toward God Is What We Call Dead Faith. "Faith without works is dead" (James 2:26). The Bible also refers to it as "unbelief" or "doubt." It does not mean that a man is not using his faith. Rather, it means that he is not using his faith *productively,* or *toward God.* He may even be using it against himself in a destructive manner.

11. Active Faith Is When A Man Uses His Believing Ability To Obtain Something He Wants From God. He usually will *do* something to prove that he has confidence in the Word of God.

The starving widow in 1 Kings 17 willingly *gave her last meal* to the prophet Elijah. Naaman, the leper, obeyed the prophet and *dipped in the Jordan River* seven times.

At the wedding in Cana, they *filled up the water pots* in anticipation of the water-to-wine miracle. Noah, though he had never seen rain, *began to build the ark* in faith.

The presence of your faith is proved by something you do in obedience to God and His Word.

12. The Ability To Believe Already Exists Within You. It is the substance called *faith.* Your faith is like a muscle. The more you use it, the stronger it will become.

I want to help you begin *using* your faith to obtain the miracles and blessings God wants you to receive.

13. You Already Possess The Seed Of Faith Within You. *Believing ability* is within every person. You choose how you will use it. Whatever you choose to believe decides whether it will be *productive or destructive* to your life. "God hath dealt to every man the measure of faith" (Romans 12:3).

14. Whenever You Use Your Faith, You Please The Heart Of God. Don't you appreciate it when others trust you? Don't you feel humiliated and a bit angry when they show *lack* of trust? Then you know how God feels about your faith in Him! "But without faith it is impossible to please Him: for he that cometh to God must believe that He is, and that He is a rewarder of them that diligently seek Him" (Hebrews 11:6).

Faith is very important to God.

Please do not take this lightly. Sometimes we make statements such as, "Well, I just don't have much faith." How would you like to hear your children talking to their little friends, "Well, my mother and dad lie to me all the time. I just don't believe anything they say." You would be crushed, insulted and humiliated.

Well, it is even more important that you trust the Word of God. God wants you to believe *every word* He speaks to you. You insult Him when you do not.

When you *use* your faith, you are pleasing to God.

When you do not trust him, you disappoint God.

It is just that simple.

I know several great men of God who are not necessarily perfect. They have made mistakes. But the principal secret of their success is that they have learned to use their faith in God.

15. You Will Change Your Circumstances When You Change The Direction Of Your Believing. "If thou canst believe, all things are possible to him that believeth" (Mark 9:23).

16. You Will Inevitably Experience What You Consistently Expect. I believe it was Henry Ford who said that men who believe they *can* do something, and those who believe they *cannot,* are *both* right.

God really wants you healed. Dare to *believe it.*
God really wants you happy. Dare to *believe it.*
God really wants to supply all your needs. Dare to *believe it.*
One of my songs on a recent album is "Dare to Believe."

"Dare to believe, and even demons tremble.
Dare to believe, and sickness must depart.
"Dare to believe, and even mountains can
be cast into the sea.
"Your world can change my friend, when you
dare to believe.

"The Seeds you have planted are not wasted.
They are ready to burst forth with new life.

"So today, my friend, let your faith be awakened.
Dare to believe that God is still alive!"

17. Your Biggest Mountain Will Succumb To Your Smallest Seed Of Faith. "If ye have faith as a grain of mustard seed, ye shall say unto this mountain, Remove hence to yonder place; and it shall remove; and nothing shall be impossible unto you" (Matthew 17:20).

You may feel as though you have little faith. I have felt that way before, too. But, Jesus did not say, "If you have faith like a *mountain* you can move a *mustard seed!*" He said that *your smallest act of faith is enough to get a mountain moved.*

But you must act on your faith. You must *speak* to the mountain. *You must tell your mountain exactly what you want it to do.* Sometimes you must *keep on* speaking to your mountain when it refuses to budge. But when you learn this secret, the mountains in your life *will* move. Jesus said it. *Believe it* and it will start working for you.

18. You Must Pursue What You Really Believe God Wants You To Possess. "If any of you lack wisdom, let him ask of God, that giveth to all men liberally, and upbraideth not; and it shall be given him. But let him ask in faith, nothing wavering. For he that wavereth is like a wave of the sea driven with the wind and tossed" (James 1:5,6).

Remember the earlier principle of desire: *The Proof Of Desire Is Pursuit.* Miracles do not just happen where they are needed. They happen where they are *wanted.* Jesus did not always go where He was needed, but where He was *wanted*.

We rarely reach for the things we really need.

But we *always* reach for those things we truly *desire*.

19. Your Guarantee Of Eternal Life Hinges Upon Your Faith In Jesus Christ. "For God so loved the world, that He gave His only begotten Son, that whosoever believeth in Him should not perish, but have everlasting life" (John 3:16).

I think we all have a built-in craving for immortality. In other words, we would love to live *forever!*

The Bible clearly teaches there is life beyond the grave. "Let not your heart be troubled: ye believe in God, believe also in Me. In My Father's house are many mansions: if it were not so, I would have told you. I go to prepare a place for you. And if I go and prepare a place for you, I will come again, and receive you unto Myself; that where I am, there ye may be also" (John 14:1-3).

I have never regretted my decision to accept Jesus Christ as my Lord and Savior. In fact, I wrote a song recently expressing my feelings about it.

> "I wouldn't want to try to live
> without the Lord in my life.

> "I wouldn't want to have to live
> in darkness when there is light.

> "And I won't trade away
> the joy I know today.

> "I wouldn't want to try to live
> without the Lord in my life."

3 Ways To Increase Your Faith

Your faith is like a Seed.

And like any Seed, it must be *watered* and *nurtured* for it to grow. As the apostles said unto the Lord, "Increase our faith" (Luke 17:5).

1. The Most Important Secret In Increasing Your Faith Is To Hear The Spoken Word Of God. "So then faith cometh by hearing, and hearing by the Word of God" (Romans 10:17).

Do you own a cassette tape recorder? Then use it. Keep it plugged in for continuous use. Keep a stack of Scripture and teaching tapes close by.

While you are shaving or bathing, *play those tapes.*

While you are waiting for your wife to get dressed, *play those tapes.*

While you are driving your car to work, *play those tapes.*

I usually keep tape recorders in every room of my house. And since I travel over 15,000 miles a month, I keep a tape deck in my motel room at all times. *Cassette tapes can feed your spirit.*

"Oh, but tapes cost too much," a little lady told me.

"Ignorance will cost you *more,*" I replied.

It is amazing how we will pay $40 for a tank of gas that is gone in three days, while excusing ourselves knowledge that could revolutionize our entire lifestyle.

Some people spend more money on their cars than they do their minds. *(Maybe that is why their cars run better than their minds!)*

Meditate on Scripture.

Memorize Scripture.

Talk about Scripture.

Compose songs with Scriptures.

2. Be Honest With God About Your Personal Needs And Desires. "He that covereth his sins shall not prosper: but whoso confesseth and forsaketh them shall have mercy" (Proverb 28:13).

"...him that cometh to Me I will in no wise cast out" (John 6:37).

It was a marvelous moment in my life when I learned to *speak* my real feelings *aloud* to God. I discovered that He would never ask me to do something that I could not do. He would not ask me to achieve something I could not accomplish.

You see, I hate to make mistakes. I really do. Any kind of mistake. Whether it is getting lost on a strange freeway or failing to spot a misspelled word in my current newsletter! And satan delights in taking advantage of that kind of conscientiousness.

He wants us to feel that we are incapable of pleasing God. I have had moments when I felt that God was simply unfair. I felt that His standard was just too high for anyone to achieve—especially me!

It is not always easy to live holy.

I sometimes have difficulty understanding the head-in-the-clouds, glib-tongued Christian who says that he never experiences adversity. Personally, I have found that the same thing happened in the lives of Joseph, Daniel and the apostle Paul.

Is it humanly possible for us to please God? *Yes, without a doubt.*

Do you really *want* to live in obedience? Then *tell Him.* He needs to hear it from your own lips.

I have found that the Holy Spirit is the easiest person to please that I have ever known. He is *consistent* in His expectations, incredibly long-suffering and unwavering in His confidence in me.

The real truth is that people are harder to please than the Holy Spirit! Subconsciously, each of us attempts to please those around us. It is impossible. *Therein is the weariness of life.*

Man-pleasing is enslaving. As Proverbs 29:25 says, "The fear of man bringeth a snare: but whoso putteth his trust in the Lord shall be safe."

I have found that one of the keys to pleasing God is to focus *only* on *24-hour achievements.* This simply means to discern *each morning* what will make Him happy for that day only. Then concentrate on His goals for *just that day.*

3. Verbally Acknowledge The Presence Of God That Is Now Within You! As a believer, you already contain the power of God within you. *Release it!* Do not bottle it up. Uncork it! "He that believeth on Me, as the scripture hath said, out of his belly shall flow rivers of living water" (John 7:38).

Do not let anyone clog up that inner river inside you. Someone near you today desperately needs the Water of Life from *your* well!

Feel Jesus. *Think* Jesus. *Talk* about Jesus!

Do not hesitate to pray for someone on the street or in a restaurant. The whole world is your turf. Dominate it!

Healing the sick is more important than accommodating a critic.

Yes, your *marriage* can be *restored.* Your *body* can be completely *healed.* Yes, God can provide the *extra finances* you desperately need at this time.

And it can begin happening the very moment you learn to use the most explosive weapon God has given you: *Your Faith.*

Faith is that invisible confidence that something exists other than what you presently see. It is that internal belief system planted by God in every human being.

Faith is simply the *ability to believe.*

Faith always draws the attention of God.

RECOMMENDED BOOKS AND TAPES:
B-24 Seeds Of Wisdom On Faith-Talk (32 pages/$3)

Your Mouth Is
    The Multiplier
Of Whatever
    Is In Your Heart.

-MIKE MURDOCK

❧ 17 ❧

FAITH-TALK

Whatever You Talk About Will Increase.
What you think about becomes larger.
Your mind and your mouth are magnifiers of anything you want to grow.

Two spies came back with faith, victory and the ability to overcome giants. Their names were Joshua and Caleb. They had been with God. They had seen the giants, but were not afraid. They had seen the grapes and decided to become champions. They had experienced too many days in the wilderness to be satisfied with failure.

They became the champions of faith. Joshua became the leader after the death of Moses. Caleb became known for "taking his mountain." Oh, the rewards of faith are sweet. The taste of victory stays in your mouth so long!

You must discern the Joshua and Caleb nearest you. Find the faith food. Listen for faith-talk. Sit under it and listen and absorb. Something within you will grow.

30 Ways To Nurture Your Faith-Talk

1. **Say What God Wants To Hear.**
   ▶ Your words affect God. Your prayers ignite God.
   ▶ Jesus taught His disciples how to pray...for provision, protection and pardon (see Matthew 6:9-13).
   ▶ Faith-talk is what God responds to favorably. Confess your sins...your desire for forgiveness...And the things you need God to do in your life.
   "If My people, which are called by My name, shall humble themselves, and pray, and seek My face, and turn from their wicked ways; then will I hear from heaven, and will forgive their sin, and will heal their land" (2 Chronicles 7:14).
2. **Talk Expectations, Not Experiences.**
   ▶ Do not drag yesterday into your future.

▶ Perhaps you have just been fired from your job. Do not meditate on your feelings of rejection. Instead, point out the possibility of promotion and changes of freedom that suddenly may emerge.

▶ Nurture the Photograph of Possibilities within your heart. Elijah gave the widow of Zarephath a picture of her potential. It stirred her expectations of a miracle Harvest in her life (see 1 Kings 17).

"And let us not be weary in well doing: for in due season we shall reap, if we faint not" (Galatians 6:9).

3. Picture Your Desired Future.

▶ Abraham had a picture of many generations of children he wanted (see Genesis 17).

▶ Joseph had a dream of himself as a leader and he remembered it (see Genesis 37).

▶ Know God's dream for your life. Get the Picture. Big. BIGGER. Fill up your mind, heart and life with it. Now make that vision consume your life...every conversation...every thought...everything around you.

"Where there is no vision, the people perish: but he that keepeth the law, happy is he" (Proverbs 29:18).

4. Listen To Mentors Of Faith.

▶ Joshua learned under Moses. Timothy learned under Paul. Elisha learned under Elijah.

▶ Observe successful lives carefully. Secrets will surface. Reasons for success will emerge.

▶ Read biographies of extraordinary people who tapped into the Fountain of Faith. Their lives will excite you to new heights of faith.

"Wherefore seeing we also are compassed about with so great a cloud of witnesses, let us lay aside every weight, and the sin which doth so easily beset us, and let us run with patience the race that is set before us," (Hebrews 12:1).

5. Respect Your Tongue.

▶ When God wanted to create the world...He spoke.

▶ Words are creative forces that bring into existence that which never existed before.

▶ Your tongue is one of the greatest gifts placed at your command by God. Use it wisely and you will discover the golden key to life.

"Behold also the ships, which though they be so great, and are driven of fierce winds, yet are they turned about with a very small helm, whithersoever the governor listeth. Even so the tongue is a little member, and boasteth great things. Behold, how great a matter a little fire kindleth!" (James 3:4,5).

6. **Talk To Yourself.**

▶ External communication is what you say to others. Internal communication is what you say to yourself.

▶ Others may not talk the God Report to you...so talk it to yourself!

▶ What you say—about your enemy, your future, your expectations—affects what you believe.

"This book of the law shall not depart out of thy mouth; but thou shall meditate therein day and night, that thou mayest observe to do according to all that is written therein: for then thou shalt make thy way prosperous, and then thou shalt have good success" (Joshua 1:8).

7. **Pursue Faith Food.**

▶ What you read affects what you believe.

▶ When you feed the Scriptures into your spirit man, faith comes alive and becomes a living force within you.

▶ Read the Bible. Read books that stir your faith in God. Nurture the Seed of Faith inside you. Acorns become oak trees.

"So then faith cometh by hearing, and hearing by the word of God" (Romans 10:17).

8. **Loosen Up And Laugh.**

▶ You are being observed today. Satan is watching to see if his tactics are working.

▶ Laugh aloud and rejoice that your circumstances are attracting the attention of God, too.

▶ Miracles are always birthed when things seem their worst. Satan is sensitive and very capable of being discouraged.

So...make the effort to rejoice.

"A merry heart doeth good like a medicine: but a broken spirit drieth the bones" (Proverbs 17:22).

9. **Keep A Journal Of Miracles.**

▶ God instructed Israel to pile stones to remind their children of the greatness of God (see Joshua 4:4-10).

▶ Look for miracles every day...unexpected, unplanned introductions to people; information that suddenly emerges; an invitation that opens great doors of opportunities.

▶ Document these experiences daily. Your written journal is your private reservoir of memories that will feed your faith.

"...The Lord said unto Moses, Write this for a memorial in a book, and rehearse it in the ears of Joshua" (Exodus 17:14).

10. Savor Each Moment.

▶ Savor means to taste, feel and extract all the pleasure and benefit...of each moment.

Someone has well said, "You are going to be on the journey longer than you will be at the destination...so, enjoy the journey."

▶ Always be where you are. Do not permit your mind to race miles ahead of where your body is. Taste Now...it is the future you have been talking about your entire life.

"...Now is the accepted time; behold, now is the day of salvation" (2 Corinthians 6:2).

11. Make Today A Major Event In Your LIfe.

▶ Do not be passive today. You are Alive! Act like it! Talk like it! Celebrate yourself!

▶ Speak a little louder today. Speak a little faster.

▶ Smile bigger...laugh aloud...exude the joy of Jesus as you spread it generously over every single hour today.

"This is the day which the Lord hath made; we will rejoice and be glad in it" (Psalm 118:24).

12. Put Faith Signs In Your Home.

▶ What You See Determines What You Feel.

▶ So, put little signs on your refrigerator, bathroom mirror and bulletin boards to stir your faith.

▶ God instructed the children of Israel to put up His Word as signs before their eyes on the door posts of their homes (see Deuteronomy 11:18-25).

"Mine eye affecteth mine heart" (Lamentations 3:51).

"Therefore shall ye lay up these My words in your heart...and bind them for a sign upon your hand,...And thou shalt write them upon the door posts of thine house" (Deuteronomy 11:18,20).

13. Focus On The Rewards Of Finishing A Task.

▶ Every task has an unpleasant side...but you must cultivate focus on the end results you are producing.

▶ Complaining people focus on the wrong things...the effort, toil or responsibility.

▶ Champions talk faith because their focus is on the finished results.

"He that endureth to the end shall be saved" (Matthew 10:22).

14. Refuse The Role Of The Victim.

▶ The Victim Vocabulary includes, "I do not have an education," "I was abused in my childhood," and "My father deserted my mother."

▶ Do not adopt this attitude. Fight it. Yesterday is over. Act like it.

▶ You have the anointing of God wrapped around you. You are not a captive, but a Deliverer. You are not a victim, but a Victor.

"Ye are of God, little children, and have overcome them: because greater is He that is in you , than he that is in the world" (1 John 4:4).

15. Pinpoint Your Support System.

▶ Nobody succeeds alone. Nobody.

▶ Friends differ. Some correct you. Others direct you. Some make you think. Others make you feel.

▶ Pinpoint those who truly stimulate you...educate you...placate you. Meticulously build your foundation for friendship...a support system that is the result of thought instead of chance.

"Two are better than one...For if they fall, the one will lift up his fellow: but woe to him that is alone when he falleth; for he hath not another to help him up" (Ecclesiastes 4:9,10).

16. Reflect On The Victories Of Bible Champions.

▶ David, with a simple slingshot, killed Goliath and eventually became king (see 1 Samuel 17).

▶ Joseph overcame the hatred of his brothers, and false accusation and became second in power to Pharaoh (see Genesis 37-41).

▶ Ponder and meditate on the lives of such champions...it will unleash energy, enthusiasm and faith.

"The people that do know their God shall be strong, and do exploits" (Daniel 11:32).

17. Replay Successes In Your Mind.

▶ Think about your past battles and struggles.

▶ David remembered and replayed his victories over the bear and lion...before he ran toward Goliath (see 1 Samuel 17:37).

▶ Yesterday is your history of successes. Remember them. Talk about them. Satan is the only one you will irritate!

"Joshua said, take you up every man...a stone upon his shoulder... That this may be a sign...that when your children ask...What mean ye by these stones? Then ye shall answer them, That the waters of Jordan were cut off before the ark of the covenant...and these stones shall be for a memorial unto the children of Israel for ever" (Joshua 4:5-7).

18. Make It A Point To Be Thankful.

▶ Thankfulness produces joy.

▶ It does not take a genius to locate, discern and detect flaws.

However, it takes great awareness to see the good things of life.

▶ Savor God's every day blessings. Your eyesight, your hearing, your ability to speak...and the thousands of other things to be happy about.

"For the joy of the Lord is your strength" (Nehemiah 8:10).

"When they knew God, they glorified Him not as God, neither were thankful; but became vain in their imaginations, and their foolish heart was darkened" (Romans 1:21).

19. Turn Little Blessings Into Celebrations.

▶ Gorgeous sunsets. Laughter of children. Hot bubble baths. Vacant parking spaces at the mall. Celebrate each little blessing.

▶ Life is a journey. Focus on all the little things that make it pleasurable. Do not take today for granted.

▶ You have already received...and received...and received so much from God. Talk it up!

"Giving thanks always for all things unto God and the Father in the name of our Lord Jesus Christ;" (Ephesians 5:20).

20. Pour The Word Over Your Mind Daily.

▶ Your mind gathers the dirt, grime and dust of human opinion every day.

▶ Renew your mind to the TRUTH—God's Word. Schedule an appointment with the Bible *daily*. The *renewing* of your mind is the key to *changes* within you.

▶ The Words of God are like waterfalls...*washing* and purifying your mind.

21. Look On The Bright Side Of A Problem.

▶ Learn to make lemonade out of every *lemon experience*.

▶ When my plane is delayed, I think of it as an extra hour to *read or catch up on correspondence*.

▶ Think...about all the *potential advantages* a problem might produce.

22. Ask A Different Question.

▶ Stop asking yourself questions that do not have answers such as *"WHY* did this happen to me?" Or, *"WHY* do they treat me this way?"

▶ Ask yourself creative questions such as, *"WHAT* can I do immediately to create changes?" Or, *"HOW* can I improve the situation?"

▶ Your mind will struggle to produce answers to every question you ask it. So do not exhaust it. Ask the *right* questions.

23. Assess Your Atmosphere.
▶ Indians used to wet their fingers and hold them in the wind to discern the direction of air currents.
▶ So you must learn to observe and *diagnose* the currents, climate and emotional atmosphere others are creating around you.
▶ Their words are poison or power. Their words are destructive or creative. Their words are doubt or faith-building. Assess them *accurately*.

24. Screen Doubters And Refuse Conversation With Them.
▶ Screen doors prevent obnoxious insects from entering your home.
▶ You must assertively screen out people who are *carriers* of the virus of doubt and unbelief.
▶ Boldly protect your ears and life from absorbing talk that does not edify and build.

25. Mark Contentious People And Avoid Them.
▶ Note those who always create conflict, complain and are hostile toward everything.
▶ Do not give them an opportunity to air their grievances and inject their poison into the conversation.
▶ *Take Charge.*

26. Identify Complainers And Withdraw From Them.
▶ You will hear a lot of garbage and unbelief dumped into your ears today. *Name it for what it is.*
▶ Discern complainers. Recognize the spirit of murmuring that has entered someone, poisoning every conversation.
▶ *Do not participate.* Take the conversation upward by stating, "What an opportunity for God to perform a miracle!"

27. Make Yourself Unforgettable To God.
▶ Conversations *reveal.* What you love, hate, crave or despise is exposed by your words.
▶ Faith is confidence in God.
▶ When you speak confidently of God's integrity and victoriously exude your anticipation of miracles...God is pleasured. God will remember you for the pleasure you created.

28. Recognize Doubt Produces Tragedies.
▶ God has *feelings.* Some words grieve His heart. Some words excite His heart. Unbelief brings God great pain. Faith brings Him great pleasure.
▶ Twelve spies analyzed Canaan for 40 days. Moses and the people accepted the Report of Doubt from the 10 spies

instead of the Report of Faith from Joshua and Caleb (read Numbers 13).

▶ *Each day of doubt brought 365 days of heartache. Doubt is as contagious as faith.*

29. Do Not Feed An Argumentative Attitude.

▶ You will be challenged today. Someone will be wanting to start an argument, a quarrel.

▶ Do not fall for it. *Refuse* to feed a contentious spirit. It erodes your keenness and *breaks your focus.*

▶ *Re-direct the conversation* to the power of God, and the potential miracle about to be birthed!

30. Learn To Linger In The Presence Of God.

▶ Those who surround you influence what you become.

▶ Something happens in the presence of God that does not happen anywhere else. *Commands* take a moment. *Plans* take time. Linger long enough to *hear His plans.*

▶ Your views will change *in His presence.* Your perceptions are corrected *in His presence.* Your faith explodes *in His presence.*

≈ 18 ≈

FASTING

Champions Use The Weapon Of Fasting.

27 Important Facts About Fasting

1. **Fasting Is A Force In The Spirit World.** When the disciples could not cast out the dumb and deaf spirit of the young son, they asked Jesus, "Why could not we cast him out? And He said unto them, This kind can come forth by nothing, but by prayer and fasting" (Mark 9:28,29).

2. **Unusual Warfare Requires Unusual Weapons.**

3. **Jesus Embraced Prayer And Fasting As Effective Weapons.** Demon powers always succumb to these weapons. I am so thankful that the body of Christ is awakening again and becoming aware of the remarkable influence we can have when we pray and *set aside time to fast.* "Then was Jesus led up of the Spirit into the wilderness to be tempted of the devil. And when He had fasted forty days and forty nights, He was afterward an hungred" (Matthew 4:1,2).

4. **You Should Fast Between Major Events Of Your Life.** *Jesus did.* When He was baptized by John he saw "the Spirit of God descending like a dove, and lighting upon Him: And lo a voice from heaven, saying, This is My beloved Son, in Whom I am well pleased" (Matthew 3:16,17). Then, Jesus fasted. His next major event was the selection of His disciples. "And Jesus, walking by the sea of Galilee, saw two brethren, Simon called Peter, and Andrew his brother, casting a net into the sea: for they were fishers. And He saith unto them, Follow Me, and I will make you fishers of men. And they straightway left their nets, and followed Him. And going on from thence, He saw other two brethren, James the son of Zebedee, and John his brother, in a ship with Zebedee their father, mending their nets; and He called them. And they immediately left the ship and their father, and followed Him" (Matthew 4:18-22).

5. **You Should Fast To Influence The Judgments Of God Away From Your Children.** David did. "David therefore besought God for the child; and David fasted, and went in, and lay all night upon the earth. And the elders of his house arose, and went to him, to raise him

up from the earth: but he would not, neither did he eat bread with them" (2 Samuel 12:16,17).

6. You Should Fast Habitually. Anna did. Anna, an 84 year old widow and prophetess never left the temple, but fasted continuously. "And she was a widow of about fourscore and four years, which departed not from the temple, but served God with fastings and prayers night and day" (Luke 2:37).

7. Your Fasting Follows The Examples Of Great Champions. The Apostle Paul fasted. "But in all things approving ourselves as the ministers of God, in much patience, in afflictions, in necessities, in distresses, In stripes, in imprisonments, in tumults, in labours, in watchings, in fastings;" (2 Corinthians 6:4,5).

8. You Should Fast Often. "In weariness and painfulness, in watchings often, in hunger and thirst, in fastings often, in cold and nakedness" (2 Corinthians 11:27).

9. You Should Fast For The Healing Of Your Children. David did. "David therefore besought God for the child; and David fasted, and went in, and lay all night upon the earth. And the elders of his house arose, and went to him, to raise him up from the earth: but he would not, neither did he eat bread with them" (2 Samuel 12:16,17).

10. You Should Fast To Create Favor In A Political Crisis. Esther did. She requested that many join her in a fast for three days without eat or drink, and she got her employees to do so likewise. "Then Esther bade them return Mordecai this answer, Go, gather together all the Jews that are present in Shushan, and fast ye for me, and neither eat nor drink three days, night or day: I also and my maidens will fast likewise;" (Esther 4:15,16).

11. You Should Fast To Create Acceptance And Influence With Those In Leadership And Positions Of Power. Queen Esther did (see Esther 4:15,16).

12. You Should Fast During Times Of Unusual Attack And Isolation. David did. "When I wept, and chastened my soul with fasting, that was to my reproach" (Psalm 69:10).

13. Your Fasting Will Produce Humility. "I humbled my soul with fasting;" (Psalm 35:13).

14. You Should Fast To Influence Three Areas Of Your Life. Ezra, the priest, did. 1) Direction. 2) Family. 3) Finances. "Then I proclaimed a fast there, at the river of Ahava, that we might afflict ourselves before our God, to seek of Him a right way for us, and for our little ones, and for all our substance" (Ezra 8:21).

15. Your Fasting Is Wasted Effort If You Lack Integrity Or Proper Motives. "Then said the Lord unto me, Pray not for this people for their good. When they fast, I will not hear their cry; and when thy offer burnt offering and an oblation, I will not accept them: but I will consume them by the sword, and by the famine, and by the pestilence" (Jeremiah 14:11,12).

16. You Should Fast To Avert The Judgments Of God Upon Your Life. "Sanctify ye a fast, call a solemn assembly: for the day of the Lord is at hand, and as a destruction from the Almighty shall it come" (Joel 1:14,15).

17. Your Fasting Affects Your Supernatural Provision. "Blow the trumpet in Zion, sanctify a fast:...Yea, the Lord will answer and say unto His people, Behold, I will send you corn, and wine, and oil, and ye shall be satisfied therewith: and I will no more make you a reproach among the heathen" (Joel 2:15,19).

18. Your Fasting Is Wrong If It Is Done Publicly To Impress Other People About You Spiritually. "And when thou prayest, thou shall not be as the hypocrites are: for they love to pray standing in the synagogues and in the corners of the streets, that they may be seen of men...Moreover when ye fast, be not, as the hypocrites, of a sad countenance: for they disfigure their faces, that they may appear unto men to fast" (Matthew 6:5,16).

19. Your Fasting Should Be A Private And Silent Posture Before God. "But thou, when thou fastest, anoint thine head, and wash thy face; That thou appear not unto men to fast, but unto thy Father which is in secret: and thy Father, which seeth in secret, shall reward thee openly" (Matthew 6:17,18).

20. Your Father Guarantees To Reward You Openly For Private Fasting. "But thou, when thou fastest, anoint thine head, and wash thy face; That thou appear not unto men to fast, but unto thy Father which is in secret: and thy Father, which seeth in secret, shall reward thee openly" (Matthew 6:17,18).

21. Your Fasting Moves God To Destroy Your Enemy. "Blow the trumpet in Zion, sanctify a fast, call a solemn assembly...and I will no more make you a reproach among the heathen: But I will remove far off from you the northern army, and will drive him into a land barren and desolate, with his face toward the east sea, and his hinder part toward the utmost sea, and his stink shall come up, and his ill savour shall come up, because he hath done great things" (Joel 2:15,19,20).

22. Your Fasting Births A Season Of Restoration After Loss. "Blow the trumpet in Zion, sanctify a fast, call a solemn assembly:...and He will cause to come down for you the rain, the former rain, and the latter rain in the first month. And the floors shall be full of wheat, and the fats shall overflow with wine and oil. And I will restore to you the years that the locust hath eaten, the cankerworm, and the caterpillar, and the palmerworm, My great army which I sent among you. And ye shall eat in plenty, and be satisfied, and praise the name of the Lord your God, that hath dealt wondrously with you: and My people shall never be ashamed" (Joel 2:15,23-26).

23. Your Fasting Can Cause An Outflowing Of The Holy Spirit Toward Your Life. "Blow the trumpet of Zion, sanctify a fast, call a solemn assembly: And it shall come to pass afterward, that I will pour out My Spirit upon all flesh; and your sons and your daughters shall prophesy, your old men shall dream dreams, your young men shall see visions: And also upon the servants and upon the handmaids in those days will I pour out My Spirit" (Joel 2:15,28-29).

24. God Commanded Us To Fast. "Therefore also now, saith the Lord, turn ye even to Me with all your heart, and with fasting, and with weeping, and with mourning: And rend your heart, and not your garments, and turn unto the Lord your God: for He is gracious and merciful, slow to anger, and of great kindness, and repenteth him of the evil" (Joel 2:12,13).

25. Various Fasts Are Possible. Some people fast from food and water for three days. Some simply fast without food for three days, seven days, twenty-one days or forty days. The important thing is to be *led by the voice of the Holy Spirit.* (It is always wise to have a physician oversee fasts for the purpose of keeping your health strong.)

26. The Purpose Of Fasting Is Not To Destroy Your Health. It is to deprive yourself of something you love, to move the hand of God to provide something you do not have. I have fasted three days per week for many months of my ministry and life. I have discovered the importance of total focus during meal times. Rather than sit at the restaurant table with friends during a dinner, it is better to *withdraw yourself from* the company of others and focus in private prayer time *with Him.*

27. Your Geographical Location For Your Assignment Can Be Revealed Following A Fast. "As they ministered to the Lord, and fasted, the Holy Ghost said, Separate me Barnabas and Saul for the work whereunto I have called them. And when they had fasted and prayed, and laid their hands on them, they sent them away. So they, being sent forth by the Holy Ghost, departed unto Seleucia; and from thence they sailed to Cyprus" (Acts 13:2-4). So the same Holy Spirit that revealed the city and country for their Assignment following a fast is not a respecter of persons. He will honor this Seed of love and deprivation.

Every champion of faith knows the power of prayer. Those who embrace the extra weapon of *fasting* see *increased* results beyond their imagination.

❧ 19 ❧

FATHERS

31 Qualities Of An Uncommon Father

1. **The Uncommon Father Highly Esteems The Word Of God.** The most important book on earth is the Bible. It is *truth*. The Uncommon Father knows this. His wife and children see him daily reading, studying and applying its principles to his life and business. The world changes. The Word does not. So, the Uncommon Father refuses to be influenced, intimidated or manipulated by the ungodly environment around him. He is settled, decisive and peaceful knowing that the Word of God is the only thing that will last forever.

"For ever, O Lord, Thy word is settled in heaven" (Psalm 119:89). "Heaven and earth shall pass away, but My words shall not pass away" (Matthew 24:35).

2. **The Uncommon Father Teaches His Children To Pray.** Prayer is *visiting with the Father*. It always attracts the attention of God. The Uncommon Father knows this. Every morning he keeps his personal daily appointment with God. His children observe him. He teaches them how to approach God, knowing that protocol is often the difference between answered prayers and unanswered prayers. He meets with his children at the same time every morning in The Secret Place. He knows that his children cannot change until they enter the presence of God, their Creator. He pursues the presence of God.

"God forbid that I should sin against the Lord in ceasing to pray for you:" (1 Samuel 12:23).

3. **The Uncommon Father Refuses To Focus On Mistakes.** Yesterday is over and must be forgotten. The Uncommon Father focuses on the *future*. He refuses fruitless discussions of his own and other's mistakes. He pours his energy into creating the dream he wants in his future. Forgiveness comes easy. Rebuilding becomes a joy. The focus of the family is on the sunrises, not the sunsets. He is an Uncommon Father and creates an uncommon life for his family because of it.

"Remember ye not the former things...Behold, I will do a new thing; now it shall spring forth; shall ye not know it? I will even make a way in the wilderness, and rivers in the desert" (Isaiah 43:18,19)

4. The Uncommon Father Is Willing To Change His Opinion. It is not always easy to make an important change. Habit is powerful. Opinions often become permanent, even though contradictory information arrives. It is an Uncommon Father who willingly listens, evaluates and adapts accordingly. His willingness to *become* is felt by tomorrow and is unlike any yesterday that existed. *Change is proof of humility.* Like a holy fragrance, it turns every home into a palace.

"Behold, I will do a new thing; now it shall spring forth; shall ye not know it? I will even make a way in the wilderness, and rivers in the desert" (Isaiah 43:19).

5. The Uncommon Father Mentors His Children On The Power Of Forgiveness. Everybody makes mistakes. Everybody. This is not a perfect world. The Uncommon Father knows this and shows his children the *rewards* of forgiveness. He does not hold grudges. He does not sulk and withdraw. Rather, he becomes the personal example of rebuilding the Bridge of Mercy. He breathes life into his family because he removes the need to *hide*.

"And be ye kind one to another, tenderhearted, forgiving one another, even as God for Christ's sake hath forgiven you" (Ephesians 4:32).

6. The Uncommon Father Avoids Unnecessary Confrontation. Conflict is exhausting, distracting and unproductive. It moves you away from your future and toward your past. The Uncommon Father knows this. So, he creates a climate of peace, gentleness and security. Kindness is treasured because the Uncommon Father has taught its importance to his family.

"If it be possible, as much as lieth in you, live peaceably with all men" (Romans 12:18).

7. The Uncommon Father Knows His Seeds Of Patience Will Grow Greatness In His Children. Great things take time. An oak tree. A child. Impatience is costly. The greatest mistakes on earth occur because of hasty decisions. The Uncommon Father listens, meditates and ponders. The Seeds of Time always pay off. *Always.* The Uncommon Father will taste the rewards.

"Rest in the Lord, and wait patiently for Him" (Psalm 37:7).

8. The Uncommon Father Chooses His Words Carefully. Words create wars. Words create peace. Words are bridges into tragedy or triumph. Words can birth unforgettable pain or eternal pleasure. The Uncommon Father knows this. When he speaks into the heart of his child, his words are like *drops of gold* creating waves of greatness and hope in his family. Because his words are so important to him, they become important to his family. He uses his words like water on a parched desert, breathing life into those he loves.

"He that hath knowledge spareth his words: and a man of understanding is of an excellent spirit. Even a fool, when he holdeth his peace, is counted wise: and he that shutteth his lips is esteemed a man of understanding" (Proverbs 17:27,28).

9. The Uncommon Father Rejoices When His Children Achieve Their Goals. Everyone has a different dream. What excites one often offends another. The Uncommon Father loves to see his children obtain a goal they have treasured. Their dreams matter. Their hopes matter. So, he listens, interviews and gathers information that makes that achievement possible. Then, the Uncommon Father teaches his children the attitude of gratitude and thankfulness for the successes God has created through them.

"Rejoice with them that do rejoice, and weep with them that weep" (Romans 12:15).

10. The Uncommon Father Leaves An Uncommon Legacy For His Children. Your legacy is your last gift to those you love. The Uncommon Father makes decisions that create long-term success for his children. His investments are cautious, careful and wise. He anticipates difficult times and prepares accordingly. Though he has endured difficult seasons, he has *learned* from them. His plans reveal his deep understanding of pain. His deep love for his family is revealed through his planning ahead and making their lives much easier.

"A good man leaveth an inheritance to his children's children" (Proverbs 13:22).

11. The Uncommon Father Praises Quickly And Criticizes Slowly. Life can be harsh. People can be cruel. Words are hurled daily like daggers, penetrating the soft heart of a child. The Uncommon Father anticipates the attack. So, he uses praise freely, lavishly and generously. He knows that his child is worthy, deserving and needy. His moments of criticism are cautious, measured and gentle. Wrapped with kindness, he gently focuses his child's attention on his own potential, not his weakness.

"Death and life are in the power of the tongue: and they that love it shall eat the fruit thereof" (Proverbs 18:21).

12. The Uncommon Father Is An Uncommon Listener. Words matter. But, silence matters just as much. While the world screams for attention, the Uncommon Father becomes a harbor for the fragmented heart. Using two Golden Tools, *words and silence,* he carefully sculptures his children into great champions. He listens for pain and *heals.* He listens for confusion and *explains.* He listens for arrogance and *warns.* He listens when nobody else is willing to take the time. He is an *Uncommon* Father.

"The hearing ear, and the seeing eye, the Lord hath made even both of them" (Proverbs 20:12).

13. The Uncommon Father Withholds His Judgment Until All The Facts Are Known. Nothing is ever as it first appears. Information is often confused, distorted and inaccurate. The Uncommon Father knows this. He will not penalize nor jump to conclusions until guilt is proven without a doubt. He is approachable, forgiving and wise. He is *Uncommon.*

"Therefore thou art inexcusable, O man, whosoever thou art that judgest: for wherein thou judgest another, thou condemnest thyself; for thou that judgest doest the same things" (Romans 2:1).

14. The Uncommon Father Seeks To Know His Children Well. Pain, doubts and fears are often hidden Seeds deep in the heart of a child. The Uncommon Father knows this. So, he questions, observes and meditates on the conduct and behavior of those he loves—his children. His knowledge of their *weaknesses* gives him the ability to *protect* them. His knowledge of their *strengths* helps him become a master at *encouragement.* His knowledge of their *friends* enables him to *anticipate* problem moments. His children matter to him more than anything on earth. He is *Uncommon.*

"Lo, children are an heritage of the Lord: and the fruit of the womb is his reward. As arrows are in the hand of a mighty man; so are children of the youth" (Psalm 127:3,4).

15. The Uncommon Father Is A Harbor, Not A Storm. The winds of competition, jealousy and rivalry blast daily across this earth. Millions of children dread the entry of their father. But, the Uncommon Father is different. He chooses to become their *harbor,* not their storm. He is their life jacket, not the hurricane that blows through the door. In his presence, life becomes restful.

"And the servant of the Lord must not strive; but be gentle unto all men, apt to teach, patient," (2 Timothy 2:24).

16. The Uncommon Father Lavishes Affection, Love And

Approval On His Children. Love restores. Affection energizes. Kindness heals. It is impossible to receive too much caring on the earth. The Uncommon Father knows this. So, he reaches, pursues and holds his children close to him. His love is like the Rock of Gibraltar, unchanging and unmoving in a world of uncertainty. Because of this, his children flourish.

"Be kindly affectioned one to another with brotherly love; in honour preferring one another" (Romans 12:10).

17. The Uncommon Father Will Not Permit Disrespect From His Children. Disrespect is cancerous. It is contagious and deadly. It will destroy the fragrance of a palace in a single day. Nothing is more destructive than words of disrespect, bitterness and retaliation. The Uncommon Father knows this. His home is his life. His family is his future. He will not tolerate, for a single moment, unholy and unwholesome words of anger directed to belittle him. Because of it, his children develop a respect for themselves, their mentors and their friends.

"Train up a child in the way he should go: and when he is old, he will not depart from it" (Proverbs 22:6).

18. The Uncommon Father Continually Evaluates The Friends His Children Choose. The Uncommon Father's children are his life. He knows how quickly wrong associates can destroy them, so he studies carefully those who surround his family. Anticipating potential damage, he stands as the Watchman of his home, guaranteeing its safety.

"And have no fellowship with the unfruitful words of darkness, but rather reprove them" (Ephesians 5:11).

19. The Uncommon Father Mentors His Children On The Danger Of Uncontrolled Anger. Anger is a powerful force when harnessed and focused appropriately. It is devastating in the life of an unwise child. Unspoken or spoken anger has filled our penitentiaries and graveyards. Millions cannot sustain friendships because of their inability to focus their anger correctly. The Uncommon Father knows this. He invests time, Wisdom and his own personal example to salvage his child from potential disaster.

"Be ye angry, and sin not: let not the sun go down upon your wrath: Neither give place to the devil" (Ephesians 4:26,27).

20. The Uncommon Father Is Unafraid To Pursue Personal Counseling. Nobody is perfect. Nobody succeeds alone. Everything arrives damaged on the earth. The Uncommon Father knows this.

When he faces a problem he cannot solve, he does not arrogantly withdraw. He reaches for wise counsel. It is the proof of his humility. Sitting at the feet of those who care, he is changed, healed and restored. He is an Uncommon Father. He reaches out, regardless of his mistakes, to set recovery in motion.

"Where no counsel is, the people fall: but in the multitude of counsellors there is safety" (Proverbs 11:14).

21. The Uncommon Father Never Quits Believing In His Children. Failure is not a conclusion. It is the half-way mark to success. The Uncommon Father knows this. Endurance is the quality of champions. He never quits praying, reaching and believing that his children are becoming great. He moves them toward their future instead of their past. His tenacity produces his desired result. He is an Uncommon Father.

"Blessed is the man that endureth temptation: for when he is tried, he shall receive the crown of life, which the Lord hath promised to them that love Him" (James 1:12).

22. The Uncommon Father Pursues Spiritual Mentorship. You Will Never Possess What You Are Unwilling To Pursue. The most important knowledge on earth is the knowledge of God. The Uncommon Father knows this. Every week, he sits in the presence of God, at the feet of a spiritual pastor. He is not too proud to recognize his limitations. His children are affected by it. Because of it, they become mentored, motivated and successful. Anyone who pursues the presence of God becomes changed.

"Not forsaking the assembling of ourselves together, as the manner of some is; but exhorting one another: and so much the more, as ye see the day approaching" (Hebrews 10:25).

23. The Uncommon Father Will Not Permit Strife In His House. Conflict distracts, destroys and divides. Strife is the door to every evil work of satan. It wounds, fragments and divides churches and homes. The Uncommon Father knows it. He exposes it and deals with it promptly. Because of this, his house becomes a place of peace and restoration.

"A soft answer turneth away wrath: but grievous words stir up anger" (Proverbs 15:1).

24. The Uncommon Father Refuses To Grieve And Offend The Holy Spirit. The Holy Spirit created you. He mentors you. In His presence, greatness is birthed. Joy is only possible in His presence. When He is offended, He withdraws. The Uncommon Father knows this. He builds his day, his business and his home around pleasuring the Holy Spirit.

"Let no corrupt communication proceed out of your mouth, but that which is good to the use of edifying, that it may minister grace unto the hearers. And grieve not the Holy Spirit of God, whereby ye are sealed unto the day of redemption" (Ephesians 4:29,30).

25. The Uncommon Father Always Tells The Truth. Always. Integrity is a force. It will outlast every lie. Deception is always exposed. God honors righteousness and honesty. The Uncommon Father knows it. He pays his bills. He does not flatter. He refuses to lie under any circumstances. He can be trusted and his home is prosperous because of it.

"Recompense to no man evil for evil. Provide things honest in the sight of all men" (Romans 12:17).

26. The Uncommon Father Is Always Accessible To His Children. Accessible means capable of being reached, used, seen or known. It simply means obtainable. The greatest need of a child is *access*. The Uncommon Father knows this. Though his schedule is full, the demands are great, he always welcomes the entry of his child into the room. His child can telephone, talk or reach him any time of the day. He is an Uncommon Father and is creating uncommon children.

"Call unto Me, and I will answer thee, and shew thee great and mighty things, which thou knowest not" (Jeremiah 33:3).

27. The Uncommon Father Teaches His Children To Respect Money. Money is important. It solves problems. Money is merely a reward for solving a problem for someone. When you solve problems, you generate finances in your life. The Uncommon Father knows this. He teaches his children the laws of prosperity, total dependency upon God, and how to use money effectively and wisely.

"Money answereth all things" (Ecclesiastes 10:19).

28. The Uncommon Father Prays For His Children Daily. Traps are everywhere. Deception can be fatal. Wrong people enter our lives daily. Every child needs an intercessor. Nobody loves children more than their parents. The Uncommon Father knows this. He also knows the power of the Holy Spirit. Each morning, he calls the names of his children to God. As their mediator, he creates the bridge between their problems and the presence of God. He is an Uncommon Father, creating an uncommon future for those He loves.

"God forbid that I should sin against the Lord in ceasing to pray for you:" (1 Samuel 12:23).

29. The Uncommon Father Is Concerned About The Quality Of Man His Daughter Chooses To Marry. The Uncommon Father is protective, concerned and wise regarding the man who enters the heart of his daughter. Knowing that he is sowing the Seed of his daughter into the vision of another man, he interrogates and evaluates the quality of that man. He is staunch, firm and militant in guarding her from a deceiver, a manipulator and user. The daughter feels this love, and because of it moves toward her future with joy and confidence. What you love, you protect.

"Lest satan should get an advantage of us: for we are not ignorant of his devices" (2 Corinthians 2:11).

30. The Uncommon Father Is The Personal Success Coach Of His Family. Everybody needs a coach. The Uncommon Father wants his children to succeed. He encourages, coaxes and inspires them like the coach of a winning football team. He is their cheerleader, their coach and their greatest fan. Because of this, his family is an uncommon family. He is an Uncommon Father.

"A wise son heareth his father's instruction: but a scorner heareth not rebuke" (Proverbs 13:1).

"Correct thy son, and he shall give thee rest; yea, he shall give delight unto thy soul" (Proverbs 29:17).

31. The Uncommon Father Sows Wisdom Continuously Into The Hearts Of His Children. Ignorance is the greatest enemy on earth. Wisdom is the principal thing. The Uncommon Father knows this and looks for opportunities to sow the Seeds of Wisdom into those he loves. He exposes his family to the greatest minds and influences of his day. His home contains "The Wisdom Room" where his family meets daily to read, study and become wise. *The future of his children depend on the Wisdom they receive.* The Uncommon Father knows this and continuously invests in their Wisdom.

"Wisdom is the principal thing;" (Proverbs 4:7).

The Wise Father Trains An Obedient Child.

RECOMMENDED BOOKS AND TAPES:
B-35   The Father's Topical Bible (378 pages/$10)
B-51   One-Minute Pocket Bible For Fathers (132 pages/$5)
B-77   The Gift Of Wisdom For Fathers (32 pages/$10)
TS-07 Secrets Of The Greatest Achievers Who Ever Lived (6 tapes/$30)

20

FEAR

Fear Is Tormenting.

Fear increases the size of your enemy *mentally*. Fear causes your hope to shrivel and die. Fear is a devastating tool of satan that has robbed millions of a victorious life.

The Israelites' journey toward Canaan has been told countless times. They left Egypt with a flurry of miracles. God had used painful and devastating situations to persuade Pharaoh. His determination to keep the Israelites in Egypt withered under the awesome power of God. Moses was a remarkable leader. His patience is legendary. The Israelites hated the days of Egyptian slavery.

At last, they were headed toward Canaan, the Land of Promise. The grapes were huge. The land was luscious. The supply was limitless.

But, there were giants in their Land of Promise.

Twelve spies were chosen to review and evaluate the land of Canaan. Ten returned full of doubt and unbelief. Two returned with great faith—Joshua and Caleb. However, when the ten spies began to talk about the size of the giants and said, "We are like grasshoppers in their sight," the hope of the Israelites died within them.

They wept all night. The faith of the two spies was totally disregarded. The Israelites forfeited the incredible promised land of Canaan.

Forty more years of wandering occurred, not because of the giants, but because of their *fear* of the giants.

▶ Giants *cannot* destroy you.

▶ *Your fear* of your giants can destroy you.

Imagine being one of the children of the Israelites. Your ear is listening at the campfire of your parents while they discuss their fear of the giants—people they had never even yet seen. They have toiled and labored as slaves. Now, they seem to have forgotten those days.

Their pain of the past is gone.

They have forgotten the tears of slavery.

Their focus is the giants—their obstacles in the Land of Promise.

What a picture of life! God has given us many promises of miracles, Harvests and supernatural blessings. Yet, the giants are

always there that *require conquering.*
> ▶ Champions are not crowned for *desiring* to be champions.
> ▶ Champions are crowned *after* they defeat *an enemy.*
> ▶ You have no right to a victory for which you have not *fought.*
> ▶ You do not have a right to anything you have not *pursued.*

Warfare is necessary for your victory.

Victory qualifies you for rewards.

Overcomers are the only people the Holy Spirit will reward in eternity. "He that overcometh, the same shall be clothed in white raiment; and I will not blot out his name out of the book of life, but I will confess his name before My Father, and before His angels" (Revelation 3:5).

"Him that overcometh will I make a pillar in the temple of My God, and he shall go no more out: and I will write upon him the name of My God, and the name of the city of My God, which is new Jerusalem, which cometh down out of heaven from My God: and I will write upon him My new name" (Revelation 3:12).

"To him that overcometh will I grant to sit with Me in My throne, even as I also overcame, and am set down with My Father in His throne" (Revelation 3:21).

Fear torments. "Fear hath torment" (1 John 4:18).

Love is an enemy of fear. When love fills your heart, fear has no place in your life. "There is no fear in love; but perfect love casteth out fear: because fear hath torment. He that feareth is not made perfect in love" (1 John 4:18).

The fruit of the Holy Spirit is love. "But the fruit of the Spirit is love, joy, peace, longsuffering, gentleness, goodness, faith," (Galatians 5:22).

So, your life in the Spirit will cause fear to dissolve and be dispelled from your life.

The disciples lost their fears after the coming of the Holy Spirit. Peter denied the Lord. Thomas doubted Him. Judas betrayed Him and committed suicide. Every disciple fled and ran away during the crucifixion. The disciples were embarrassed, humiliated, shamed and confused.

Think about it. When the maiden at the home of the high priest questioned Peter, he crumbled. Perhaps, this was the experience Jesus referred to earlier when He spoke to Peter. "Simon, Simon, behold, satan hath desired to have you, that he may sift you as wheat: But I have prayed for thee, that thy faith fail not: and when thou art converted, strengthen thy brethren" (Luke 22:31,32). Jesus warned him of an enemy. He saw satan setting the trap.

Anything close to Jesus receives attack.

Yet, Jesus truly believed that Peter would overcome every pitfall of satan. He anticipated the success of Peter. "When thou art converted." Jesus did not say..."if." He said..."when."

Then, He provided Peter *another focus.* "Strengthen your brethren." What was He saying?

▶ Stop your introspection.

▶ Do not over-analyze the attack of satan against you.

▶ Do not boast to everybody about your great ability to overcome.

Now, *focus on others.* Many are experiencing fear, unbelief and weakness like yourself. Focus on *their overcoming.*

This is the incredible work of the Holy Spirit. "For God hath not given us the spirit of fear; but of power, and of love, and of a sound mind" (2 Timothy 1:7).

The disciples did not even fear while they experienced beatings. They rejoiced and were happy that they were considered worthy to suffer for the name of Jesus. "When they had called the apostles, and beaten them, they commanded that they should not speak in the name of Jesus, and let them go. And they departed from the presence of the council, rejoicing that they were counted worthy to suffer shame for His name" (Acts 5:40,41).

The disciples intensified their obedience and evangelism after the beatings. "And daily in the temple, and in every house, they ceased not to teach and preach Jesus Christ" (Acts 5:42).

Dreams have been dashed on the Rocks of Fear for hundreds of years. Champions carrying the Seeds of Greatness within them have lost their grip on incredible goals and dreams...because of fear.

I heard someone say that a baby is born with two basic fears. But, by the time the child is 20 years old, over 172,000 fears have been documented.

14 Facts You Should Know About Fear

1. **Fear Changes Your Focus.**

2. **Fear Weakens Your Resolve, Determination And Will Power.**

3. **Fear Breaks The Golden Connection Of Choice Friendships.**

4. **Fear Has Crushed The Hopes Of A Young Man And Woman About To Be Married.**

5. **Fear Has Sabotaged A Million Promotions.**

6. **Fear Prevents You From Making Important Changes In Your Life.**

7. **Fear Wears Various Disguises.** It wraps itself in the Robe of Reality, Honesty, Caution and Logic.

8. **Fear Is A More Deceptive Enemy Than Satan.**

9. **Fear Is Within You.**

10. **Fear Stops You From Reaching—Thinking That Rejection Will Await.**

11. **Fear Stops You From Asking For Forgiveness—Afraid That Mercy Will Not Be Offered.**

12. **Fear Stops You From Admitting Your Guilt And That You Are Wrong—Afraid That Grace Will Not Be Returned.**

13. **The Holy Spirit Is An Enemy To Fear.** The Holy Spirit is the One Who sustained Jesus in the Garden of Gethsemane when He prayed concerning "the cup of suffering."

14. **The Fear Of Man Can Stop Physical Healings From Occurring In Your Body.** Look at the blind man. He cried out, "Jesus, Thou son of David, have mercy on me." The crowd around him told him to hold his peace (read Mark 10:48). But, he refused to fear the opposition of men around him. And, he received his miracle.

Do not let this happen to you today.

Come into His presence. Reach out toward the Holy Spirit. Ask Him to dispel every ounce of fear within you. Begin to thank Jesus for paying the price, making you an overcomer and interceding for you before the Father.

▶ Somebody is fighting hell for you today.

▶ Somebody will defeat fear for you today.

▶ That Somebody is the Holy Spirit.

Many fears exist: the fear of loss...failure...poverty...false accusation...sickness and disease...cancer...rejection. But, you have a Friend, the Comforter, the Holy Spirit.

Always remember, the Holy Spirit can eliminate all fear of man.

Our Prayer Together...

"Heavenly Father, I boldly come to You in the Name of Jesus. You have commanded me to ask largely of You, anything regarding the work of Your hands. Today, I ask You for holy boldness like the disciples experienced during the days of the outpouring of the Holy Spirit. Father, I reject fear. I receive faith. Your love fills my heart today. I know You love me. You know that I love You. So, I walk as an overcomer today. In the Name of Jesus, I agree with Your Word that fear cannot remain in me. I open the door of my heart to faith, confidence and full trust in You. You will not disappoint me. Thank You for the promise of victory. You are my victorious Healer and Best Friend. In Jesus' name. Amen."

❧ 21 ❧
FOCUS

━━━➤❖◄━━━

The Only Reason Men Fail Is Because Of Broken Focus.

While traveling around the world for more than thirty years and speaking more than fourteen thousand times, I have listened to the details of the personal battles and conflicts of many hurting people. And as I have listened, I have learned a very important truth: An important goal of satan is to simply break the focus of God's people from off of their Assignments. Focus is anything that consumes your time, energy, finance and attention. So if satan can blur the focus of your Assignment, he can master you. And if he can master you, he can bring pain to the heart of God, Who is his only true enemy.

How important is your focus?

Listen to the words of God concerning those who would tempt His people to go to another god:

"If thy brother, the son of thy mother, or thy son, or thy daughter, or the wife of thy bosom, or thy friend, which is as thine own soul, entice thee secretly, saying, Let us go and serve other gods, which thou hast not known, thou, nor thy fathers; Namely, of the gods of the people which are round about you, nigh unto thee, or far off from thee, from the one end of the earth even unto the other end of the earth; Thou shalt not consent unto him, nor hearken unto him; neither shall thine eye pity him, neither shalt thou spare, neither shalt thou conceal him: But thou shalt surely kill him; thine hand shall be first upon him to put him to death, and afterwards the hand of all the people. And thou shalt stone him with stones, that he die; because he hath sought to thrust thee away from the Lord thy God, which brought thee out of the land of Egypt, from the house of bondage" (Deuteronomy 13:6-10).

Now listen to how *Jesus* addressed *broken focus* in the New Testament:

"And if thy right eye offend thee, pluck it out, and cast it from thee: for it is profitable for thee that one of thy members should perish, and not that thy whole body should be cast into hell. And if thy right hand offend thee, cut it off, and cast it from thee: for it is profitable for thee that one of thy members should perish, and not that thy whole body should be cast into hell" (Matthew 5:29,30).

Jesus encouraged *His disciples* to keep *their focus* on the kingdom of God. He assured them that their financial provisions and everything they needed would be produced through absolute focus upon Him:

"But seek ye first the kingdom of God, and His righteousness; and all these things shall be added unto you" (Matthew 6:33).

How do you destroy someone's goal? Give him another goal. How do you destroy another's dream? You give him another dream. Why? It fragments his focus. It dilutes his energy. So to avoid this in your Assignment, there are twelve Wisdom principles on Focus that can make a real difference in your life: *see pages 57-59 on "Distractions."

6 Keys That Will Help You Protect Your Focus

1. Recognize That Broken Focus Will Destroy Your Dreams. Distraction from your Assignment will create an unending parade of tragedies and disasters in your life.

2. Take Personal Responsibility. Be the gatekeeper of your eyes, ears and heart. Nobody else can fully protect you. You will be protected by God, as you yield yourself to Him.

3. Control The Music And Teaching That Enters Your Ears. What You Hear Determines What You Feel. What you hear also determines what you fear.

"And all Israel shall hear, and fear, and shall do no more any such wickedness as this is among you" (Deuteronomy 13:11).

4. Keep Continuous Praise On Your Lips And Music Throughout Your Home. I keep music playing twenty-four hours a day on my property and in my house. The rooms throughout my home have sound, and there is music to the Holy Spirit being sung and played every minute. I have twenty-four speakers on the trees in my seven-acre yard. I am determined to protect my focus.

5. Starve Wrong Friendships. Wrong friends do not feed, fuel or fertilize the total focus of your Assignment. So, let those friendships die. Samson did not have to date everyone to get his hair cut. It only required one wrong person to destroy his future.

6. Pursue And Permit Only Those Relationships That Increase Your Focus On Your Assignment. It was late one night in southern Florida. The service had ended, and several ministers wanted to go to a restaurant. As we sat there, I listened to their conversation. I have two major interests in my life: learning and teaching. And both must take place continuously for me to have pleasure!

So, I sat there and listened as everyone discussed ball games, politics and tragedies. I kept listening for worthy Wisdom Keys that might be imparted, and for important questions that might be asked. But neither took place. Several times I even attempted to change the direction of the conversation, but it seemed to be ignored. The Holy Spirit was not the focus, and I was too tired to force the conversation in an appropriate direction. So, I quietly stood and said, "I must leave. God bless each of you." Then I left. I wish I could have that kind of courage every year of my lifetime, every day of my life.

Focus Is The Master Key To The Golden Door Of Success.

RECOMMENDED BOOKS AND TAPES:
B-91 The Leadership Secrets Of Jesus (196 pages/$10)

When You Replay
The Past,
You Poison
The Present.

-MIKE MURDOCK

≈ 22 ≈

FORGETTING THE PAST

━━━━━➤∘⋘━━━━━

Forgetting Is A Weapon That God Gives Us.
It is a tool given to us by God.
Forgetting is not the inability to recall or retrieve a memory. It is not amnesia. Joseph saw his brothers, he remembered.

He knew who they were, but he retrieved the memory without pain because something had replaced the pain, and that was the purpose for the pain. Purpose was bigger to him than the pain. The purpose for it. He said, "What you meant for evil, God meant for good. You meant to destroy me. God used that to salvage all of you."

How do you forget? You forget by displacement. You displace that memory with something. Joseph had this picture of his brothers treating him wrong. It was wrapped with pain. *So, he wrapped something else around it that covered up the pain and that was the purpose.* There was a reason for that. And the reason has a benefit that the pain cannot eradicate and do away with. There is a purpose.

20 Facts About The Weapon Of Forgetting

1. Forgetting Is The Hidden Weapon That Wins The Battles. Against satan...it is the hidden weapon. It is the secret weapon. It is the weapon that has kept marriages together. It is the weapon that has won the battles, won every fight. It is the weapon that almost nobody is willing to use in a war. It is the weapon almost nobody remembers in a war. It is the weapon almost nobody remembers in conflict...the weapon of forgetting.

Peter almost lost his life...he was bitter, he was crying. But he used the weapon of forgetting, he was restored. He became the great preacher on the day of Pentecost.

Judas forgot the weapon. He committed suicide. He could not forget his own mistake, could not forgive himself, could not walk away.

Forgetting, we think, is a sign of weakness. We think of forgetting as concession. Giving up something. Okay, I will forget. I am going to do this for you. We forget it is a weapon whereby we win a battle.

Whoever forgets wins.

2. When You Forget, You Win Your Own Battles, And Then, Enable Others To Win Theirs. Think of the time that we have been fragmented. I thought of it today...as a boss...we think of being fragmented. We say, "Well, but they have not forgotten." They have got to find their weapon. But you can do the forgetting and you win your battle, and then enable them to win theirs.

3. Forgetting Keeps People Together. *Think of the times that we have all made mistakes.*

What has kept us together? That weapon of forgetting.

A wife and husband, their home is like a storm, if you have seen the movie, *Twister.* Their home is like a twister. It is emotional. In the home, they are yelling, they are screaming, there are accusations, there is fussing, there is anger. And suddenly, the woman reaches inside of her purse, her heart, and pulls out the weapon of forgetting. It subsides. Love is restored. An hour later, they are eating lunch together. The home is kept together, because she used a weapon... forgetting as a weapon.

A teenage daughter screams at her mother, "I hate home. I can't wait to leave." And the mother reaches inside of her, pulls out the weapon of forgetting, reaches over and pulls her up close, and says, "I brought you into this world. I'll fight every devil for you, baby. You can't make me quit loving you." "...Forgetting those things which are behind," (Philippians 3:13). "Remember ye not the former things, neither consider the things of old" (Isaiah 43:18).

A church is about to splinter. A member has been angry, and a pastor goes to that member and says, "I love you. I prayed for you to come into my life. I don't know what is wrong, but those things are past." And all the anger and the bitter things that were spoken, he gets the weapon out of his arsenal called forgetting. And the member stays. The church is kept together and restored.

4. Deliberately Use The Weapon Of Forgetting To End The Conflict. *Deliberately use this weapon to win war, knowing that when you use that weapon, you will give birth.* First you will end conflict. You will end confusion. You will end unproductivity because unforgiveness is exhausting. It demands your repeated attention. Unforgiveness means you have to continuously work. Some of you notice, you even have to work on remembering some things.

5. Forgetting Is A Weapon That Hell Dreads For You To Use. It is how nations can get along. It is how people can get along. It is not a concession. It is not something you give up. It is not something you lost. Forgetting is a weapon that hell dreads for you to use. Use it today. Use it frequently. Use it with joy. Use it with purpose.

6. There Is No Hope Of Succeeding In Life Without The Weapon Of Forgetting. *I do not believe there is a hope of us succeeding without the weapon of forgetting.* I do not think a family will be sustained without using the weapon of forgetting.

Success requires forgetting offenses. Forgetting your own mistakes. Forgetting your own flaws. Forgetting the mistakes of those close to you. Forgetting attacks.

7. God Uses The Weapon Of Forgetting To Get You Into His Family And Keep You There. *It is what has made God...the Bible says our sins are in the sea of forgetfulness.* The Bible says as far as the east is from the west He has thrown our sins behind His back.

"He hath not dealt with us after our sins; nor rewarded us according to our iniquities. For as the heaven is high above the earth, so great is His mercy toward them that fear Him. As far as the east is from the west, so far hath He removed our transgressions from us. Like as a father pitieth his children, so the Lord pitieth them that fear Him" (Psalm 103:10-13).

8. Forget The Past And Give Birth To Your Future. "Brethren, I count not myself to have apprehended: but this one thing I do, forgetting those things which are behind, and reaching forth unto those things which are before, I press toward the mark for the prize of the high calling of God in Christ Jesus" (Philippians 3:13,14).

Unforgiveness is exhausting. Useless. Unproductive. It takes you away from what you are really wanting. Even when you have got an enemy and they have done you wrong, learn from it. Retrieve information from it, and then give yourself to your future.

9. God Uses The Weapon Of Forgetting To Keep Us In Contact With Him. "I, even I, am He that blotteth out thy transgressions for Mine own sake, and will not remember thy sins. Put Me in remembrance: let us plead together: declare thou, that thou mayest be justified" (Isaiah 43:25,26).

So, I am going to have to use that same weapon to keep relationships restored. Keep breathing life into them.

10. The Weapon Of Forgetting Brings Victory. Joseph became second in command because he chose to forget the injustices of the past.

Jesus forgot and received millions.

Thousands of marriages are healed today because somebody found in their armory the weapon of forgetting.

11. Forgetting Is An Instant Weapon You Can Use To Get Immediate Results. It is an instant weapon that you can use instantly...and it is your choice.

12. Nobody Can Keep You From Using The Weapon Of Forgetting. Your enemies cannot stop you from using that weapon.

It did not stop Jesus from using the weapon when Peter denied that he even knew Jesus. There is Joseph...his brothers hated him... despised him, but it did not stop him from using the weapon.

13. When You Forget, God Forgets And Blesses. "With the merciful thou wilt shew thyself merciful;" (Psalm 18:25).

"Blessed are the merciful: for they shall obtain mercy" (Matthew 5:7).

"Be ye therefore merciful, as your Father also is merciful. Judge not, and ye shall not be judged: condemn not, and ye shall not be condemned: forgive, and ye shall be forgiven:" (Luke 6:36,37).

Joseph named two of his sons...one Manasseh and one Ephraim. The word Manasseh means to forget. The word Ephraim means to be blessed, prosperous, bountiful, fruitful. He named Manasseh first, before he named Ephraim. Ephraim was after his forgetting, after Manasseh. He had to forget and then God began to bless. And he used the sequence of naming his sons, I think, in a strategic and obvious way. He did not say if God will bless me, I will be able to forget. He said, no, my forgetting unlocks my blessing. My forgetting unlocks the door to my blessing.

"I have surely heard Ephraim bemoaning himself thus; Thou hast chastised me, and I was chastised, as a bullock unaccustomed to the yoke: turn thou me, and I shall be turned; for thou art the Lord my God. Surely after that I was turned, I repented; and after that I was instructed, I smote upon my thigh: I was ashamed, yea, even confounded, because I did bear the reproach of my youth. Is Ephraim my dear son? is he a pleasant child? for since I spake against him, I do earnestly remember him still: therefore my bowels are troubled for him; I will surely have mercy upon him, saith the Lord....for I will forgive their iniquity, and I will remember their sin no more" (Jeremiah 31:18-20,34).

14. Forgetting Does Not Erase The Memory. *Forgetting is not the erasure of a memory.* It is adding something to it that obliterates that. God has a purpose. God has a reason. God has a product involved.

Paul wrote to Philemon and said, "Onesimus was an unworthy servant." Onesimus was the slave for a friend of Paul's. Years later Onesimus runs away from his master and gets locked into the same prison as Paul. They get to meet each other and know each other. Paul writes Onesimus' master, who is his close friend, a letter about Onesimus, to let Onesimus' master take him back as a brother, not as a slave. But he said this thing could work for both of us, because before he was an unprofitable servant, but now, he is not a servant. He is our brother.

15. Do Not Ever Forget The Weapon Of Forgetting. If you are going to remember anything, remember to forget.

So, when you have shot your arrows and your enemy keeps coming, you have shot the arrow of praise and you have shot the arrow of Wisdom and you have shot every arrow, say, "There is one more." And no enemy can withstand the weapon of forgetting.

16. Forget By Remembering How God Has Forgotten Your Offenses. Joseph used forgetting because he remembered God had a purpose, that all pain can be productive.

Jesus learned obedience through the things He suffered. Paul said if we suffer with Him, we will reign with Him. So, He saw purpose in the pain. He saw a future after the pain. He saw something past that.

"Remember ye not the former things. I'll do a new thing" (see Isaiah 43).

Now, how do I forget? We call it the Law of Displacement. How do I forget that? By remembering something else. Remember Calvary. Remember your future. Remember that God forgot your sins. Remember that God has forgotten your offenses. And the last thing you want to be like is the servant who was forgiven a mountain of debt.

It was impossible for that servant to repay the debt and the man he owed came to him and said, "You're forgiven." And the man turned and went to someone who owed him and began to look for him to kill him. He had him locked up. And the man who had forgiven his debt came to him and said, "How dare you. How dare you not duplicate what I have done for you."

"Then his lord, after that he had called him, said unto him, O thou wicked servant, I forgave thee all that debt, because thou desiredst me: Shouldest not thou also have had compassion on thy fellowservant, even as I had pity on thee? And his lord was wroth, and delivered him to the tormentors, till he should pay all that was due unto him" (Matthew 17:32-34).

17. Through God's Word, Through Praise And Through Forgetting, We Are Going On. I believe it was the secret of Paul who held the coats of the men who stoned Stephen, and watched Stephen bleed and his face come apart with strips of flesh, bruises. People stoned him until he was covered, and he died. And Stephen said, "Forgive them. They do not know what they are doing."

And Saul...I think that is why he could accept prison. "What You Make Happen For Others God Will Make Happen For You" (Ephesians 6:8). He put people in prison. He got prison.

18. The Blood Of Jesus Is The Weapon God Used To Enable Him To Forget Our Sins And Iniquities. In Malachi, when the period of Maccabees, the kings that ruled Malachi 400 years and Matthew, it was so dark during those 400 years...the priesthood was so deteriorated that God was incensed. And suddenly, Matthew breaks forth and God says, "I've got a new plan. I've got a better covenant. We're going to forget all of that and start with Calvary and the blood, and you don't have to have any blood of bulls and goats and sheep and lambs and meal and pigeons and turtledoves. There's one sacrifice."

And when you see Jesus hanging on Calvary, there is the weapon that God used. He found a way to forget. Forget our sins...our mistakes.

"But in those sacrifices there is a remembrance again made of sins every year. For it is not possible that the blood of bulls and of goats should take away sins. Wherefore when He cometh into the world, He saith, Sacrifice and offering Thou wouldest not, but a body hast Thou prepared Me: In burnt offerings and sacrifices for sin Thou hast had no pleasure. Then said I, Lo, I come (in the volume of the book it is written of Me,) to do Thy will, O God. Above when He said, Sacrifice and offering and burnt offerings and offering for sin Thou wouldest not, neither hadst pleasure therein; which are offered by the law; Then said He, Lo, I come to do Thy will, O God. He taketh away the first, that He may establish the second. This is the covenant that I will make with them after those Days, saith the Lord, I will put My laws into their hearts, and in their minds will I write them; And their sins and iniquities will I remember no more" (Hebrews 10:3-9,16,17).

God has every reason to remember our sins. He has every day to remember them. Not only that, He has us to keep fertilizing the memory. And every time we make a mistake, we sustain and keep, and

repeat and perpetuate, and give life and breathe life into something...
and He takes the weapon again.

19. Forgetting Is A Permanent Weapon God Has Put In Your Ammunition Chest. The weapon of forgetting is a permanent tool He has put in your ammunition chest. So when nothing else seems to work in your life, say, "I'm going to get the weapon nobody's been using." Take out the weapon of forgetting.

20. Your Enemy Is Powerless Against The Weapon Of Forgetting. Your enemy...is powerless against the weapon of forgetting. Hallelujah. Hallelujah. This is almost a book, isn't it? It is almost a book..."Mentor's Manna Library On Forgetting."

After the weapon of forgetting, it annihilates yesterday and gives birth to a future.

Our Prayer Together...

"Father, Thank You for the weapon of forgetting that obliterates the memory of the enemy. That breaks his arrows in two when it shoots memories of yesterday toward us. It is a defensive weapon. It is the weapon that satan is helpless against.

"Thank You for forgetting, forgetting our sins because You have remembered our desired end. You said You knew that they were but flesh. You knew men are but dust. And You had a conclusion that You had decided. So, You refused to let the events en route toward the conclusion to blind You, to stop You. Thank You, Father, for Your obsession with our conclusion. Thank You for Your obsession with our conquering. You keep looking toward our end result. No wonder You promised the overcomer in Revelation so many rewards.

"Holy Spirit, You are the One that brings things to our remembrance, so bring to our remembrance the weapon of forgetting. The purpose of memory is to retrieve an understanding of our weaponry. Thank You for the weapon of forgetting. We will not go back to yesterday. We will not revisit yesterday's sorrows. We will not build a monument to yesterday's pain. We build tomorrow.

"Father, it is the difference between a Judas and a Peter. One was suicide, the other was a successful preacher. Because one used the weapon of forgetting. Thank You for making yesterday's diary unreadable, blurred, destroyed, eradicated from our life. Amen."

Greatness Is
The Willingness
To Embrace
Uncommon Responsibility.

-MIKE MURDOCK

❧ 23 ❧

GREATNESS

Greatness Is Usually Camouflaged.

Few recognized Jesus "in swaddling clothes" in a manger. Few recognized Him in the Temple as the Son of God.

Two thieves died next to Christ at the crucifixion. One did *not* recognize Who He was and cursed Him. The other *recognized* Him...and requested "...remember me" (Luke 23:42).

Several years ago, a man that I respect and admire very much gave me this secret.

"Mike, never permit greatness in your presence without celebrating it, recognizing it and acknowledging it in some way." Then, I observed him. If an incredible athlete was eating in the same restaurant, my friend would write him a note of gratitude or even pick up his restaurant tab on the way out. Today, my friend is seen in magazines with the greatest names in human influence. Kings, presidents of nations and the greatest leaders of our world are with him on a regular basis.

He cultivated the habit of recognizing greatness whenever he saw it.

The scriptures are full of examples of greatness.

Some had great *Faith.*

Some had great *Endurance.*

Some had great *Gifts.*

Some had great *Influence.*

Some had great *Wisdom.*

Jonathan recognized greatness in David. Some sons often see greatness overlooked by their fathers. Saul never saw it in David.

The servant of Abraham discerned the greatness of Rebekah. He had asked the Lord to reveal the mate of Isaac. "And let it come to pass, that the damsel to whom I shall say, Let down thy pitcher, I pray thee, that I may drink; and she shall say, Drink, and I will give thy camels drink also: let the same be she that Thou hast appointed for Thy servant Issac;" (Genesis 24:14).

Ruth discerned the greatness of Naomi. It linked her to Boaz, the financial champion of Bethlehem.

Abigail recognized the greatness of David. He avoided the

bloodshed of Nabal because of it. Abigail later became the wife of David.

Elisha knew greatness when he got in the presence of it. So, he asked Elijah to let him stay by his side and reap the benefits of that mantle of anointing.

Joshua knew greatness when he got in the presence of it. That is why he called Moses the servant of the Lord and followed his instructions even when it was contrary to his own heart.

One of the greatest evangelists that God ever placed in Christianity told me something interesting one day. He related how he had often been in the presence of young ministers who had just entered their ministry. During two hour lunches or times together, not one question was ever asked him relating to the healing river of ministry that flowed through him and how to make it happen in their own ministry and lives.

If there is any cry that ought to erupt from our hearts during these days, it should be the cry for God to give us the ability to recognize greatness.

Recognition Of Greatness Guarantees Consistent Access To It.

8 Facts You Should Remember About Greatness

1. Greatness Is Not The Absence Of Weakness. Everyone has weaknesses. Job said, "Great men are not always wise:" (Job 32:9).

2. Greatness Is Often Camouflaged. All Men Fall, The Great Ones Get Back Up. When you think of greatness, do not think of unmarred, unscarred, unbattered and perfect human specimens. Everyone has scars—invisible or visible. Scarred generals inspire the troops.

3. Fathers Sometimes See Greatness Ignored By Their Sons. David recognized the unforgettable loyalty of Jonathan.

4. What You Respect, You Will Attract. What You Respect Will Come Toward You. What You Do Not Respect Will Move Away From You. It does not matter if it is a miracle, a dog or a person!

5. Greatness Is When Someone Walks Away From The Temptation Of Pleasure To Protect Their Integrity. Joseph never sought to retaliate against Potiphar's wife. On the other side of the door of pain is promotion.

6. Greatness Is When Someone Willingly Confronts An Enemy Nobody Else Wants To Fight. David was an example. When King Saul and David's own brothers were afraid, David willingly confronted their enemy, Goliath.

7. We Rarely Discern Greatness In Others Accurately.

Almost every conclusion we have about others is flawed, inadequate and insufficient. We quit on others, because we cannot see *what* God *is seeing.* God has not quit. He placed something inside them that we cannot see.

8. Those Closest To You Often Have An Incredible Future. It might intimidate you if you knew how great it really is. In fact, you would probably be investing more time and energy in knowing them if you really could see what God is planning to do through their lives!

13 Keys In Discerning Greatness In Others

1. Look Twice At Your Brothers And Sisters Again. (Think of Joseph!) The brother who agitates you might become Prime Minister. So, create memories that will foster *respect.*

2. Look Past Outward Appearances. The thin wall of clothing is so deceptive. Remember Ruth? She is a peasant bowed low, gathering barley. Her stringy hair and tattered clothes *conceal* her *future.* She will become the future wife of her boss, Boaz! She will someday sign your paycheck. So, leave those *handfuls of purpose to bless her* (see Ruth 2:16).

3. Look Beyond The Distraction Of Beauty. Remember the beautiful Queen Esther? Consider the fool, Haman. He has misjudged the beautiful woman sitting by the king. She knows something he does not know. Within her is the knowledge that will bring about his death. It is just a matter of time. You never know how much is really occurring inside the minds of those around you.

4. Take A Second Look At The Person Others Are Despising. Remember Jesus at the crucifixion? Thousands are jeering. Look twice. His eyes are still focused. His voice is still clear. He is *the Son of God.* One thief on the cross next to Him looks again at Jesus, and enters Eternity forgiven. In minutes the thief will be with Him in Paradise. "And he said unto Jesus, Lord, remember me when Thou comest into Thy kingdom. And Jesus said...To day shalt thou be with Me in paradise" (Luke 23:42,43).

5. Look Again At A Situation You Do Not Yet Understand. Imagine Mary, the Virgin Mother of Jesus. See her huddled over on the small donkey? The blanket is covering a small child. The child is Jesus, the Son of God, Who will give His life for this world. She needs a place to sleep. Someone has the opportunity of a lifetime to bless the Son of God.

6. Look Again At Someone Who Appears Out Of Place. Picture David, the teenage shepherd, talking to his soldier brothers on the battlefield. He has a slingshot. In minutes Goliath will fall dead at his feet. *The only thing between insignificance and fame was his enemy* (see 1 Samuel 17:41-51).

7. Look Again At A Helpless Situation. Imagine the little boy in the crowd following Jesus. See him in the corner? Look again. His lunch basket contains five loaves and two fishes that will feed this entire crowd within the next 30 minutes (see John 6:8-13).

8. Look Again At An Unreasonable And Illogical Request. Imagine the scenario Joseph created with his brother in the palace. I can imagine the shock when Joseph told his brother to bring Benjamin to him. Look at this man again. He is giving you an instruction. Bring back your baby brother. He wants to see him face to face. Do not get angry. This man is the brother you wronged but mercy will flow from him *as you complete his instruction.* He is capable of providing for you and your family the rest of your lives. He is offering to do it. Follow his instruction (see Genesis 42:18-24).

9. Look Again At An Enemy That Appears Unchangeable. Imagine Saul the tormentor of the church. Note his passion. He is dead wrong, but he does not know it yet. The same Holy Spirit Who empowered you to preach today, Stephen, is looking at this man. God is about to throw him on the ground (give him a new heart) and make him blind for three days. That man holding the coats of those stoning you is only hours from a dramatic transformation. Soon he will become the apostle of apostles, the Apostle Paul! The man attacking your anointing is about to receive the same victory and breakthrough!

10. Look At Joseph. He had dreams. He could interpret them. He knew their value. He saw greatness in discerning the future. He was articulate in his description. He had the integrity, honesty and openness to share it with his own brothers. *Yet his own brothers never sensed what destiny was on the head of their baby brother.* Yet, he was the master key to their future survival. He was the only reason they would have a future. He would provide for their father in his old age. His Wisdom would be pursued by the Pharaoh of Egypt. He would design the food plan for millions of people. Yet, his own brothers never grasped it.

11. Look At Those On Your Job. Someone in your office has seen something you have never seen. They contain information you have not yet tapped into. *What is it?*

12. Look Twice At The Mentors Who Are Crossing Your Life. What have they accomplished? What battles have they won? What hurdles have they jumped? What difficult rivers have they crossed? What mountains have they tunneled through? *They have survived. How?*

Interrogate. Interview. Extract information from their lives.

What *financial* devastation have they tasted and overcome? What *false accusations* have been hurled, and yet they withstood them? What *misunderstandings* have occurred, and yet they kept their focus? What *traps* have they miraculously avoided?

▶ Every mentor has *defeated a different enemy.*

▶ Every mentor uses *different weaponry.*

▶ Every mentor has a *different focus.*

13. Look At King Saul. He was a very foolish man in many ways. But, he had enough sense to know when the mantle of greatness was on a shepherd boy. He knew that it was more than a miracle slingshot that brought Goliath down. He quickly perceived that a supernatural hand was upon the shoulder of the young shepherd. He saw the power of his music. It did not take him long to discover satanic spirits were uncomfortable when David played the harp. Even King Saul *pursued* greatness, when he felt inferior to everything around him.

12 Keys In Recognizing Personal Greatness

1. You Contain An Uncommon Treasure. It is invisible but irrefutable. It is your difference, your dominant gift and the magnet drawing others.

It is your *greatness.* "But we have this treasure in earthen vessels, that the excellency of the power may be of God, and not of us" (2 Corinthians 4:7).

God knows it. He created you. He has always known the invisible purpose for which you were created.

2. Your Assignment Was Decided In Your Mother's Womb. "Before I formed thee in the belly I knew thee; and before thou camest forth out of the womb I sanctified thee, and I ordained thee a prophet unto the nations" (Jeremiah 1:5).

3. You Are Not An Accident Waiting To Happen. "I will praise Thee; for I am fearfully and wonderfully made: marvellous are Thy works; and that my soul knoweth right well" (Psalm 139:14).

4. Everything Inside You Is Known, Treasured And Intended For Full Use By Your Creator. "My substance was not hid from Thee, when I was made in secret, and wondrously wrought in the lowest parts of the earth" (Psalm 139:15).

5. Your Flaws Do Not Necessarily Prevent God From Using You. They exist to motivate your pursuit of Him. "Thine eyes did see my substance, yet being unperfect; and in Thy book all my members were written, which in continuance were fashioned, when as yet there was none of them" (Psalm 139:16).

6. Your Very Existence Excites God. "How precious also are Thy thoughts unto me, O God! how great is the sum of them! If I should count them, they are more in number than the sand: when I awake, I am still with Thee" (Psalm 139:17,18).

Picture an author exulting over his book. The book exists. The author created it. He is excited about it whether anyone else is or not. Imagine a composer, exhilarated over a completed song. He knew its beginning and its ending. Its potential excites him.

7. Your Very Presence Energizes God. He saw your beginning and His desired conclusion.

▶ God is looking at something within you *that you have never seen.*

▶ God is looking at something inside you that even *satan cannot discern.*

▶ God is looking at something you contain that *you have not yet discovered.*

▶ God will tell you secrets satan will never hear.

▶ The mercies of God have not been wasted on you and your ministry. He has big plans for your life.

8. The Forgiveness Of God Has Validated Your Life. You are becoming a *monument* and trophy of His grace. *God boasts about you and your life to every demon who enters His presence* (see Job 1:8).

▶ You are looking at your *beginning.*

▶ God is looking at your *end.*

▶ You are studying your *flaws.*

▶ God is studying your *future.*

▶ You are studying your *enemies.*

▶ God is studying your *eventuality.*

▶ You are *awaiting* your *destiny.*

▶ God is awaiting *your discovery of it.*

9. Never Consult Those Who Have Not Discovered The Greatness Within You. Their focus will be different, their conclusions inaccurate, their counsel useless.

10. Stay In The Presence Of The One Who Created You. You will never quit feeling good about yourself when you stay in His presence. He is looking at something He considers to be remarkable. He planted this greatness within you while you were yet in your mother's womb.

David discerned his greatness and willingly confronted Goliath.

Soldiers saw brashness; the Holy Spirit saw *boldness.*

Soldiers saw anger; God saw justice.

Joseph discerned his greatness.

His brothers saw pride; God saw *passion.*

The brothers saw a threat; God saw a *throne*.

11. The Opinion And Observation Of Others Is Not The Foundation For Your Greatness. So, stop pursuing their approval. God is looking at something inside you they *cannot see, refuse* to see and may *never* see.

The brothers of Jesus could not discern *His Divinity*.

The brothers of Joseph could not *interpret his dream* properly.

The brothers of David could not *imagine him* as a soldier.

The friends of Job could not discern the satanic scenario before his crisis.

Haman could not even *discern* the nationality of Esther.

Nobody is completely accurate in their assessment of you. *Nobody*.

Your flaws are *much less* than they imagine.

Your greatness is *far greater* than they will ever discern.

12. The Holy Spirit Alone Has Accurately Assessed Your Future, Your Passion And The Willingness Of Your Heart To Become Great. That is why He keeps reaching, pursuing and developing you in the midst of every attack and crisis.

God never *gives up* on you.

God never *quits looking at you*.

God never *changes His plans* toward you.

God never quits believing in your future.

Remember this continuously, God is seeing something inside you that keeps Him excited and involved. It is something nobody else can see.

Find Your Greatness.
It is One of the Secrets of The Uncommon Life.

RECOMMENDED BOOKS AND TAPES:
B-74 The Assignment (The Dream And The Destiny) Vol. 1 (176 pages/$10)
B-75 The Assignment (The Anointing And The Adversity) Vol. 2 (192 pages/$10)
B-97 The Assignment (The Trials And The Triumphs) Vol. 3 (161 pages/$10)
B-98 The Assignment (The Pain And The Passion) Vol. 4 (144 pages/$10)

Men Do Not Decide
Their Future.
They Decide Their Habits
And Their Habits Decide
Their Future.

-MIKE MURDOCK

❧ 24 ❧

HABITS

Great Men Simply Have Great Habits.

A well known billionaire said, "I arrive at my office at 7:00 a.m. It is a habit." Recently a best selling novelist who has sold over one million books said, "I get up at the same time every morning. I start writing at 8:00 a.m. And I quit at 4:00 each afternoon. I do it every day. It is a habit."

11 Facts About Your Habits

1. **Habit Is A Gift From God.** *It simply means anything you do twice becomes easier.* It is the Creator's key in helping you succeed.

Jesus stayed busy. He traveled. He prayed for the sick. He taught and ministered. He supervised His disciples. He spoke to large crowds. However, He had an important custom and habit. "And He came to Nazareth, where He had been brought up: AND, AS HIS CUSTOM WAS, He went into the synagogue on the sabbath day, and stood up for to read" (Luke 4:16).

2. **Uncommon People Do Daily What Common People Only Do Occasionally.** Daniel prayed three times a day (see Daniel 6:10). The psalmist prayed seven times daily (see Psalm 119:164). The disciples of Jesus met on the first day of each week (see Acts 20:7).

3. **Habits Are Stronger Than Desires.** Look in the eyes of a drug addict and you will know that. Look in the eyes of an alcoholic that wishes he did not succumb to the bottle, but his habit has taken over.

A habit is a good word. Discipline is a good word, but they are two distinct and different things.

4. **The Purpose Of Discipline Is To Birth A Habit.** *It takes 30 days to birth a habit.* You have to do something 30 consecutive days at the same time to birth a habit. Some of you are going through your life trying to be disciplined, and you cannot. Discipline only needs to be 21 to 30 days. And then you birth a habit, and then a habit takes over.

5. **Everything You Are Doing Today...Is Becoming A Habit.** Look at the loose change on your dresser. Where did you place it? You have probably placed it there every morning or night.

Look at your bed. If it has stayed unmade today, you probably left it that way yesterday. If you make it this morning...you will probably make it tomorrow morning.

What you do first every morning...is habitual.

Who did you telephone first this morning? It is probably who you think about calling first...every morning.

Everything in your life is a habit.

If you ate breakfast this morning...it is probably an habitual thing you do every morning.

What you read first everyday...is probably what you read first every morning.

If you do something different every single morning...you may think you do not have a habit...but, your habit is doing the first thing "that crosses your mind."

Whatever you put off every morning...is probably something you put off every morning.

Where did you lay your clothes after removing them last night? Probably the same place...you always do!

I could not find my microcassette this morning.

I looked around at several places...my briefcase, etc.

As I glanced in my closet, I noticed it on top of some socks in a drawer. Had I broken a habit? Not really. You see, one of my habits is to lay whatever is in my hand close to me when I am doing another task. When I was hanging up some clothes, I simply laid my microcassette there...the habit of "convenience"...was stronger than the habit of placing it back in my briefcase or pocket.

One habit will usually override another habit...in certain situations.

6. Your Habits Are Creating Your Future...Problems Or Pleasures. *Whatever you are doing today...habitually...is creating a marvelous pleasure in your future...or a problem.*

7. You Can Break A Bad Habit. *Some habits are easier to break than others.*

Breaking a habit will require your total focus...and a reason and benefit for doing so.

Some habits seem almost impossible to break.

8. You Can Only Break A Strong Habit When There Is A Strong Reason Or Benefit To Do So. Many who felt it impossible to break the habit of smoking...did so immediately through great pain...or when a doctor told them they were going to die in six weeks if they did not.

9. What You Consider A Bad Habit...Another May Not. I have a habit of leaving my bed unmade...*Why?*

I have lived my whole life in hotels and motels...where maids come in and change the sheets. That is all I know.

And...I sleep in one place...without "tearing up" the bed!

10. The Habits Of Those You Love May Sometimes Be In Total Opposition To Your Own Habits. That is why it is hard for us to understand other people and their "unwillingness" to make changes. It may be the putting down of the seat of a toilet for a man, and his wife cannot understand it...but it is a habit.

11. Your Habits Determine The Kinds Of Friends You Develop. If you have a habit of going to a local gym, your friends are probably going to be those in the gym...or those who admire you for going and want to be a part of it.

If you have a habit of drinking every evening from 7:00-9:00...your buddies are going to be those that drink with you.

When you choose your habits, you choose your friends.

When you choose your friends, you will choose your habits.

12 Daily Habits That Will Bring You To Uncommon Greatness

1. The Habit Of Rest. When you are rested, you assess life totally differently and accurately.

▶ You will assess your friends accurately.

▶ You will assess your enemies accurately.

▶ You will address others appropriately.

▶ You will plan logically.

Tired Eyes Rarely See A Bright Future.

When Fatigue Walks In Faith Walks Out.

2. The Habit Of Health Consciousness. Eat only those things that build your strength and energy, etc.

Drink water continuously. It is the second best thing you can do each day.

Take deep breaths and breathe properly.

Walk one hour a day. It will revolutionize your life...your emotions...your focus.

Every day that you move toward health, you increase your joy, your peace and your well-being.

Be ruthless in asserting your posture and position on health.

3. The Habit Of Order. Order means the accurate arrangement of things.

The purpose of order is to create comfort. When you walk into a room where there is order, you feel comfortable and do not want to leave.

When you walk into a room where there is disorder, you feel

discomfort and want to leave.

You must build the habit. I forget how many janitors and people they have working at Disney World, but it is incredible how you can hardly find trash on the ground. You cannot find a cigarette butt on the ground. It is incredibly clean, and people go there by the millions. Why? You go into a room where there is order, you want to stay. Go into a room where there is disorder, you want to leave.

Keep one item for one place...do not have several places for the same kind of thing in your home. For example, do not have five different places for pencils. Have a specific place for supplies.

Order Increases Productivity.

Order is difficult for creative people and spontaneous people. So, they often hire people to keep things in order around them while they create.

I have noticed that people who have uncommon success are meticulous and attentive to order. You go to the homes of people who have uncommon success and their shirts are in one place, ties in one place, their dresses are in order. There is order.

You say, "Well, Mike, that is just not me."

Slow your life down and do things right. And right will multiply. Only do what you want to increase in your life.

4. The Habit Of Wisdom-Consciousness. Always look for Wisdom in any situation you are in. It is there. You simply have to look for it. You can be in a crisis. You may run out of gas. You may be pulled over by a policeman and given a ticket. But, look for the Wisdom that is in any situation that you are in.

Always listen for Wisdom in every conversation. It is there. A lawyer may be talking about a situation in a courtroom. A cook may be describing something she puts in a recipe. Your friend may be describing the latest development in computers. Somebody is speaking Wisdom around you...it is your personal responsibility to listen for it, absorb it, pursue it, interrogate and ask about it.

5. Boldly Pursue Wisdom In Others Around You. Keep a book handy at all times. Never be without a book that you can be absorbing. Your mind is capable of trillions of facts. Constantly wash your mind with Wisdom.

Keep an appointment with the Wisdom of God...by keeping the Word of God handy and convenient. Keep a schedule for reading the Bible. Determine the topic that you want to become an expert at in the Word of God. I encourage everybody to become an expert on at least one topic in the Bible. It might be the Holy Spirit, Healing or Love. Whatever it is, become an expert.

Here are my suggestions for becoming an expert on anything in

the Word:
- ▶ It should be a topic in which you have a continuing interest and desire.
- ▶ Circle 365 scriptures from the Bible on that topic and memorize one scripture a day.
- ▶ Keep those 365 scriptures with you at all times to look over and review.
- ▶ Tell everyone around you what your passion is to know about in the Bible and have them to give you gifts at Christmas and your birthday...relating to that topic. For example, if you have an obsession to know about healing, go to a Christian bookstore and make a list of all the books on healing that you wish you owned. Make a list of the book, its cost, the publisher and the bookstore where it is available. Then, when your friends ask you what you want for your birthday or Christmas, hand them your book list and say, "This is my desired library in my future."

But there must be a habit...something you are doing daily...about your Wisdom. Do not schedule one day a week merely just to read... make it a part of your daily habit.

6. The Habit Of Holiness Consciousness.
- ▶ Have a place to meet with the Holy Spirit.
- ▶ Pray in the Spirit for one hour a day...when you walk or whenever.
- ▶ Wrap every telephone conversation with a prayer about the Holy Spirit.
- ▶ Include something about the Holy Spirit in every letter that you write.
- ▶ Memorize 365 scriptures about the Holy Spirit from the Word of God...one a day.
- ▶ Stay Spirit conscious.
- ▶ Read The Word Of God Aloud Daily.

Abraham Lincoln read the newspaper aloud each morning in his office. It agitated the others, but he discovered that he remembered much more and remembered it longer than when he read silently.

7. The Habit Of Financial Consciousness. Wealthy men negotiate everything...because they are financially conscious.

Uncommon millionaires will argue over a penny...because of their financial consciousness. They are not cheap. They are not poor.

They are financially conscious.

Financial consciousness is a cultivated habit.

Many people stay poor by trying to appear wealthy. They want to look wealthy...when they are actually dirt broke and have bounced checks every month. But, they want everybody else to think they have plenty of money.

The wealthy are continuously evaluating everything from a financial standpoint.

They refuse to pay retail...they want wholesale or less.

They will buy something used before they buy something new...so as to eliminate all the wasted expenses. One of the wealthiest men I know refuses to buy a new car. He says, "I can buy two cars for the price of one if I will buy a two year old car." He is simply financially conscious. He is not trying to impress anybody. He simply wants to keep his money.

Sam Walton's son said about his father, "Mother and dad just refused to ever spend any money."

They are financially conscious when they buy a house.

They are financially conscious when they purchase their car...looking for long-range benefits.

They are financially conscious when they buy their clothes...people worth millions will find the discount and wholesale clothing stores and refuse to go to some retailers. Why? They are simply financially conscious.

8. The Habit Of Doing Your Assignment That Day. You must know the center of your Assignment. If you are going to be a professional basketball player, then every morning you would spend an hour at the free throw line...doing something specific about your Assignment.

If you are a heavyweight boxer, you would get up at 4:30 every morning and do roadwork for three hours...that is linked to your Assignment.

You have to do something every day toward the center of your expertise or your habit...it compounds your success.

It cannot be something you do erratically. For instance, if you want to become an expert at public speaking, then your daily habits would include carefulness in everything that you said so that in your normal conversation, each dialogue would become a practice session for your speaking and enunciation.

9. The Habit Of Planning Your Day. Write out a plan for each day. Writing it out keeps you on course. A plan keeps you focused. I give out to my staff a sheet of paper every day. It is called "Schedule and Successes." On the left hand side, it is from 7:00 to 7:00, 12 hours.

Then the first section is Schedule. What they schedule to do. I want to know what they plan to do. If they do not turn in a plan for that day, they do not get paid for that day. An unplanned day costs me money, so I do not pay my staff for a day they have not planned.

On the right hand side is "Successes." Schedule is what you intended to do. Successes is what you really did. Let's say under Schedule side 10:00 they said, "I'm going to meet with Bill Jones." But Bill cancelled. Then go straight across. I want to see what did you do then when he did not show up. I want to see the successes. What are the four phone calls you made when he did not show up?

Take to heart creating a plan for every day. If you just want to do nothing. Write that out. From 2:00 to 6:00 I am going to do nothing. But at least you have planned it, and you have followed your plan. If you are going to lay out by the pool for 12 hours, say, "Lay by the pool." Put that down. Cultivate the habit of planning a day.

I am talking about habits that will take you to greatness...uncommon greatness. Because all of your efforts should be focused.

10. The Habit Of Managing Your Time Daily. You have to manage your time daily. Make your time count. Your appointments should always have purpose. Do not ever set an appointment with somebody without a deadline. I will meet with you from 1:00 to 1:20. Do not say I will meet you in the afternoon or I will meet you at 1:00. Set an appointment from 1:00 to 1:20, and if they come at ten after 1:00, they have ten minutes left in their appointment. If you will start valuing your time, others will be educated by it. Everything you do educates others.

Managing your time will require four things.

You will have to have an uncommon goal. Your goals must be visual, clear and you must feel passion about your goals. Do not set a goal you do not feel passionate about. Goals are borrowed or born. You will never pursue long a goal you have borrowed from somebody else.

Set goals small enough to achieve. Set a goal you can achieve today so you can create progress and a sense of momentum. You do not have to lose 40 pounds to feel good. You can lose 2 pounds and you will feel great. How many have noticed you have not had to learn everything, just some things that made you feel good.

I did not write a book today, but I dictated about 8 or 10 chapters. So I am on my way. Progress creates a pleasure, not arrival. Completion rarely creates joy; progress creates joy.

You were created for movement. You have eternity in you. You will never arrive where you are going. You have got to enjoy the journey because in Him you live, you move and you have your being. Eternity is in you. Life is in you. And the proof of life is movement.

Be meticulous about access to you. Do not let just anybody have your telephone number. When you go to bed at night, turn your phone off so you can sleep. "Well, I am afraid I'm going to miss something."

When? You will not miss anything. Turn that phone off. Limit those who have access to you.

11. The Habit Of Precision And Accuracy. *Precision creates confidence.*

Example—I have driven by stores and watched people lined up at 9:00 a.m...fully confident that the store will open at that precise time. Why? It is their habit. Many are en route to work. They count on that precision...they need that precision...their entire flow of tasks for that day is dependent on the precision of that store to open up.

Suppose the store was erratic in the procedure? Some mornings, they would open at 8:30, and other mornings at 9:45. They would lose customers...the confidence factor is powerful in achieving uncommon goals. People must feel confident toward your life—you will do what you say.

You will do what they expect you to do.

Accuracy creates comfort. Why are people comfortable talking outside of a theatre, or a store, or a restaurant...while waiting for it to open? They are comfortable because they can count on the precise opening time. It removes stress. They can anticipate a need being met.

Accuracy portrays competence. When you see great precision, you begin to feel that the person is competent and capable about his work.

Yesterday, a worker at my home finished putting in a waste system plant. When I asked him to give me the details of what happened, his precision was remarkable. He spit out statistics and facts and was quite comfortable in doing so. His precision about every detail was a portrait of competence and capability. I felt that he knew what he was talking about whether he did or not! I felt it.

Accuracy reflects integrity. When someone is exact and specific, a sense of honesty and integrity is created. When a newspaper article reads, "At 12:17 a.m. this morning, a man was robbed at 1423 Third Street..." a sense of honesty is implied and felt.

Precise people are often misread as hard to please, picky, perfectionist and a task master. Yet, the same people who are upset over precision in the workplace...examine their paycheck carefully to make sure every penny they worked for is truly coming to them.

Details matter.

Details matter when uncommon greatness is pursued and desired.

When an important goal is achieved, precision was a major factor.

When a goal fails, its failure can be traced to someone involved who lacked precision.

Precision requires extra time. While filing and processing many papers this morning, I noticed that each paper required careful scrutiny and a decision. It is time consuming. But, when I need that paper, it will be accessible and readily retrieved.

Precision in clothing will require extra time and attention. Precision in your spiritual life will require meticulous review of the Word of God.

Everybody requires precision in some things. I have watched sloppily dressed men meticulously review a car engine with a mechanic. They were not precise and careful in their clothing, but would spend hours making sure a car engine was everything promised.

Precision in everything will produce an uncommon life of greatness.

12. The Habit Of Relationship Consciousness. Do something for your inner circle of relationships daily.

I call them your "Love Circle."

I call my parents every day (my father now).

I did it for my mother when she was alive.

Talk to your protégés daily.

Build on your inner circle and do something every day to nurture the worthy relationships in your life.

▶ Appreciate their difference from others around you. Stop making one friend be like another friend. Each is contributing a different asset.

▶ Assess how God is using each person in your life. Is it for conversation, motivation or inspiration?

▶ Lavish your love on those you love and care about.

▶ Create ways to express your affection and caring for them.

You Will Never Change Your Life Until You Change Something You Do Daily.

RECOMMENDED BOOKS AND TAPES:
B-80 The Greatest Success Habit On Earth (32 pages/$5)

The Proof Of Humility Is The Willingness To Reach.

-MIKE MURDOCK

❧ 25 ❧

HUMILITY

Humility Intrigues God.
The Scriptures continuously divide two categories of people:
▶ The Proud
▶ The Humble

Humility Is The Golden Key To Receiving.
Your needs do not attract God. Your *recognition* of your need attracts God. Every blind man did not receive the attention of God. Blind men who *wanted to see* attracted Jesus.

Poor widows did not receive all the miracles. A poor widow who *admitted she needed a miracle* received it (see 1 Kings 17).

Pride is a thief.

Arrogance will shut the door on your Harvest.

Many become poor trying to appear rich. I have known people who were months late on their house payments, lost their car, but still they are telling everybody around them, "Things are going great."

Humility is the recognition of your own limitations and the worthy qualities in another.

Anything You Do Not Possess God Has Stored In Someone Close To You, And Love Is The Secret Map To The Treasure.

Your miracle will not begin until you recognize that you need one.

3 Proofs Of Humility

1. The Humble Recognize Pride As An Enemy To Their Receiving. Pride is a horrible tragic and poisonous thing. It is deceptive. A young couple buying a house they cannot afford shows pride. Oh, I have had the poison of pride in my own life so many times. There have been times that I needed a financial miracle, but I was ashamed to discuss it. I refused to tell a pastor or even my partners, because I believed in "prosperity." If I had admitted I needed a miracle Harvest, they would wonder, "Where's your prosperity that you have been teaching all this time?"

Remember the Pharisee who announced to God that he was glad

he was not like the other man? But, across the synagogue was a publican kneeling before Him, pounding his chest and crying out for mercy? Pharisees were too proud to admit they needed a savior.

2. The Humble Admit That They Need Help. Several years ago, I experienced the greatest financial crisis of my life. It happened suddenly. For a good while, my songs were sung everywhere. My royalty checks were incredible. Several hundred thousand dollars came into my hands quickly. I gave expensive gifts to my family, my friends and my staff. I took all my friends on vacations. I had more money than I had ever had in my lifetime.

Suddenly, a crisis came. I will spare you the details, but I will simply say that I was suddenly in debt several hundred thousand dollars. As I said before, I could not even afford to pay $1,500 to a close friend, my CPA, to get a financial statement from him. (I was going to use this statement to get a loan from the bank.) But, he refused to work for me and get my financial statement so that I could get a loan!

I felt like a hypocrite. Here I was traveling and ministering about the Laws of Blessing. I had been swimming in the River of Plenty. Suddenly, it dried up. I was washed up on the Shore of Nothing.

My miracle began when I went in to the presence of God and admitted that I needed supernatural intervention. I did not have a wealthy board to stand with me. My family did not have any money. My partners were sowing everything they could.

Prayerlessness is proof you do not really believe God can help you.

3. The Humble Rely Upon The Voice Of The Holy Spirit. They get alone with Him. Confess everything you believe you should open up before Him. Do not be fearful. Do not be timid. Do not be protective of yourself. Confess everything.

The moment I cried out to God to show me a plan that would bring me out of trouble, the Holy Sprit began to walk me into my miracle. But, it did not happen until I confessed my need.

10 Facts About Humility

1. Humility Is Not What You Think About Yourself—But What You Think Of Others. True humility is not viewing yourself as worthless. It is the recognition of the worth and value of others. It is the willingness to help someone else succeed even if it requires you to step aside.

2. Humility Is Not Thinking You Are Worthless. *That is inferiority...*a Tool of satan.

3. **Those Who Remain Humble Are Usually Promoted In Rulership.** Read the story of Joseph (see Genesis 41:37-42).

4. **The Truly Humble Are Truly Great.**

5. **Humility Does Not Care Who Gets The Praise And Recognition, Just So The Job Gets Done.**

6. **Humility Will Always Be Recognized And Honored At The Appropriate Time.** Mordecai exposed the plan of Assasikoh.

7. **Humility Is A Quality You Develop In Yourself.** "Humble yourselves therefore under the mighty hand of God, that He may exalt you in due time:" (1 Peter 5:6).

8. **Humility Is Your Willingness To Focus On The Success Of Others.** For example, when Job prayed (read Isaiah 58 and Ephesians 6:8,9). *Humility Is Expected By God.*

"Humble yourselves therefore under the mighty hand of God, that He may exalt you in due time:" (1 Peter 5:6).

10. **Humility Is Recognition Of The Worth And Value Of Others Around You.** Jesus says to "love your neighbor as you love yourself" (read Leviticus 19:18).

RECOMMENDED BOOKS AND TAPES:
B-91 The Leadership Secrets Of Jesus (196 pages/$10)

Memory Replays
The Past.

Imagination Preplays
The Future.

-MIKE MURDOCK

❧ 26 ❧

IMAGINATION

Imagination Is The Key To Your Future.

19 Facts About Imagination

1. You Will Always Move In The Direction Of Your Strongest And Most Dominant Thought.

2. Your Imagination Is An Invisible Machine Inside Your Mind That Creates Pictures Of Something In Your Future. Pictures of those things you *desire.*

One of the most beautiful gifts God has given you is your *mind.* There are two major functions of your mind. One is your *memory,* the other is your *imagination.* Both are God-given gifts that can help or hurt you. Your *memory* will *photograph, file and replay* pictures of your *past.* Your *imagination,* on the other hand, *creates and replays pictures of things you want to happen in your future.*

3. Uncommon Achievers Have Learned How To Use Their Imagination Effectively. Great achievers usually have learned to *replay* the memories of their past *triumphs* and *preplay* the pictures of *their desired successes.*

When David faced the giant Goliath, he mentally *replayed* his previous victories in killing the bear and the lion. Then he used his imagination to *picture* and *preplay* his impending victory over Goliath.

4. Miracles Begin In The Soil Of Your Imagination. God plants a dream within you. Then, that *dream* is *incubated* in the room of your imagination.

Abraham carried a *dream* planted by God. It was a picture of countless generations of children.

"And I will make thy seed as the dust of the earth: so that if a man can number the dust of the earth, then shall thy seed also be numbered" (Genesis 13:16).

"And I will make thy seed to multiply as the stars of heaven," (Genesis 26:4).

5. Abraham Used His Imagination To Strengthen His Faith. Yes, he was human, like you and me. He fought a constant stream of doubts regarding his *dream.* His wife, Sarah, 90 years old and long past her childbearing years, even laughed!

Their faith for a son did not happen overnight. They carried their dream in their *imagination,* and Isaac was conceived.

6. God Even Acknowledged The Power Of An Evil Imagination. A fascinating story in Genesis 11 illustrates the power of imagination. The Babylonians wanted to build a city with a tower that would reach into Heaven. Apparently, it was an exaltation *against* God. He was displeased. So, He confused their tongues and scattered them abroad.

But there is a remarkable observation in Genesis 11:6, about these people and their ability to picture the goals they had set for themselves.

"And the Lord said, Behold, the people is one, and they have all one language; and this they begin to do: and now nothing will be restrained from them, which they have imagined to do."

God *acknowledged* the gift and the power of imagination He had given to them. Unfortunately, they had chosen to misuse it.

7. God Has Given Every One Of Us This Incredible Gift.

8. Your Imagination Can Unleash Unexpected Energy. I am sure you have seen a similar scenario at your house.

You arrive home from work. Your wife is sprawled on the sofa, appearing totally exhausted.

"Honey, what are we having for supper tonight?" you ask.

"Oh, Marcus, I can't prepare supper tonight," she replies. "It's been a really terrible day at the office. My feet are killing me. My back is acting up again, and I feel a migraine coming on. Would you mind fixing something for yourself?"

You stumble around the kitchen, opening the refrigerator and searching for something to satisfy your hunger pangs.

Suddenly, the phone rings.

"Hi, Marcus, this is Tammie. May I speak to Jena?" asks the voice on the other end.

"Well, Tammie, she is really too tired to talk to anyone right now, but I will tell her you called."

"Oh, Marcus, this is too important. Please let me talk to her for just one minute," Tammie implores.

So you call your wife. "Tammie's on the phone for you, she says it's important."

Sluggishly, your wife gropes for the telephone. "Yes, Tammie?" she mutters.

"Oh, Jena, you won't believe it. Do you remember that gorgeous red dress we saw last week at Bloomingdale's? They have just marked all those dresses down to half-price. For tonight only! You've got to go with me!"

Instantly, your wife leaps to her feet. "Oh, my, yes, Tammie!" she exclaims. "I'll be ready in 20 minutes."

You stand in the kitchen, stunned, as your wife sweeps like a tornado into the bathroom, shouting over her shoulder, "Oh, honey, this is what I've been waiting for. You're going to love this dress! They're having a half-price sale till 9 tonight. I just have to go!" And before you can grab your checkbook, she's gone like Elijah the Second in a whirlwind!

Was your wife exaggerating her fatigue and weariness earlier?

Probably not. But a *new photograph* had been placed in her mind. A different picture had suddenly *dominated her imagination,* instantly creating new energy and motivation. It happens to all of us, doesn't it?

God has given you the gift of your imagination. He wants you to use your imagination productively. So start now and grow the Seeds of good health, favor, faith and financial prosperity in the soil of your imagination.

9. Jesus Used His Imagination To Picture The Future Rewards Of His Suffering.

Jesus Saw Beyond The Cross

Jesus was acquainted with sorrow. He knew pain. He experienced rejection. But something kept drawing Him toward the cross.

Or, did He see something *beyond* the cross?

"Looking unto Jesus the author and finisher of our faith; Who for the joy that was set before Him endured the cross, despising the shame, and is set down at the right hand of the throne of God" (Hebrews 12:2).

His mind was on the *Resurrection,* not just Calvary.

He endured the pain of the cross by concentrating on *what was to follow* His death.

His *focus was the Resurrection* on the *other* side of the Crucifixion. It was evident that *Heaven was often on His mind* while He was on earth.

"In My Father's house are many mansions: If it were not so, I would have told you. I go to prepare a place for you" (John 14:2).

Some call it goal-setting...visualization...imagining. You may call it anything you will. But it is a basic law in achieving great successes. *Your life will always move in the direction of your dominating thought.*

Your imagination is the workshop of your mind. You can *Dream, Design and Determine* what you want to happen in your life. Whatever dominates your imagination *today* will very likely be experienced in your life *tomorrow.*

10. Winning Athletes Use Their Imaginations. A major university conducted an experiment with its basketball team. They divided 10 men into two teams to determine an average percentage of free throws scored. Team A was instructed to practice free throws for an hour each day for 30 consecutive days.

However, Team B had a different Assignment. The men were told to remain in the locker room and, *using their imagination only,* visualize themselves shooting free throws and mentally picturing the basketball dropping through the net. This imagining was to be practiced for the same time period as Team A—one hour each day for 30 consecutive days.

The results were remarkable.

Members of Team A, after actually practicing on the court every day, improved their free throw score by 23 percent. Members of Team B, *using only their imaginations* for 30 days, improved their score by 22 percent! Almost identical improvement! It is hard to believe, isn't it?

11. Your Imagination Controls You. "Whatsoever things are true, whatsoever things are honest, whatsoever things are just, whatsoever things are pure, whatsoever things are lovely, whatsoever things are of good report; if there be any virtue, and if there be any praise, think on these things" (Philippians 4:8).

12. It Is Your Responsibility To Protect Your Mind And Imagination. Thoughts will invade your imagination from almost everywhere. Thoughts of *fear* and *unbelief* are what I call *Disaster Seeds* planted by satan.

Thoughts of *miracles* and *blessings* are *Dream-Seeds* planted by God.

Your imagination is *not* a referee. It will not judge whether the Seeds going into your mind are good or bad. It will simply *grow* whatever Seeds you decide to water and nurture.

This is one of the reasons we need the Holy Spirit and the Word of God in our lives. The Holy Sprit will help you harness and focus your imagination to grow your *Dream.*

13. You Can Change Disaster Seeds Into Dream-Seeds In The World Of Your Imagination. In 1 Kings 17, God sent the prophet Elijah to the home of an impoverished widow.

"What are we having for supper tonight?" he asked the woman.

"Two pancakes for me and my boy, and then we are going to die," she replied. (This is the Mike Murdock version of course!)

She had a Disaster Seed: a *picture* of her approaching *starvation.*

Elijah, however, had a *Dream-Seed:* a *picture* of her *supply.*

He said, "Give me a meal first." Then he added, "Your meal will never run dry."

Elijah planted a picture of supply in her imagination to help stimulate her faith.

God sent Elijah to paint a picture on the walls of her mind—*a picture of supply instead of starvation.* That picture—the invisible photograph of her needed supply—*unleashed* her faith and gave her an incredible miracle of provision during the famine.

14. Your Imagination's Mate Is Your Memory. Your memory keeps files of the past: photographs of past *painful* experiences and those of past *pleasurable* experiences.

I am sure that you can remember many *pleasurable experiences* in your past. You can probably remember the day you were married or received your high school diploma or the day you passed the test for your first driver's license. I am sure you can well remember the moment you gave your life to Christ.

Replaying these past triumphs and victories in your mind is a powerful way to *motivate* yourself toward your *Dreams.*

David did this when he faced Goliath. He replayed his memory of victory over the lion and the bear. His *mental rehearsal* ignited the fire of courage within him to face and conquer the giant Goliath.

On the other hand, be careful in conversations and associations with people who provoke painful memories.

One of the most productive life principles in the writings of Paul is found in Philippians 3:13,14: "Forgetting those things which are behind, and reaching forth unto those things which are before, I press toward the mark for the prize of the high calling of God in Christ Jesus."

The prophet Isaiah commanded the same principle of forgetting.

"Remember ye not the former things, neither consider the things of old. Behold I will do a new thing; now it shall spring forth; shall ye not know it? I will even make a way in the wilderness, and rivers in the desert" (Isaiah 43:18,19).

The *healing* of your memories will not remove your ability to recall your past, but rather give you the ability to *replay* the past *without the accompanying pain.*

Joseph experienced this in Genesis 42. He *recognized* his brothers who had wronged him in his past, but he felt no animosity toward them. He had discerned the *purpose* of the pain and realized that God had actually *used* his unfortunate experience to *promote* him!

15. You Can Begin Using Your Imagination Productively Today. Every great achiever has used the Master Key of Imagination to unlock the door to his miracles and blessings. God wants you to use your imagination the same way.

Your marriage is being restored. *Picture it.*

Your memory is being healed. *Picture it.*

The healing power of Jesus is flowing through your body this very moment. *Receive it.*

Money is being placed in your hands to pay your bills. *Expect it.* Your Heavenly Father wants to bless you beyond anything you have ever experienced.

Oh, will you dare to believe this? Will you dare to shake off the mistakes of the past—and reach for the miracles God desires to place in your hands?

16. You Can Change What Has Been Happening In Your Life By Focusing Your Imagination. You can *reverse* yesterday's wrong decision by making a *good* decision today. You can turn the tide. *Nothing is impossible.* Nothing.

Jesus said, "If thou canst believe, all things are possible to him that believeth" (Mark 9:23).

Refuse the chains of past injustices. Do not waste your time analyzing those who have wronged you. Use your energy to create new roads ahead of you, not repairing the old roads behind you! Start *focusing* on your own *immediate* goals and the *Dreams* ahead that God has planted within you.

17. Refuse To Misuse Your Imagination. Some people *misuse* and *misdirect* their imagination. They feed their imaginations destructive pictures, *Disaster Seeds.* This happened in Noah's generation.

"And God saw that the wickedness of man was great in the earth, and that every imagination of the thoughts of his heart was only evil continually" (Genesis 6:5).

The Apostle Paul recognized its misuse.

"Because that, when they knew God, they glorified Him not as God, neither were thankful; but became vain in their imaginations, and their foolish heart was darkened" (Romans 1:21).

Dealing With Disaster Seeds

Each of us face daily temptations. Advertisers stir and awaken our physical appetites via billboards, magazines and television. Overeating has almost become a way of life in America. Illicit sexual gratification is promoted in the same manner.

These *pictures* are *planted* as Seeds into our minds and imaginations continually. These Seed-pictures are *destructive.* I call them Disaster Seeds because they destroy your faith in God. They must be confronted and uprooted from the soil of your imagination.

"Casting down imaginations, and every high thing that exalteth itself against the knowledge of God, and bringing into captivity every thought to the obedience of Christ;" (2 Corinthians 10:5).

Your imagination will grow any Seed that you plant in it. Good or bad. This is why David said, "I will set no wicked thing before mine eyes:" (Psalm 101:3).

18. Jesus Rejected From His Imagination Any Person Or Picture That Could Be A Distraction To His Desired Goals. Jesus warned about these Disaster Seeds entering through the eye-gate. "The light of the body is the eye: if therefore thine eye be single, thy whole body shall be full of light. But if thine eye be evil, thy whole body shall be full of the darkness, If therefore thy light that is in thee, how great is that darkness!" (Matthew 6:22,23).

Remember, your imagination is the room of incubation for your Seeds of Faith. And you can experience unlimited miracles when you allow God to rule your imagination.

19. The Imagination Of Joseph Moved Him From The Pit To The Palace. Joseph, in Genesis, received a *Dream* from God. He *chose to believe it,* and saw himself destined for the throne. His brothers hated him for it, and planted Seeds of confusion, hatred and jealously into his life.

But Joseph refused to nurture those Disaster Seeds of unforgiveness and hostility. He refused to doubt his *Dream* and years of nurturing that *Dream* in his imagination eventually promoted him from slave boy to prime minister.

What God did for Joseph He can do for you. You may be misunderstood by someone close to you right now. Bitter words may have been hurled at you this very day. You may feel like giving up your dreams. Those are normal feelings we all have occasionally.

But I pray for you, my friend, in the precious name of Jesus, this very moment, that your *Dream* will be ignited again. *What God spoke to you in the light, do not doubt in the darkness.*

Make up your mind to stand your ground.

Dare to dream again. Start dreaming *bigger* than you have ever dreamed before. Just like Joseph chose to grow the *Dream* from God, you, too, can start growing the *Dream* God has planted within you.

Jealousy Occurs
    When You Believe
Someone Else Received
What You
Should Have Received.

-MIKE MURDOCK

⋙ 27 ⋘

JEALOUSY

Somebody Will Despise You Because Of Your Success.

You see, somebody will compare your success with their own. It is unwise, unnecessary and ungodly. But, it happens every day. Paul warned, "but they measuring themselves by themselves, and comparing themselves among themselves, are not wise" (2 Corinthians 10:12).

Success will deplete you. It requires so much of your time, your energy and life that when you look at it, *you* see struggle, tears and pain. *Others do not.* They were *not* there when you wept and interceded through the night. They did *not* taste the threat of bankruptcy. No, *they never see what you see in your successes.*

You see *responsibility.*

They see *rewards.*

You see *cost.*

They see *compensation.*

You see *tears.*

They see *triumph.*

Envy is a deadly poison which breaks up friendships, wounds marriages and stains the beauty of progress. Solomon wrote, "jealousy is cruel as the grave: the coals thereof are coals of fire, which hath a most vehement flame" (Song of Solomon 8:6).

David became the target of intense envy. After he defeated Goliath, women came out of all the cities of Israel, singing and dancing, with taberts, with joy, and with the instruments of music and said, "Saul hath slain his thousands, and David his ten thousands" (1 Samuel 18:7).

Jealousy overcame Saul. "And Saul was very wroth, and the saying displeased him; and he said, They have ascribed unto David ten thousands and to me they have ascribed but thousands: and what can he have more but the kingdom? And Saul eyed David from that day and forward...and Saul cast the javelin; for he said, I will smite David even to the wall with it" (1 Samuel 18:8,9,11).

Think about it. *Jealousy births the spirit of murder and destruction.*

7 Keys In Overcoming Envy And Jealousy

1. Realize That You Have Something Another Admires. A fascinating verse explains it all: "And Saul was afraid of David, because the Lord was with him, and was departed from Saul" (1 Samuel 18:12).

2. You Cannot Stop Envy In Others. It is their own problem. You see, their emptiness has been exposed because of something God has given to you. *You have received something from God that they wish they possessed.*

3. Never Belittle Yourself To Generate Favor. You will be tempted to belittle and down play your own successes and blessings to appease and satisfy a jealous and angry friend or foe. Do not waste your energy. "Make no friendship with an angry man; and with a furious man thou shalt not go: Lest thou learn his ways, and get a snare to thy soul" (Proverbs 22:24,25).

David did this. "And David avoided out of his presence twice" (1 Samuel 18:11).

4. When Envy Arises, Your Presence Usually Fuels And Nurtures The Envy. Keep your words kind and humble. "A soft answer turneth away wrath: but grievous words stir up anger" (Proverbs 15:1).

5. You Cannot Solve A Problem For Envious People. "Wrath is cruel, and anger is outrageous; but who is able to stand before envy?" (Proverbs 27:4)

6. Envy Requires The Surgery Of The Holy Spirit. He will have to put such love within them for Him and you that change emerges. "Charity suffereth long, and is kind; charity envieth not;" (1 Corinthians 13:4).

7. Reserve Your Enthusiasm To An Appropriate Audience. Wait until you are in the presence of someone who truly rejoices with you. Avoid boasting in your own achievement. "Let another man praise thee, and not thine own mouth; a stranger, and not thine own lips" (Proverbs 27:2).

I have felt attacks of envy within myself toward others. Several years ago, I saw the incredible buildings and sanctuary of a friend of mine. I looked around and thought, "I cannot even get a newsletter published on time and here he is with a television studio, 4,000 loyal church members and a gorgeous home!" I felt so small. I felt unimportant. I felt unnecessary.

Then, I flew across the country and visited with several of my dear friends who have world renowned ministries I would be able to influence. Their budget was more than $150,000,000 each year. They could have anything they wanted, any time of the day. They could speak and major leaders of America would fly to their city to meet them.

As I stared at my little pebbles next to their mountains, I felt so insignificant. Then, the Father reminded me.

My pebble had pebble responsibilities.

Their mountain had mountain responsibilities.

I could not see the depth of their pain, stress and warfare. It was a lesson in understanding *my* Assignment. "Do you want me to increase the welfare and difficulties of your life?" Of course not.

If you suffer, you *reign*.

If you reign, you *suffer*.

While the *childless couple looks* longingly at the *mother with five children,* they may be unaware of the great difficulties and burdens that mother carries.

Jesus said it clearly, "What is that to thee? Follow thou Me" (John 21:22). Your own Assignment will require *all of you*.

Reject jealousy.

Despise envy.

Do *not envy others* and *do not let their jealousy break your own focus.*

Your happiest days are just ahead.

What You Respect
You Will Attract,
What You Do Not Respect
Will Move Away From You.

-MIKE MURDOCK

❧ 28 ❧

MARRIAGE

Nothing Feels Better Than A Good Marriage.

Nothing hurts worse than an unhappy one.

Someone has said that the home can be like Heaven or like hell. Your home and marriage affect you more than anything else. A man can have an old car and still enjoy life. A woman can live in a small, cramped apartment and still be glad she is married. But when the marriage is crumbling, there is nothing else to fill that particular "emptiness." God created man for a mate (see Genesis 2:18).

What are some of the *keys* to a better marriage? There are hundreds of suggestions from everywhere. In my office, as I write this, my shelves are filled with books about marriage, the home, and the husband and wife's expectations of each other. One husband writes as though the cure-all in a marriage is to bring roses every week to his wife or wash the dishes for her. One wife thinks all the husband really wants is for her to be beautiful and sensuous when he comes home from work.

It can be a bit ridiculous. Personally, I do not think what works with one marriage will necessarily work for another. All of us have *different needs* at *different times and stages* in our lives.

Know Your Mate.

Your mate is affecting you.

Your mate grows your weaknesses or your strengths.

Your mate multiplies your agitation or your peace.

Your mate is helping create the climate of torture or triumph at your house. "Two are better than one; because they have a good reward for their labour" (Ecclesiastes 4:9).

You must invest the time to understand and know your mate if you want to maximize your life.

5 Things You Should Know About Your Mate

1. Know The Wounds Of Your Mate. A pastor sat in my home weeping. "My wife has not touched me in six months," he wept. "Mike,

I can't take it much longer. I want to be held, touched and loved."

A childhood experience of molestation is a powerful influence that often goes undetected while destroying many marriages.

2. Know The Fears Of Your Mate. A young wife tearfully admitted that her father's infidelity and unfaithfulness to her mother had left her embittered. She falsely accused her husband when any behavior reminded her of her father.

3. Know The Closest Friends Of Your Mate. Your children are always affected by their friendships at school. They react differently to you after they have been with their friends. Your mate will, also.

"I wouldn't put up with that from my husband," a friend told a pastor's wife. She returned home with volcanic anger. Her friend had only heard one side of the argument. Yet, she embraced the counsel of that uninformed friend.

4. Know Those Who Counsel Your Mate. Never, never, never again will I permit someone I love to receive counsel without me being present. I was shocked and horrified to hear the counsel received by someone I loved several years ago. *Do not send your mate or children to a counselor you do not know well.* In fact, I would urge you to sit in on every counseling session to protect those you love from unwise and distorted counsel.

5. Know The Weaknesses Of Your Mate. Lust? Lying? Imagination? Jealousy? Inferiority? Prevention is often possible when you understand the flaws and weaknesses of your mate. You can protect and build a wall around them.

The 20 Success Keys I have included here are things to observe as you look at your marriage through the eyes of God. Remember: Success is achieving the goals *God* has for you. You know that His goal for you is a good marriage.

The Golden Key To Success Is Understanding—which is the ability to interpret a situation or person as God does. A marvelous miracle would be to see your wife or husband as *God* sees them today.

20 Success Keys To A Better Marriage

1. Recognize The Value God Places On Your Marriage. If marriage were not a powerful tool for your success in other areas of your life, God would not have ordained it. Do you truly value your family life? God does. He knew it would affect your relationships with other people (read Genesis 2:18).

2.   Recognize That Satan Hates A Good Marriage. A good marriage is a powerful force against evil.   In a good marriage, a husband and wife will strengthen one another for God. They will teach their children how to discern between good and evil.

3.   Discern Undesirable Influences And Protect Yourself From Them. Do you have certain friends that have an unsettling effect on your home life?   One woman noticed her marriage pressures were not nearly so great when a particular friend left town or went on vacation, so she limited her time spent with that person (read 1 Corinthians 15:33).

4.   Rebuild Good Influences Into Your Home Climate. Christian music and Christian friends should be brought into your home circle frequently.   Good books should be picked up regularly for the family to read.   Christian bookstores are everywhere.   Take advantage of your local bookstore. I thank God for my own parents who constantly bought books, records and tapes for me over the years. They influenced me greatly. They took me to youth rallies and youth camps. They continually looked for ways to expose my heart to the climate of God.

5.   Make Church The Center Of Family Activities. Make it the hub of life. If there must be a limitation in your activities, let it be the job or school, but never the church life. Let your *pastor* be an *important man* in your home life. If Bible questions arise, let it be a natural thing to consult church leaders who are "mentoring" your family.

6.   Respect The Opinions Of Others In Your Home And Prove It By Asking Worthwhile Questions And Listening To The Answers. All of us crave respect. We want to feel we count—that what we say *will* matter!   Obviously, we cannot follow all the advice given, but sometimes just merely considering it will be of tremendous value. Respect the *privacy* of other family members. Respect *their time.*

7.   Discern The Favorable Qualities In Your Mate. *Notice what others like about your mate and verbalize it.* If others enjoy your mate, why do you focus on the things you do *not* like? Ask your friends and notice the qualities *they* admire—then express those qualities to your mate: "I really appreciate the time you spend at work making us a living." "You keep a clean house!" Their significance can be found through focusing on their *strengths,* not on their *weaknesses.*

8.   Use The Irritating Traits Of Your Mate As A Stepping Stone To A Higher Spiritual Goal In Your Life. Let them be like "sandpaper" removing your rough edges. Patience can be built into your life. God is allowing them as a test to your life. Do not run from them. *Develop...grow...mature...*through pressure on you!

9. Establish A Daily Family Altar Time. I will not pretend this is easy. It is *not,* but it is possible and unbelievably powerful. I remember when I saw my own parents reading the Bible and praying, I thought subconsciously: "This must be important. God must really talk to them." Most children will not rebel nearly as much when they see and hear their parents praying and reading the Word. I think wives who see their husbands disciplined in this way are most apt to respect them as the scriptures teach.

10. Take Authority Over Every Attack Of Satan In Your Home. Learn to recognize satanic attacks upon your family and use your authority as a born-again Christian, and child of the King. You can take control of satan by using the name of Jesus. This is your privilege as a believer.

11. Minimize The Problem Areas Of Your Marriage. Everyone has them. Some just know how to "play the rough edges down." *Do not talk to just anybody and everybody about problems in your marriage.*

12. Focus At Least Once A Week On The Possibilities Of Your Mate, Not The Problems. This is definitely not easy. But *try it!* Help your mate to develop a good *self-image.*

13. Maintain A Faith-Talk Level In Your Daily Home Life. Do not permit doubt and unbelief to fill discussion in your house. When someone starts talking about the bad weather, another of how he dreads to go to school, another about the new boss who is not so nice—such talk will affect the climate and atmosphere of your home! *Stop it!* Talk about the *blessings* of God, the *good* things that are happening.

Never talk "divorce."

Do not pave the road to failure. Do not make it easy for yourself to slip and slide. If something negative is never talked, it probably will not be easy to do (see James 3:2).

14. Work Toward Financial Freedom Not Accumulation. Stress that *possessions* bring will become *pressures* if they are not acquired in God's *timing.* If too many purchases are made, the appreciation level is usually much lower and short-lived.

15. Assign Tasks And Require Accountability For Household Responsibilities. Most people are not strongly self-motivated. Do not expect more than family members are capable of.

Homes that have clear and defined responsibilities for each child and parent are free from confusion.

16. Keep Confidences And Respect Privacy. I think sometimes home is where we learn distrust instead of trust. A husband and wife should not betray each other's confidence in front of children. Neither should they expose one child's inner world to another. *Confidentiality is one of the most treasured gifts you can give to another.*

Discretion is more than the evidence of Wisdom.

Discretion Is The *Proof Of Love*.

17. Pray For Specific Methods To Meet The Needs Of Those In Your Family. You may be their *only key* to inner happiness. Let God give you the proper "burden and compassion" for those around you.

18. Keep Filled With The Spirit. Maintain an inner relationship with God. Learn to pray often *in the language of the Holy Spirit*. Constantly build yourself and edify yourself in the Holy Spirit (see Jude 20).

19. Maintain Recreation Time Together. This is just as important as any other part of your life. Enjoy life together. Have fun in each other's company. God ordained the family for your *pleasure*.

20. Never Give Up. Keep *trying* to make your home a *happy* place. Review these Keys continuously. There will always be crisis experiences and moments of setbacks. *Minimize the bad times. Maximize the good times.*

"Lo, children are an heritage of the Lord: and the fruit of the womb is his reward. As arrows are in the hand of a mighty man; so are children of the youth. Happy is the man that hath his quiver full of them: they shall not be ashamed, but they shall speak with the enemies in the gate" (Psalm 127:3-5).

RECOMMENDED BOOKS AND TAPES:
B-55 Twenty Keys To A Happier Marriage (32 pages/$5)
B-114 The Law Of Recognition (248 pages/$10)

Your Reaction
   To Your Parents
Determines God's Commitment
   To Your Prosperity.

-MIKE MURDOCK

≈ 29 ≈

MOTHERS

Mothers Decide The Greatness Of Their Children.

31 Qualities Of An Uncommon Mother

1. The Uncommon Mother Encourages Her Children To Pursue Their Dreams. Every dream is born or borrowed. An Uncommon Mother knows this. So, she invests time in helping her children *discern the Dream* God has planted within them. She listens, *interviews* and *gathers information relative to that dream.* She will *make any investment* necessary in books, seminars or materials that unleash faith and confidence to achieve it. She bathes and guards that dream with *her daily intercession* in her private place of prayer, "The Secret Place."

"Without counsel, purposes are disappointed: but in the multitude of counselors they are established" (Proverbs 15:22).

2. The Uncommon Mother Teachers Her Children To Trust God During Seasons Of Battle. Nothing Is Ever As Bad As It First Appears. The Uncommon Mother knows this, and she patiently focuses the attention of her children on the power and presence of God. She explains, from the life of Joseph, that opposition is usually the wave that moves them from the pit to the prison to the palace. The master key is total faith in the promises of God.

"In God have I put my trust: I will not be afraid what man can do unto me" (Psalm 56:11).

3. The Uncommon Mother Is Patient, Knowing Her Children Are Becoming Something Greater. Seasons change. The acorn becomes the oak tree. Babies become leaders. The weak become strong. Patience is the Golden Key that unlocks the greatness of a child. The Uncommon Mother knows that her longsuffering will produce permanent rewards.

"And let us not be weary in well doing: for in due season we shall reap, if we faint not" (Galatians 6:9).

4. The Uncommon Mother Always Celebrates Every Tiny Success Of Her Child. Love is excited when another excels. Others will envy. Many will criticize. Knowing this, the Uncommon Mother creates a climate of enthusiasm and excitement around every small step of progress. This fuels the confidence of her children, enabling them to endure any season of opposition in their future.

"Death and life are in the power of the tongue: and they that love it shall eat the fruit thereof" (Proverbs 18:21).

5. The Uncommon Mother Knows When To Speak And When To Be Silent. Words matter. Silence matters, also. Studying her child continually, the Uncommon Mother knows when right words can heal, strengthen and calm. She also uses silence when a child longs for a listening ear. These two golden tools, words and silence, have sculptured many great champions.

"The Lord God hath given me the tongue of the learned, that I should know how to speak a word in season to him that is weary:" (Isaiah 50:4).

6. The Uncommon Mother Always Hears A Matter Out Before Judging. Information is sometimes distorted. Details are limited. Accurate conclusions are impossible when something is unknown. The Uncommon Mother knows this. She refuses to penalize anyone until guilt is proven.

"Therefore thou art inexcusable, O man, whosoever thou art that judgest: for wherein thou judgest another, thou condemnest thyself; for thou that judgest doeth the same things" (Romans 2:1).

7. The Uncommon Mother Always Seeks To Know Her Children Well. Every child is different. Each has fears unspoken and unknown. Each one is birthing dreams that others do not grasp. What causes one to cry causes another to become angry. The Uncommon Mother knows this and carefully ponders how to solve those needs in each child.

"Lo, children are an heritage of the Lord: and the fruit of the womb is His reward. As arrows are in the hand of a mighty man; so are children of the youth" (Psalm 127:3,4).

8. The Uncommon Mother Is Always A Harbor Of Gentleness. Life becomes stormy. The winds of rivalry and the waves of jealousy blast daily. Like a warm harbor, the Uncommon Mother always welcomes her children with gentleness, pouring the oil of compassion. The broken become healed in her presence.

"And the servant of the Lord must not strive; but be gentle unto all men, apt to teach, patient," (2 Timothy 2:24).

9. The Uncommon Mother Always Lavishes Affection On Her Children. It is impossible to receive too much warmth, caring and affection. Affection heals. Love restores. Kindness strengthens. The Uncommon Mother knows this. She reaches, comforts, loves and holds her children close to her. Stroking, caressing and hugging her children is as normal and necessary as breathing. Her children become whole.

"Be kindly affectioned one to another with brotherly love; in honour preferring one another;" (Romans 12:10).

10. The Uncommon Mother Always Warns, Cautions And Corrects Her Children When Necessary. Disasters occur daily. Millions are crashing on the rock of rebellion. The Uncommon Mother wants her children to succeed. She sees, fears and warns when a pitfall is observed. She will risk their anger in order to guarantee their success. She is a true watchman on the wall.

"Poverty and shame shall be to him that refuseth instruction: but he that regardeth reproof shall be honoured" (Proverbs 13:18).

11. The Uncommon Mother Evaluates And Qualifies The Friendships Of Her Children. Children are easily influenced. The opinions of others matter greatly. Children often alter their conduct and behavior dramatically if it attracts others to them. The Uncommon Mother understands this potential danger. She studies those who are speaking into the life of her children. She refuses to permit the presence of a destroyer.

"And have no fellowship with the unfruitful works of darkness, but rather reprove them" (Ephesians 5:11).

12. The Uncommon Mother Teaches Her Children How To Harness Their Anger Effectively. Prisons are filled with children who could not control their anger. Murders occur because of unharnessed anger. Millions destroy friendships because of their inability to focus their anger appropriately. The Uncommon Mother shows her child how to channel rage into a project, a career and become a solution. Anger is an energy that needs an appropriate focus. The Uncommon Mother reminds her children continuously of the devastating results of uncontrolled rage.

"Be ye angry, and sin not: let not the sun go down upon your wrath: Neither give place to the devil" (Ephesians 4:26,27).

13. The Uncommon Mother Helps Her Children Grow Powerful Faith. Faith is confidence in God. It enters your heart when the Word of God is heard, spoken or read. Faith is the powerful magnet that attracts miracles into your life. The Uncommon Mother nurtures faith by reading the Scriptures aloud, helping her children memorize them and maintaining their daily appointment with the Word of God. She knows that their faith can produce everything in their future they will ever need.

"If ye have faith, and doubt not,....ye shall say unto this mountain, Be thou removed, and be thou cast into the sea; it shall be done" (Matthew 21:21).

14. The Uncommon Mother Knows The Power And Influence Of Anointed Music In The Home. Music is powerful. It is an industry worth billions. Music is the most powerful current of influence on earth. The Uncommon Mother knows this. So she provides Godly music throughout every room of her home and automobile to create a climate for miracles and faith. She educates her children on the power of worship and praise, knowing that they will become warriors and overcomers because of it.

"But now bring me a minstrel. And it came to pass, when the minstrel played, that the hand of the Lord came upon him" (2 Kings 3:15).

15. The Uncommon Mother Always Teaches Her Children To Dream Again. Failures happen. Mistakes are common. But God is the God of the second chance. He will always outlast your storms. Always. The Uncommon Mother knows this. So she encourages her children to stop looking at where they have been and start looking at where they are going. She knows the incredible power of dreaming again.

"The glory of this latter house shall be grater than of the former, saith the Lord of hosts: and in this place will I give peace, saith the Lord of hosts" (Haggai 2:9).

16. The Uncommon Mother Always Visualizes Her Children Succeeding. What Happens In Your Mind Usually Happens In Time. Visualization works. It affects your faith, your conduct and your decisions. The Uncommon Mother knows this. So she keeps a picture of the potential of her children. She uses her imagination to visualize their future successes. Because of this, her words strengthen and impart faith and confidence in her children.

"And He brought him forth abroad, and said, Look now toward heaven, and tell the stars, if thou be able to number them: and H e said unto him, So shall thy seed be" (Genesis 15:5).

17. The Uncommon Mother Teaches Her Children The Principles Of Financial Prosperity. Gifts, genius and skills are not enough to succeed. Principles must be taught. The Uncommon Mother carefully plants an understanding of the principles of integrity, diligence and work in the heart of her children. She insists on honesty. She exposes lies. She provides a list of chores. She insists on diligence. Laziness is penalized. Accomplishment is rewarded. The Uncommon Mother is the first mentor that decides the financial future of her children.

"Beloved, I wish above all things that thou mayest prosper and be in health, even as thy soul prospereth" (3 John 1:2).

18. The Uncommon Mother Always Keeps A Private Place

For Prayer...The Secret Place. Places matter. Where you are determines what you experience. You experience legal matters in a law office; medical examinations in a hospital. In the presence of God, you will see God and learn His laws and ways. His secrets belong to those who pursue Him. The Uncommon Mother becomes great because she stays in His presence habitually and teaches her family to do so as well.

"He that dwelleth in the secret place of the most High shall abide under the shadow of the Almighty" (Psalm 91:1).

19. The Uncommon Mother Manages Her Time Wisely. Time is the currency on earth. You must trade it for anything else you desire. Whatever you presently own—you traded your time for it. Whatever you do not have, you have been unwilling to trade time for it. The Uncommon Mother schedules her day carefully. She insists on punctuality and teaches her children how to make each hour count in their lives by the daily use and habit of a Time Use notebook.

"Redeeming the time, because the days are evil" (Ephesians 5:16).

20. The Uncommon Mother Teaches Her Children The Necessity Of Forgiveness. Retaliation always multiplies pain. It guarantees an enemy. The Uncommon Mother knows this. So she continuously reveals the inevitable Harvest when the Seed of Forgiveness is planted in others. Mercy always multiplies. *What you sow into others, God always sows back into you.*

"For if ye forgive men their trespasses, your heavenly Father will also forgive you: But if ye forgive not men their trespasses, neither will your Father forgive your trespasses" (Matthew 6:14-15).

21. The Uncommon Mother Requires That Her Children Accept The Responsibility For The Problems They Create. Blaming others multiplies our problems. Millions sabotage their own lives because they refuse to accept the responsibility for their own mistakes. The Uncommon Mother helps her children avoid this tragedy. She names their weaknesses. She confronts her children with them. Then she shows them how to experience the power of God to overcome those weaknesses.

"If we say that we have no sin, we deceive ourselves, and the truth is not in us. If we confess our sins, He is faithful and just to forgive us our sins, and to cleanse us from all unrighteousness" (1 John 1:8,9).

22. The Uncommon Mother Is Unafraid To Reach For Help. Nobody succeeds alone. Everything created requires something else created. The Uncommon Mother knows that reaching will birth a miracle. Reaching is not a sign of weakness. It is the proof of humility. She sits at the feet of a spiritual mentor, stays linked to those who encourage her, and refuses the trap of pride.

"When thou art in tribulation, and all these things are come upon thee, even in the latter days, if thou turn to the Lord thy God and shalt be obedient unto His voice; (For the Lord thy God, is a merciful God;) He will not forsake thee, neither destroy thee, nor forget the covenant of thy fathers which He sware unto them" (Deuteronomy 4:30,31).

23. The Uncommon Mother Never Quits. Endurance is the quality of champions. The Uncommon Mother never quits believing. She trusts God completely. She never quits praying. Tenacity is always rewarded. She never quits reaching. Focus always births obsession. An obsession births tenacity. Tenacity always produces the desired results.

"Blessed is the man that endureth temptation: for when he is tried, he shall receive the crown of life, which the Lord hath promised to them that love Him" (James 1:12).

24. The Uncommon Mother Helps Her Children Break The Chains Of Bad Habits. Alcohol ruins. Drugs destroy countless lives. Illicit sex has sabotaged the relationships of millions. The Uncommon Mother despises these chains that enslave. She cries out to God for the deliverance of her children. She insists on breaking these chains through her intercession, warnings and wise counsel.

"If the Son therefore shall make you free, ye shall be free indeed" (John 8:36).

25. The Uncommon Mother Is Always Faithful To The House Of God. Spiritual mentorship is necessary for survival. The house of God is where the Seeds of Righteousness are sown. The presence of God creates memories of peace, joy and strength that cannot occur anywhere else on earth. The Uncommon Mother insists that her children sit continuously under the influence of truth.

"Not forsaking the assembling of ourselves together, as the manner of some is; but exhorting one another: and so much the more, as ye see the day approaching" (Hebrews 10:25).

26. The Uncommon Mother Reads The Word Of God Daily To Her Children. Truth affects us. It destroys error. It burns away falsehood. It purifies. The Uncommon Mother knows this. So she daily mentors her children by reading the Word of God aloud, insisting on their memorization of scripture and consistently evaluating their understanding of it.

"Thy word have I hid in mine heart, that I might not sin against thee" (Psalm 119:11).

27. The Uncommon Mother Helps Her Children Discover Their Assignment On Earth. Everything created is a solution. Your Assignment is decided in your mother's womb. It is always to a person or a people. The Uncommon Mother does not decide what her children will do with their lives—she helps them discern their Assignment in the presence of God.

"Before I formed thee in the belly I knew thee; and before thou camest forth out of the womb I sanctified thee, and I ordained thee a prophet unto the nations" (Jeremiah 1:5).

28. The Uncommon Mother Will Not Permit Strife In Her Presence. Strife is the door to every evil work of satan. It divides churches, causes divorce and wounds the hearts of children permanently. It can turn a billion dollar company into bankruptcy within months. The Uncommon Mother will not permit the very seed of strife in her presence. She exposes it and deals with it immediately.

"A soft answer turneth away wrath: but grievous words stir up anger" (Proverbs 15:1).

29. The Uncommon Mother Is Totally Dependent Upon God. Men fail. Husbands fail. Fathers are not always right. The Uncommon Mother knows the Source of everything she needs to succeed—the Holy Spirit Who created her. She does not depend upon her own education, influence or skills. She lives relaxed, because Someone greater than anyone else lives within her. The Holy Spirit never fails her.

"Greater is He that is in you, than he that is in the world" (1 John 4:4).

30. The Uncommon Mother Always Chooses Her Words Carefully. Words create tragedies or triumphs. Words birth fear or faith. The world was created by the words that God spoke. Knowing this, the Uncommon Mother educates her children in the carefulness of words. Every success you experience begins with the words in your mouth. The Uncommon Mother mentors her children in the wise selection of words that heal instead of hurt.

"For by thy words, thou shalt be justified, and by thy words thou shalt be condemned" (Matthew 12:37).

31. The Uncommon Mother Always Teaches Her Children The Secret Of Blessing. The secret of blessing is not merely what you know, but what you sow. The Uncommon Seed always produces the Uncommon Harvest. It is the hidden mystery of supernatural increase. The Uncommon Mother shows her children how to multiply, increase and produce their desired Harvest. She explains the reason she tithes and the Harvest she expects in return. It causes her children to completely depend upon God.

"Honour the Lord with thy substance, and with the firstfruits of all thine increase: So shall thy barns be filled with plenty, and thy presses shall burst out with new wine" (Proverbs 3:9,10).

RECOMMENDED BOOKS AND TAPES:
B-36 The Mother's Topical Bible (468 pages/$10)
B-57 31 Secrets Of An Unforgettable Woman (140 pages/$9)

You Will Never Leave
Where You Are
Until You Decide
Where You Would Rather Be.

-MIKE MURDOCK

⊗ **30** ⊗

MOTIVATING YOURSELF

It Happens To Everyone.

Your happiest moments *dissipate.*

Your energy suddenly *dissolves...*in a moment.

Your excitement over accomplishing the Dream suddenly is *gone...*as you wake up one morning.

Many people with great potential and great dreams have *lost their motivation* to achieve them. When you drive by a graveyard, remember this...many are inside those graves with buried dreams, buried treasures, buried potential...that never was fulfilled...because they lost their motivation.

It is not enough to have a great dream or skills.

You must learn the steps to take...what to do...when all the reasons, drive and enthusiasm for a worthwhile goal have *dissipated.*

It matters to me...because I understand what this is like.

Divorce can be *wrenching,* destroying all motivation to live.

Loss of a loved one can birth uncommon grief.

Disappointment in a love relationship can make you literally want to die and wish you could disappear.

Loss of confidence in others can ruin you.

It is *possible* to regain lost motivation.

It is *necessary* to regain lost motivation.

It is *easier* than you think...to regain your motivation.

You can *dream* again.

You can *launch* and *birth* your dreams again.

7 Keys To Motivating Yourself

1. Everything Can Break Down, Burn Out Or Crash. *The television advertisement was astounding.*

I viewed the advertisement, glued to the screen. This company had exciting people, passionate and enthusiastic about their computer saying that it was the best thing on earth that ever happened. It showed them in the workplace and at home. It was so simple that even children could run the computer! Such enthusiasm affected me.

So, I picked up the phone. I asked my assistant to order me that individualized and customized computer from this great company. The company itself was praised everywhere. I was ecstatic. When it arrived a few days later...so many things I had ordered were supposed to be on it.

However the list I had given was not completed. Several things were missing.

So, I sent the computer back. They added what had not been put on. They sent it back to me.

It started "crashing" every five to ten minutes.

I had spent thousands of dollars. But, it continuously gave me problems.

Anything bought eventually breaks.

Anything created eventually crumbles.

Anything born can die.

That is why motivating yourself again is so valuable.

When I awoke this morning, I was very concerned over my loss of motivation...for several goals.

▶ *Loss of motivation for my morning workouts.* My enthusiasm of three months ago was completely gone. I did not want to do another thing toward health.

▶ *Loss of motivation toward nutrition or proper eating.* I was tired of reading about right foods, eating right portions, exercising and developing health.

▶ *Loss of motivation toward book writing.* As I meditated on my loss of motivation, I thought about my book writing. It has been several months since I really focused on writing a new book. That concerned me. My first love in the area of productivity...is my book writing.

▶ *Loss of motivation towards my personal prayer life.* It has been to The Secret Place...for my four-hour prayer time.

Motivating myself towards these four goals...has been at an all time low.

I thought on this and realized the importance, more than ever, of keeping motivated toward a worthwhile goal.

Oh, I have accomplished many things the last several weeks and months. My life has been *continuous* productivity, *daily, hourly.* But, I have not received great fulfillment from the things that have been accomplished. The things that generate my greatest pleasure and joy...have gone *undone, unfinished* and *not attended to.*

As I thought on this, I felt a little flicker of desire to dictate this book to you and discuss my feelings as I am experiencing them.

So, I reached for my microcassette recorder. It is the most expensive one in the world. The company is famous. I have experienced problems with the last five recorders I have owned. As I picked up my new one, it did not work. I am supposing it is the batteries. At any rate, nothing moved.

So, I reached for my beautiful digital recorder. It has never failed me. It has been good when I have used it. But, it only flickered a little sign, "Low battery!"

So, I telephoned my transcriber. She has a machine hooked up to a specific phone number that I can call and record my personal dictation. She, in turn, types it out and returns it to me via e-mail.

The codes for using the phone failed to work. We finally secured the correct codes and started the process. So, I called the telephone number. It rang and rang and rang.

New equipment has been installed in her home, and something has gone wrong with her recording telephone number.

Everything can break down.

Everything can burn out.

The best of the best...can crash.

So, when you are tempted to feel inferior, discouraged and depressed over your loss of motivation...simply laugh out loud!

Everything burns out. Everything breaks down. Everything crashes.

You must simply repair it.

You must face it, confront it and correct it.

Permitting yourself to remain unmotivated will *compound* your problems...until you lose everything including your health, your family and your very life itself.

The greatest among us lose motivation. If you read the biographies of Uncommon Achievers and leaders, you will discover seasons where they felt incredible discouragement and despondency. They felt like giving up.

But, their difference was their ability to *renew* their motivation and enthusiasm.

You keep going...until you hit the vein of gold again. It may not happen automatically. You must take the necessary steps toward it.

History is full of chaotic and horrifying deaths, painful situations because the people did not regain their motivation.

Jesus Himself experienced moments of lost motivation. Look at His behavior in the Garden of Gethsemane for a moment. He even prayed, "Father, if it be Thy will, let this cup pass from Me." He sweated as it were drops of blood. This was His *crisis hour.* His moment of lost motivation.

Jeremiah experienced lost motivation.

Micah experienced great loss of motivation.

Jonah lost his motivation and even refused to obey the command to go to Nineveh. Jonah experienced the horrifying belly of the fish. He cried out in his anguish until he got back on track.

What happens when you lose motivation?

You must realize the potential *pain* and *eventuality* of lost motivation.

Suicide can happen to those who do not regain their motivation for life. Some of the wealthiest and most famous people in the world committed suicide...because they refused to take the important steps to recapture their motivation.

2. Your Success Is Determined By Your Ability To Stay Motivated. *It will happen.* That day will come...that you lose your incentive, your energy and enthusiasm for your dreams, your goals and even the relationships that matter.

Motivation is possessing incentive and reward for pursuing a desired goal.

In embezzlement cases, investigators search for an employee who is having financial difficulties. They know that if someone is experiencing blackmail, bankruptcy or great grief, they will do desperate things. As the saying goes, *desperate people do desperate things.* Why do they look for someone experiencing financial devastation as a person who may embezzle money? That person who desperately needs money...will do desperate things to generate money. They are looking for someone who has a reason or incentive for risking this behavior.

In murder cases, the same procedure is followed. Who was the *beneficiary* on the life insurance? When was the life insurance taken out? Was anyone vindicative toward the victim? They are looking for someone with the *motivation*...the *reason* for *doing it.*

Motivation is your *energy, incentive, passion* or *reward* for specific conduct or behavior.

It is incredibly important and a necessary ingredient in the life of every achiever.

Mothers and *fathers* require motivation to continue to rear their children properly.

Teenagers must maintain motivation...to stay in school, finish...graduate.

Every *pastor* requires continuous motivation...to maintain his spiritual vigil over his flock.

Every *employee* must learn to nurture his motivation...or he will look for reasons to stay home from work.

Sometimes, the motivation for doing something is to avoid *pain.*

Sometimes, the motivation for a task is to experience *gain* or *reward.*

It is generally accepted that most of our conduct occurs to avoid pain. Financial pain. Social loss. Pain of rejection. But, almost everything we do is to avoid pain.

Your *Financial Success* depends on your ability to stay motivated and be productive on your job.

Your *Relationship Success* depends on your ability to stay motivated...to keep communicating, to make necessary changes and adjustments, to listen and honor those around you.

Your *Career Success* will require constant motivation before you can experience promotion, improvement and dramatic success.

Your *Spiritual Success* will require the ability to stay motivated...toward God, the Word of God and even your prayer life. As my father often says about prayer, "The secret to a prayer life is to get something when you pray. That will bring you back to the place of prayer. If you do not receive something when you pray, you will lose your motivation to return."

Many people experience births, surges and dramatic beginnings of enthusiasm.

Have you ever gone to a football game? You sat there. Your mind was on many things. But, as the team began to play, and the fans around you began to rally and scream, little by little your focus was brought to the game at hand. The worries about your job dissolved. The anxieties about rearing your children dissipated. You became totally focused on that game.

Your Focus Determines Your Feelings.

Those around you helped reinforce your focus on that game...and you recaptured enthusiasm and excitement for it. You recaptured that enthusiasm...though the circumstances of your life never changed for one single moment. Your family problems remained unsettled. Your job situation did not change. What happened? *Your focus changed.*

That is why I want you to read and understand this incredible Wisdom Study on Staying Motivated...because your motivation is not decided by the changing circumstances around you.

▶ The *atmosphere you create* around you affects your motivation.

▶ The *people you associate with* affects your motivation.

▶ Your *focus* determines your motivation.

As you see, your success in life is completely determined by your ability to stay focused, keep motivated and retain your enthusiasm for worthwhile dreams.

You are the creation of God. You will experience great moments of inspiration, surges of enthusiasm and victorious moments of launching worthwhile dreams. Those dreams are worthy, lawful and ideal. Those dreams are worth the investment of your time, your energy and your life.

God births these Uncommon Dreams within you...for a *reason*...and for a *season*.

Others will respond to your motivation, your passion and the fulfillment of your life.

Thousands can be affected by you. The Law of 250 in relationships proves this. I read some time back that the average person influences 250 others. Those 250 affect another 250 each and so on. The waves of your influence are limitless.

Somebody *broken*...needs your motivation.

Somebody *confused*...needs your motivation.

Somebody *misdirected* and *unfocused*...needs your motivation.

Somebody will *fail*...unless you stay motivated.

Somebody will *die* an untimely death...unless you stay motivated.

You may ask this question, "Why should I fight to stay motivated when it seems easier to stay depressed, uninvolved and just quit?"

If quitting brings you joy, then quit.

If quitting generates peace, then quit.

If quitting is your answer, why are you so miserable?

Quitting does not produce the desired result...so there is no reason to quit!

There is nothing to go back to!

Replay the happiest moments of your life. They were *productive* moments. They were hours and days of *uncommon enthusiasm* toward a worthwhile goal. You had a picture that you were pursuing. You saw an internal Portrait of Possibilities. You *focused* on it.

The circumstances of your life may not change as much as you think...but, it is your *focus* that requires adjustment.

Every successful businessman had days of little motivation. I think it was Abraham Lincoln who said, "Success is the ability to go from failure to failure without losing your enthusiasm." He should know! Think of all the losses that he experienced in his pursuit of political office, the presidency of the United States, before he became the president. He experienced great adversity, continuous losses. He experienced continuous rejection of the majority of people who were voting for him.

But, he learned how to stay motivated.

Motivating yourself is one of the *Master Secrets to Success.*

3. You Will Fail With Your Life Unless You Learn How To Motivate Yourself. Failures occur daily.

Thousands fail with their life...weekly, hourly and daily. They fail to achieve their potential, their greatness and their dreams.

Millions fail in their *family life,* because they do not know how to stimulate dormant love.

Millions fail in their *business* because they lose enthusiasm to produce and achieve a great goal.

Many *ministers* have failed in their ministry because of broken focus. Instead of staying focused on something they could achieve, the pain of rejection and the confusion over unmotivated saints brought distress and stress.

The *hospitals* are full of people who failed...because they lost their motivation to keep their health.

The *divorce courts* are full of people who lost motivation...to develop adequate communication skills in their relationships.

The *bankruptcy cases* are plentiful...because of those who lost their motivation to learn, make adjustments and develop customer relationships.

You, too, will fail unless you sit down and evaluate the losses you will experience without this great skill...the art of *motivating yourself.*

Your destiny will require your own decision-making.

Destiny is not the inevitable occurrence of fate.

Destiny necessitates your involvement. Your decisions. Your own passion.

3 Basic Philosophies Exist On The Earth

1.   God Is In Control Of Everything That Happens On The Earth. Is this true? Are my decisions unnecessary? If everything that happens is planned and ordered by God, you cannot legally prosecute a rapist...nor a murderer...nor a child abuser. Why? If you believe God is in control, that person is not responsible for their own conduct and behavior. God is responsible. Is that possible? *Of course not.* Jesus said He was not willing that any should perish but that all should come to repentance...yet people are perishing every day. In Matthew 23:37 He looked across Jerusalem and said, "How often would I gathered thy children together, even as a hen gathereth her chickens under her wings, and ye would not!"

God did not predestine your decisions; God only predestined the *consequences* of your decisions.

2.   Satan Is In Control Of Everything On The Earth. If he is, why is there so much success, enthusiasm, passion, miracles happening on the earth? If satan were in control of the earth, nobody would serve Christ. No preacher would ever preach the gospel. No man would get saved. No, satan is not in control of the entire earth or terrorism would rule.

3.   Your Personal Decisions Are Creating Your Personal Circumstances. It is documented 331 times in scripture. Review Isaiah 1:19,20, "If ye be willing and obedient, ye shall eat the good of the land: But if ye refuse and rebel, ye shall be devoured with the sword:"

This indicates and proves that I am involved in the decisions of my life.

> ▶ *The Quality Of Your Wisdom Determines The Quality Of Your Decisions.*
> ▶ *The Quality Of Your Decisions Are Revealed In The Circumstances Of Your LIfe.*
> ▶ *Your Financial Circumstances Reveal Your Financial Decisions.*
> ▶ *Your Relationship Circumstances Reveal Your Relationship Skills...And The Quality Of Your Decision.*

You *can* succeed. You need not fail.

But, you must learn the secrets of *Motivating Yourself*...to avoid the horrifying and tragic consequences of daily failure.

4.   It Is Your Personal Responsibility To Motivate Yourself Toward Your Dreams. *You are responsible for yourself.*

Nobody else is responsible for motivating you.

Nobody else is responsible for *your* goals.

You are accountable for your own gifts and skills.

You are accountable for your opportunities.

You are responsible for your own future.

Others may motivate you. Encourage you. Or, even help out emotionally, financially and spiritually. It is wonderful to have worthwhile and caring friends to strengthen you during times of difficulty.

But, they are responsible for themselves, their own motivation and their own dreams and goals.

Someday...you will be alone.

Sometimes...others are carrying burdens too heavy for themselves anyway. Your burden is impossible for them to carry.

You must *cultivate* the gift of motivating yourself.

Stop blaming painful childhood experiences.

Stop blaming your mate for all your feelings.

Stop waiting for everybody else to correct themselves...so you can experience a moment of enthusiasm and ecstasy.

Decide *now*...the *direction* you want your life to go.

Decide *now*...the *environment* you want to cultivate and develop around you.

Decide *now*...how true *success* is defined for you personally.

Decide *now*...what you are willing to *live with* and what you are wiling to *live without*.

Freedom may be important to you.

Financial success may be important to you.

Happiness in your marriage and family may be important to you.

Does *spiritual peace* matter to you?

Does *laughter* matter to you?

Does your *legacy* that you are leaving for others really matter to you?

Then, let us get on with your life.

3 Essential Keys In Staying Motivated

1. **Identify What Matters Most To The Heart Of God.**
What does God *expect* of you?

What does God *require* of you?

What has God *spoken* to you to do with your life?

2. **Identify What Matters The Most To You About Your Life.**

3. **Identify What Matters The Least To You.** Uncommon Wisdom came from my Uncommon Mother regarding the will of God for your life. "Son, the will of God is really an attitude. You can get in the

will of God...in a single moment. The very moment that you recognize you are on the wrong track and you cry out to God and give Him your whole heart. At that moment, when you surrender your whole heart to His plan and will, you will immediately enter and be in the center of the will of God."

That has helped me beyond description.

A foolish decision may launch you into a painful season.

A single wrong relationship can batter, bruise or even break you. It may take two or three years for that wrong decision to be exposed and admitted.

Yet, in a single moment your pursuit of God positions you in His presence.

You can enter the will of God for your life.

Your past can be concluded.

Your focus can be restored toward a specific goal that generates great joy and enthusiasm again.

You can enter the perfect plan of God for your life...in a single moment.

5. Identify The Specific Factors That Create Distraction And Loss Of Motivation In Your Life. Everything has a root cause.

Years ago, I wrote a little song called, "There's A Reason For It All."

The Bible says quite simply, "...the curse causeless shall not come" (Proverbs 26:2).

When you lost your motivation, there were downward steps that you took. Identify those influences.

6. Recognize The Elements That Awaken Your Energy, Enthusiasm And Passion. I love learning.

Discovery is my greatest joy.

When I read something...or someone teaches me a new truth....I become ecstatic.

That is why the presence of God is so important to me. Every morning when I pray in The Secret Place, the Holy Spirit reveals pictures of possibilities. He unlocks truths I never saw before. My heart is awakened. My mind is on fire. My goals are adjusted and focused.

The presence of God is invaluable to me. It is where I make my greatest discoveries. You will, too.

7. Your Words And Conversations Greatly Affect Your Own Motivation. Words create currents.

Words create currents in your emotions, your home, your mind, your life and the very earth.

Words unleash war...or birth peace.

Words are the tools God has given you to create the environment you want to live in, reap from and sculpture around you.

3 Basic Reasons For Losing Your Motivation

1. Fatigue Affects Your Motivation. You can overwork yourself on a great and worthwhile dream. Fatigue and weariness of flesh can be devastating to a dream and a goal. Years ago, Michael Korda, the editor of *Time Magazine*, wrote in his book on success that energy is the first necessary ingredient for true success.

Energy is necessary for success.

Tired Eyes Rarely See A Great Future.

When Fatigue Walks In, Faith Walks Out.

I have finished great meetings and experienced great success...yet, awakened the next morning so drained emotionally and mentally that I wanted to quit the ministry.

I do not always understand this kind of emptiness. There are other times that I have felt weary in body and mind, yet for unknown reasons...I stayed motivated. I did not study those reasons. Perhaps, there were friends around me encouraging me. Perhaps, I was so focused on one thing that I kept motivated.

Whatever the reason, fatigue plays an influential role in the destruction of your joy, your motivation and your life.

Rest is an achievement.

Sleep is an achievement.

Jesus put it this way, "Come ye apart and rest a while:" (Mark 6:31).

God Himself rested on the seventh day after six days of creation. I have often been puzzled about that. Was He tired? Of course not. Was His creativity exhausted? Of course not.

Possibly...He was setting an example for us to recognize the Rhythm of Life.

Solomon wrote it this way, "There is a time to be born...a time to die..." (Ecclesiastes 3:1-8). There is a time for things.

Wrong timing...in a professional heavyweight boxing match can lose a world title.

Wrong timing...in investing in the stock market can result in your bankruptcy and financial destruction.

Wrong timing...in conversation with your mate can eventually bring you to a divorce court.

2. Attempting Too Many Things At The Same Time Will Affect Your Motivation. J. Paul Getty, the great billionaire, once said, "I've seen as many people fail from attempting too many things as attempting too few."

Paul wrote, "This one thing I do" (Philippians 3:13).

Passion and enthusiasm are magnificent traits of Uncommon Achievers. Unfortunately, it often results in attempting to help too many people at the same time. Too many requirements and demands on a doctor can result in a deterioration of his own health.

Great preachers have experienced the unraveling of their own ministry and anointing...when they attempted too much at the same time.

Decide what matters the most to you in your Future.

Decide what matters the most to you about Today.

Discern what matters Least.

Pinpoint your specific responsibilities to God.

Pinpoint your responsibilities to your Family.

Decide your limitations...your frustrations...your observations... and be willing to take the first small step toward adjustment today.

3. Unhealthy Relationships Drain You Emotionally And Mentally. Be honest with yourself. It often exists in your own family. In associates around you. Different relationships exude different energy levels.

Some of your friends will generate incredible creativity and movement in your emotions and spirit. You come alive in their presence. You dream bigger as they begin to talk to you. Other relationships will leave you empty, exhausted and focused on your problems instead of your future.

Every Friendship Does Not Have Equal Value. You must embrace this, accept it and live by it.

Everything in your life has a different value and you must learn to prioritize those things that matter most.

Who is speaking doubt into your life?

Who is making you feel inferior?

Who has demonstrated great affection and loyalty and confidence in you?

Who gives you the most gifts?

Who is willing to spend the most time with you?

What happens in your spirit in the presence of specific friendships?

Do you have a friend that requires more energy and time than your Assignment is requiring?

Do you have a friend that is angry because you invest your time and energy in your Assignment instead of them personally?

Withdraw from those who stay unhappy with you without a true reason and cause.

Withdraw from those who continuously find fault with you though you are emptying your very life out daily.

Withdraw from those who feel insulted when you do not telephone them, though your own life seems overwhelming and you cannot get everything done.

It is equally important to:

Pursue those who find moments in your presence exhilarating and invaluable to them. They prove it by counting each moment as a priceless irreplaceable gift.

Pursue those who willingly adapt to your schedule...to taste the pleasure of your company, your conversation and mentorship.

Identify Your Greatest Sources Of Inspiration

1. Who Are Your Three Favorite Conversationalists Whose Words Unlock Your Creativity And Energy?

2. What Environment Feeds Your Enthusiasm And Joy? I love shopping. I love a new shopping mall and seeing new products, new inventions and great marketing programs. Sometimes, I will go to a mall and walk through it knowing that when I finish, a great energy will have entered me because of things I saw or experienced.

3. What Hobbies Or Attractions Awaken Your Enthusiasm And Motivation? I love leather cases of all kinds. I love to see the new electronic equipment that is released and created from month to month. When I go to an electronic store, seeing the new PDA's or new gadgets that have been created excites me. New features on a computer awaken my energy and unlock a new joy in me. Nurture an understanding of what stimulates you, too.

4. What Daily Or Monthly Accomplishment Births Fulfillment And A Sense Of Significance In Your Life? When I dictate a book, I feel progress inside. When I finish a book, I feel progress inside. When I finish a book and get it published, I feel exhilarated.

When I have the finances to send a new book to over 100,000 partners, I am ecstatic. I love sowing. Sowing generates great joy in me.

When I find someone in great need who is worthy of receiving a gift, I love sowing that gift into their life. I am always looking for someone who qualifies to receive a Harvest from God.

Any movement towards order around me...brings great enthusiasm to me. Last night, I came home late to several of my staff working and getting things back in place here at my house. They had opened box after box to put back into place because of some changes and renovations here at my home. Seeing their enthusiasm and willingness to get things in order around me...meant the world to me. I was ecstatic over it. I was happy. I am agitated by all the details involved in getting things organized...but, it generates great joy in me to watch others do it!

Some tasks generate joy while you are doing them.

Some activities generate enthusiasm when you begin them.

Some activities generate enthusiasm when you finish them.

Helpful Keys To Using Words As Personal Motivation

1. Use Songs Of Worship To Cure The Deadly Disease Of Worry Within You. Worry is unproductive meditation on problems facing you. Unresolved issues.

Worship will correct that focus and bring you into the presence of God. "Serve the Lord with gladness: come before His presence with singing" (Psalm 100:2).

2. Use Words Of Encouragement And Healing To Those Around You. It is easy to find things wrong in those around you every day. Your desire to correct them may be meaningful to you, but destructive to them. Affirm them. Find something they are doing right and discuss it with them. Remind them of how different and important they are to your life.

3. Use The Vocabulary Of An Overcomer Instead Of A Victim. Stop saying, "I have a problem to solve."

Start saying, "Some issues are being resolved that will really make a difference in our company and bring much success to us all."

Stop saying, "I have made many mistakes in my life."

Start saying, "I have made many discoveries that have brought me to new successes and joy."

Stop saying, "I have too many things to do."

Start saying, "I am incredibly productive today."

You Will Start Succeeding Significantly In Your Life When You Learn To Motivate Yourself Hourly.

RECOMMENDED BOOKS AND TAPES:

B-14 Seeds Of Wisdom On Relationships (32 pages/$3)

B-24 Seeds Of Wisdom On Faith-Talk (32 pages/$3)

TS-42 School Of Wisdom, Vol. 2: "101 Wisdom Keys That Have Most Changed My Life" (6 tapes/$30)

~ 31 ~

NEGOTIATION

━━━━◆▷◉◁◆━━━━

Negotiation could be defined for the Winner as, "The ability to change opinions and circumstances or to come to agreement through a climate of favor, not force."

The Apostle Paul was a master of successful negotiation. Educated under a brilliant lawyer, Paul became incredibly skilled in the art of debate, persuasion and logic. Power, prestige and wealth did not intimidate Paul. When he spoke, kings listened and trembled. But the fiery apostle dealt with many Christians with gentleness, kindness and grace.

Paul's ability to negotiate through the spirit of love is clearly demonstrated in his letter to Philemon, a personal friend and owner of a slave named Onesimus. Onesimus had evidently stolen from Philemon, a convert of Paul's. He had run away, met Paul and became converted. The letter is an appeal from Paul to accept Onesimus, not as a servant, but as a brother. From this letter I have taken 26 proven principles that you can use, as Paul did, to win through negotiation.

Paul's 26 Principles Of Successful Negotiation

1. He Created A Climate Of Compassion. "Paul, a prisoner of Jesus Christ," (vs. 1).

2. He Included Others To Demonstrate The Widespread Effect Of The Decision. "Timothy our brother unto Philemon...and to your beloved Apphia and Archippus...and to the church in thy house:" (vs. 1,2).

3. He Revealed Appreciation Of The Relationship With Open Affection. "...unto Philemon our dearly beloved," (vs.1).

4. He Reduced A Climate Of Conflict By Establishing Mutual Objectives. "...unto Philemon our dearly beloved, and fellow labourer," (vs. 1).

5. He Gently Made Philemon Aware Of His Spiritual Responsibility. "...and to the church in thy house:" (vs. 2).

**6. He Possessed And Projected Genuine Concern For

Philemon's Well-Being. "Grace to you, and peace, from God our Father and the Lord Jesus Christ. I thank my God, making mention of thee always in my prayers" (vs. 3,4).

7. He Reminded Him That His Personal Reputation Was Involved. "Hearing of thy love and faith, which thou has toward the Lord Jesus, and toward all saints;" (vs. 5).

8. He Expressed Appreciation Of The High Quality And Good Effect Of His Past Reputation. "Hearing of thy love and faith, which thou hast toward the Lord Jesus, and toward all saints;...For we have great joy and consolation in thy love, because the bowels of the saints are refreshed by thee, brother" (vs. 5,7).

9. He Expressed Confidence In His Compassion And Concern. "Hearing of thy love and faith, which thou hast toward the Lord Jesus, and toward all saints;...For we have great joy and consolation in thy love," (vs. 5,7).

10. He Reminded Philemon Of The Power Of His Influence For Good. "For we have great joy and consolation in thy love, because the bowels of the saints are refreshed by thee, brother" (vs. 7).

11. He Approached Him With An Attitude Of Humility. "Yet for love's sake I rather beseech thee," (vs. 9).

12. He Appealed To His Tenderness By Revealing His Position Of Disadvantage. "...being such an one as Paul the aged, and now also a prisoner of Jesus Christ" (vs. 9).

13. He Clearly Defined The Subject Of Concern. "I beseech thee for my son Onesimus, whom I have begotten in my bonds:" (vs. 10).

14. He Showed The Case Was Not Optional, But Of Personal Importance. "I beseech thee for my son Onesimus," (vs. 10).

15. He Established Disadvantages Of The Previous Agreement. "Which in time past was to thee unprofitable," (vs. 11).

16. He Expected Mutual Gain From The New Arrangement. "Which in time past was to thee unprofitable, but now to thee and to me:" (vs. 11).

17. He Allowed Philemon To Make His Own Decision Based On His Understanding Of The New Advantages. "But without thy mind would I do nothing; that thy benefit should not be as it were of necessity, but willingly" (vs. 14).

18. He Showed How The Problem Was A Necessary Passport To A Greater Benefit. "For perhaps he therefore departed for a season, that thou shouldest receive him for ever;" (vs. 15).

19. He Illustrated How The New Agreement Would Help

Philemon Personally. "For perhaps he therefore departed for a season, that thou shouldest receive him for ever; Not now as a servant, but above a servant, a brother beloved, specially to me, but how much more unto thee, both in the flesh, and in the Lord?" (vs. 15,16).

20. He Stated What He Wanted And Asked For A Decision. "If thou count me therefore a partner, receive him as myself" (vs. 17).

21. He Allowed For Unknown Factors And Offered Compensation For Any Loss. "If he hath wronged thee, or oweth thee ought, put that on mine account;" (vs. 18).

22. He Proved Sincerity By Being Willing To Commit To A Written Contract. "I Paul have written it with mine own hand, I will repay it:" (vs. 19).

23. He Reminded Him Of Previous Personal Efforts Uncompensated For. "Albeit I do not say to thee how thou owest unto me even thine own self besides" (vs. 19).

24. He Expressed How Much His Personal Happiness Depended On The Decision. "Yea, brother, let me have joy of thee in the Lord: refresh my bowels in the Lord" (vs. 20).

25. He Spoke With Confidence In Philemon's Ability To Make A Good Decision And Even Planned Around It. "Having confidence in thy obedience I wrote unto thee, knowing that thou wilt also do more than I say" (vs. 21).

26. He Shared Future Projections Of Fellowship And A Working Relationship. "But withal prepare me also a lodging: for I trust that through your prayers I shall be given unto you" (vs. 22). "The grace of our Lord Jesus Christ be with your spirit. Amen" (vs. 25). Paul knew the Golden Rule of Negotiation: "And as ye would that men should do to you, do ye also to them likewise" (Luke 6:31).

RECOMMENDED BOOKS AND TAPES:

TS-10 Paul's 26 Secrets For Negotiation (6 tapes/$30)
B-44 31 Secrets For Career Success (115 pages/$10)

God Will Never Advance You
Beyond Your Last Act
Of Disobedience.

-MIKE MURDOCK

～ 32 ～

OBEDIENCE

Obedience Is The Only Thing God Will Ever Require Of You.

18 Facts You Should Know About Obedience

1. When You Ask God For A Miracle, He Will Always Give You An Instruction. Each miracle is linked to an act of *obedience.* Your obedience is the *only proof* that you truly believed His instructions to you.

Let me illustrate. Picture yourself sitting at a table. You instruct your teenage son to mow the grass the next morning. You also warn him that if he fails to do so, he will not be able to attend the football game the following weekend.

When you arrive home from work, the grass is still high. It is not mowed. You are infuriated. You walk to his bedroom only to find him propped upon his bed with his TV blaring, and he is on the telephone with his girlfriend. What happened?

He really did not believe you.

So, you speak to him and say, "You have forfeited the privilege of attending the football game next weekend."

"Oh, come on. That is not fair!" he yells out. "I am going to do it. I just do not want to do it *today!*"

This is so simple but very clear. *He did not obey your instruction because he really did not believe you would do what you said.* Now, if you yield to his clamoring, whining and complaining, and you permit him to attend the game, you will *destroy every thread of credibility* being woven around his life. Your words will never mean anything to him.

So, when the weekend rolls around, you make him stay home. Will he remember it the next time you instruct him to mow the grass? *Probably.*

2. Pain Is Sometimes Necessary For Us To Understand The Importance Of Obedience. This often happens in our relationship with God. You see, He longs to be our Companion, our Mentor, our Best Friend. He is not a military leader in our lives. He is much more than a boss. He does not enjoy punishment. In fact, He lives to show mercy. "For the Lord is good; His mercy is everlasting; and His truth endureth to all generations. Praise ye the Lord. O give thanks unto the Lord; for He is good: for His mercy endureth for ever" (Psalm 100:5; 106:1).

Unfortunately, sometimes His instructions are not taken seriously. Sometimes He is scorned, scoffed at and ignored.

3. Nobody Succeeds Who Ignores Him. He is God.

4. He Is A Holy God. "Because it is written, Be ye holy; for I am holy" (1 Peter 1:16).

5. He Is A Just God. "Tell ye, and bring them near; yea, let them take counsel together: who hath declared this from ancient time? who hath told it from that time? have not I the Lord? and there is no God else beside Me; a just God and a Saviour; there is none beside Me" (Isaiah 45:21).

6. He Is A Jealous God. "Thou shalt bow down thyself to them, nor serve them: for I the Lord thy God am a jealous God, visiting the iniquity of the fathers upon the children unto the third and fourth generation of them that hate Me;" (Exodus 20:5).

7. Obedience Is The Only Proof That You Truly Trust Him. And He longs to be believed. Two of the most wonderful truths I have discovered in my entire life are:

His Only Pleasure Is To Be Believed.

His Only Pain Is To Be Doubted.

8. He Wants To Be Believed And Obedience Is The Only Proof Of Your Faith. "God is not a man, that He should lie; neither the son of man, that He should repent: hath He said , and shall He not do it? or hath He spoken, and shall He not make it good?" (Numbers 23:19)

9. He Wants Us To Obey Him In Order To Produce Good Seasons Of Blessing And Rewards In Our Lives. "If ye be willing and obedient, ye shall eat the good of the land" (Isaiah 1:19).

10. He Offers Rewards As Incentives For Obedience. "And all these blessings shall come on thee, and overtake thee, if thou shalt hearken unto the voice of the Lord thy God" (Deuteronomy 28:2).

11. He Warns Of Penalties To Discourage Us From Disobedience. "But it shall come to pass, if thou wilt not hearken unto the voice of the Lord thy God, to observe to do all His commandments and His statutes which I command thee this day; that all these curses shall come upon thee, and overtake thee" (Deuteronomy 28:15).

12. He Expects Obedience. Jesus said, "My sheep hear My voice, and I know them, and they follow Me" (John 10:27).

13. Your Assignment Will Contain A Collection Of Instructions. Most of them are already clearly written in the Word of

God. You can read them daily. You can hear them daily on cassette tapes. Some people want to hear instructions spoken into their conscious minds or hearts that differ from what He has already established in His Word. "For ever, O Lord, Thy word is settled in heaven" (Psalm 119:89).

14. You Will Never Receive An Instruction From The Holy Spirit That Contradicts His Word. "For ever, O Lord, Thy word is settled in heaven" (Psalm 119:89).

15. God Will Permit Adversity To Enable You To Learn His Laws. "It is good for me that I have been afflicted; that I might learn Thy statutes" (Psalm 119:71).

16. His Word Prevents Disaster And Destruction. "Unless Thy law had been my delights, I should then have perished in mine affliction" (Psalm 119:92).

17. His Word Is The Only Ingredient That Cleanses Your Mind And Life. "Wherewithal shall a young man cleanse his way? by taking heed thereto according to Thy word" (Psalm 119:9).

18. God Will Destroy A Part To Preserve The Whole. "And if thy right eye offend thee, pluck it out, and cast it from thee: for it is profitable for thee that one of thy members should perish, and not that thy whole body should be cast into hell. And if thy right hand offend thee, cut it off, and cast it from thee: for it is profitable for thee that one of thy members should perish, and not that thy whole body should be cast into hell" (Matthew 5:29,30).

Mercy is very important to God.
Grace is just as important to Him.
His mercy is *forgiveness...from* sin.
His *grace* is empowerment...over sin.
His mercy is the removal...of sin.
His grace is victory...*over* sin.
Mercy is a removing of sin.
Grace is an *imparting of power.*
His grace (or power to overcome) is as accessible as His mercy.
His goal is *not* really mercy.
His goal is *relationship.*
His mercy is His bridge into *grace.*
His grace is the bridge into *relationship.*
When you ignore grace, relationship becomes impossible.
The most important thing you will do today is obey His voice...Every Hour.
Your *joy* depends on it.
Your *Assignment* depends on it.
Your life depends on it.

The Seasons Of Your Life
Will Change
Every Time You Decide
To Use Your Faith.

-MIKE MURDOCK

❧ 33 ❧

OPPORTUNITY

Opportunity Is A Gift From God.
Opportunity is any situation where your favorable qualities and skills, known or unknown, can be recognized, received and ultimately rewarded.

4 Facts You Should Know About Opportunity

1. God Is The God Of Opportunity. Throughout the Word, countless examples remind us that God gives men an opportunity to repent, rebuild and even receive miracles.

2. Opportunities Are Often Overlooked Because Of Immaturity Or Ignorance. One of my closest friends was invited to make a choice years ago: an automobile or a piece of land in Florida. He chose the automobile. Sadly, the land he rejected was connected to the famed Disney World. He lost a fortune because of it. He did not recognize the Golden Opportunity for investment.

3. An Opportunity Can Even Be Given To You During A Crisis Season Of Your Life. God spoke to Elijah to leave the brook and go to the widow of Zarephath...to give her an opportunity to use her faith (read 1 Kings 17).

4. An Opportunity Is Always Near You, Merely Awaiting Your Recognition Of It. "No good thing will He withhold from them that walk uprightly" (Psalm 84:11).

You Must Learn To Recognize These 8 Golden Opportunities

1. Recognition Of An Opportunity For Uncommon Mentorship. Elisha did and pursued Elijah. Ruth embraced Naomi, refusing to go back to Moab.

2. Recognition Of An Opportunity For A Miracle Of Healing. Blind Bartimaeus did. He cried out and received his healing.

**3. Recognition Of An Opportunity To Be Rewarded For

Destroying An Enemy. David did. He conquered Goliath.

4. Recognition Of An Uncommon Friendship That Can Bring Countless Joy. Jonathan did. He became known for his loyalty to David.

5. Recognition Of An Opportunity For Financial Breakthrough. The widow of Zarephath did.

Years ago, I received a telephone call. A friend of mine was involved in a networking organization. He flew out and assisted me. God helped me in a wonderful way. I made thousands of dollars. Yet, others around me never saw the opportunity. They were too busy complaining how hard it was to do.

6. Recognition Of An Opportunity For Significance. David did. He killed Goliath.

7. Recognition Of An Opportunity To Erase The Memory Of Every Stigma Of Your Life.

8. Recognition Of An Opportunity For Access To An Uncommon Man Of God. Oral Roberts once related to me that young preachers had spent hours with him without asking a single question about Divine Healing. How tragic!

Recognition Of A Golden Opportunity Can Turn An Empty Life Into Uncommon Success.

RECOMMENDED BOOKS AND TAPES:
B-114 The Law Of Recognition (248 pages/$10)

❧ 34 ❧

ORDER

━━━▷❂◁━━━

Order Decides Your Excellence, Increase And Prosperity.

30 Facts About Order

1. Order Is The Accurate Arrangement Of Things. Order is placing an item where it belongs. Order is keeping your shirts, ties and shoes in the appropriate place in your closet.

2. Order Increases Comfort. When you walk into a room of order, you want to stay. Things are "right." You feel clean, energized and happy. When you walk into a room of clutter and disorder, an unexplainable agitation begins. Sometimes, you are unable to even name it or understand it. But, *you were created for order,* and anything that slows you down emotionally or mentally will become a distraction.

3. When You Increase Order In Your Life You Will Increase Your Productivity. Filing cabinets, trays on the desk and special places for folders make it easier to get your tasks done *on time.* Have you ever shuffled paper after paper in search of a bill? Of course! When you finally located the bill, you were agitated and angry. It affected your entire day. *Disorder influences your attitude* more than you could ever imagine.

4. Everything You Are Doing Is Affecting Order In Your Life. Think for a moment. You get up from your breakfast table. Either you will leave your plate on the table, or you will take it to the sink. The decision you make will either increase the order or disorder around you. (Leaving it on the table increases your workload and creates disorder. Taking it to the sink *immediately* brings *order.*)

It happened last night for me. I took off my suit coat and laid it over the chair. I did not really feel like taking it over to the closet and hanging it up. But, realizing that I was going to hang it up sooner or later, I walked over to the closet and hung up my coat. I immediately increased order around me.

5. Every Moment You Are Increasing Order Or Creating Disorder Around You. Small, tiny actions can eventually produce chaotic situations.

6. Every Person Around You Is Increasing Order Or

Disorder. Some people have an attitude of disorder. They are unhappy unless everything is in disarray and cluttered. Others refuse to work in such an environment. Their productivity requires organization.

Somebody has said that the arrangement of things in your garage reveals much about your mind. Somebody asked me once, "Does this mean if I do not have a garage, that I really do not have a mind either?" (Smile!) I certainly hope that is not the case, but I am certain psychologists have come to some pretty accurate conclusions.

7. **Order Eliminates Stress And Agitation.** Every time you lose your keys, you are reminded to keep them *in a specific place*.

8. **Order Increases Accuracy.**

9. **Order Prevents Error.**

10. **Order Prevents Strife.** "And Abram said unto Lot, Let there be no strife, I pray thee, between me and thee, and between my herdmen and thy herdmen; for we be brethren" (Genesis 13:8).

"Cast out the scorner, and contention shall go out; yea, strife and reproach shall cease" (Proverbs 22:10).

11. **Order Creates Comfort.** When Lot left, Abraham prospered.

"Then had the churches rest" (Acts 9:31).

12. **Anyone Who Increases Order In Your Life Is Assisting You In The Achieving Of Your Dream.** Celebrate them and protect their role in your life.

13. **The Role Of Authority And Government Is To Increase And Maintain Order.** Policemen judge the traffic and speeding tickets are issued.

14. **Order Involves Time, Timing And Seasons.** "To every thing there is a season, and a time to every purpose under the heaven:" (Ecclesiastes 3:1).

15. **Order Involves Protocol, Approach And Ceremony.** Esther quietly respected the protocol established by the king.

16. **Order Must Precede Increase.** You must water the roots before a tree grows.

17. **Any Success In Your Life Has Been Created By A Degree Of Knowledge Or Benefit Of Order.** Joseph is a portrait of order and honoring authority.

18. **It Is The Responsibility Of Parents To Teach Order To Their Children.** Spiritual order, protocol and putting God first should be the priority of every believing parent.

19. **Maintaining Order Requires Continuous Focus And Attention To It.** Even taking notes on Order requires attention or you will write down notes *sideways* down the edge of the note

paper.

20. God's Goal Is Order, Not Soul Winning. He will withdraw His favor toward a major evangelist who is in sin, reaching millions to preserve order in the church.

21. Anyone Who Increases Order In Your Life Will Eventually Be Regarded As A Blessing To Your Life.

22. What Others View As Order May Not Be God's Order For You. Martha was agitated toward Mary for her sitting at the feet of Jesus.

Children want parents to stay home from work.

23. Order Will Require Major Decision-Making.

24. Creating Order Requires Total And Continuous Focus, Time And Discipline. It will not happen accidentally.

25. Recognize The Long-Term Chaos And Losses That Disorder Will Create. If this continues, your momentum will eventually destroy you and your productivity. Successes will become fewer.

26. Take A Long Hard And Serious Look At Your Personality. What can you do to take steps toward change?

27. Ask Others Who Are Gifted In Organization To Assist You And Keep You On Course. I read where Donald Trump said a few days ago that he hired one woman whose entire job is to keep things in order around him.

28. Do Not Berate Yourself And Become Overly Critical Because Of Your Lack Of Knowledge, Giftings Or Ability To Keep Things In Order.

29. Recognize Those Who God Puts Close To You Who Can Correct Things Around You And Keep Things In Order.

30. Do Not Try To Justify Disorder Around You. Relax, and take a small step today toward Order.

It is commendable that you are planning to take an entire week of your vacation to put everything in Order in your house next summer. However, I suggest you begin *this very moment* taking some steps to put things in place in the room.

Twenty minutes can make a major difference. Little hinges swing big doors. *You Can Get Anywhere You Want To Go If You Are Willing To Take Enough Small Steps.*

RECOMMENDED BOOKS AND TAPES:
B-44 31 Secrets For Career Success (115 pages/$10)

The Size Of Your Enemy
Determines
The Size Of Your Reward.

-MIKE MURDOCK

⇜ 35 ⇝

OVERCOMING

Never Forget Two Battle Truths!
1. *Your Battle Is Always For A Reason.*
2. *Your Battle Is Always For A Season.*

Overcomers Are The Only Ones Rewarded In Eternity. "He that overcometh, the same shall be clothed in white raiment; and I will not blot out his name out of the book of life, but I will confess his name before My Father, and before His angels. Him that overcometh will I make a pillar in the temple of My God, and he shall go no more out: and I will write upon him the name of My God, and the name of the city of My God, which is new Jerusalem, which cometh down out of heaven from My God: and I will write upon him My new name. To him that overcometh will I grant to sit with Me in My throne, even as I also overcame, and am set down with My Father in His throne" (Revelation 3:5,12,21).

"Fight the good fight of faith, lay hold on eternal life, whereunto thou art also called, and hast professed a good profession before many witnesses" (1 Timothy 6:12).

Well, go ahead and get back up and going! Something good is en route from the Father to you today!

8 Point Memo To Spiritual Soldiers

▶ *Accurately Assess Your Struggle.*
▶ *Name Your Real Enemy For Who He Is.*
▶ *Make A Quality Decision To Go On With God.* You have already been in your past. There was nothing there that you wanted, so fight to get into your future.
▶ *Make Up Your Mind To Conquer.*
▶ *Your Endurance Is Demoralizing To Satan.*
▶ *The Rewards Of Overcoming Are Worth A Thousand Times More Than Any Pain You Will Ever Experience.*
▶ *The Taste Of Victory Lasts Far Longer Than The Memory Of*

Your Struggle!

▶ *Overcomers Are The Only People Rewarded In Eternity.*

10 Facts Every Overcomer Must Remember

1. The Holy Spirit Is Very Reward Conscious. He knows the difference between obedience and disobedience; punishments and rewards. That is why He encouraged us to hear everything He had to say—"He that hath an ear, let him hear what the Spirit saith unto the churches" (Revelation 2:7). "...To day if ye will hear His voice, Harden not your heart, as in the provocation, and as in the day of temptation in the wilderness:" (Psalm 95:7,8).

2. The Holy Spirit Always Rewards The Obedient. He does not necessarily reward good people, smart people or wealthy people. He rewards *obedient* people.

3. The Holy Spirit Wants You To Become An Overcomer. "...Greater is He that is in you, than he that is in the world" (1 John 4:4).

4. Jesus Taught That The Holy Spirit Was The Secret Of Becoming An Overcomer. "But ye shall receive power, after that the Holy Ghost is come upon you:" (Acts 1:8). The Apostle Paul believed that you could be an overcomer. "I can do all things through Christ which strengtheneth me" (Philippians 4:13).

5. The Holy Spirit Gave You The Word Of God As A Weapon Against Your Enemy. "...and the sword of the Spirit, which is the word of God" (Ephesians 6:17).

6. The Holy Spirit Uses The Word To Produce The Nature Of An Overcomer Within You. "And that from a child thou hast known the holy scriptures, which are able to make thee wise unto salvation through faith which is in Christ Jesus. All scripture is given by inspiration of God, and is profitable for doctrine, for reproof, for correction, for instruction in righteousness: That the man of God may be perfect, thoroughly furnished unto all good works" (2 Timothy 3:15-17).

7. The Holy Spirit Will Reveal To You The Secrets Of Getting Along With Others. "And in those days, when the number of the disciples was multiplied, there arose a murmuring of the Grecians against the Hebrews, because their widows were neglected in the daily ministration. Then the twelve called the multitude of the disciples unto them, and said, It is not reason that we should leave the word of God, and serve tables. Wherefore, brethren, look ye out among you seven men of honest report, full of the Holy Ghost and wisdom, whom we may appoint over this business. But we will give ourselves continually to prayer, and to the ministry of the word. And the saying pleased the whole multitude:" (Acts 6:1-5). "Behold, how good and how pleasant it is for brethren to dwell together in unity! It is like the precious ointment upon the head, that ran down upon the beard, even Aaron's beard: that went down to the skirts of his garments; As the dew of Hermon, and as the dew that descended upon the mountains of Zion: for there the Lord commanded the blessing, even life for evermore" (Psalm 133:1-3). The Holy Spirit shows us that blessing flows out of the bond of unity.

8. The Holy Spirit Reveals To You The Cause Of Every Satanic Work Around You. "For where envying and strife is, there is confusion and every evil work" (James 3:16).

9. The Holy Spirit Is Able To Make You An Overcomer. You see, He empowered Jesus to overcome satan in the wilderness of temptation (read Matthew 4). The Holy Spirit knows your season of testing (see Luke 4).

10. The Holy Spirit Knows The Weaknesses Of Your Enemy (see Matthew 8). The Holy Spirit knows the *weaponry* you will need to win any battle you are facing.

Oh, you must develop an addiction to the Holy Spirit. Your dependency upon Him is the real reason you can succeed.

You can overcome any bad habit, inner grief and chaotic situation—*through the Holy Spirit.* You can overcome any financial crisis and devastation, bankruptcy and sickness and disease...through the power of the *Holy Spirit.*

Oh, decide to be an overcomer today!

Always remember, the Holy Spirit will reveal specific Wisdom you require for living an overcoming life.

Our Prayer Together...

"Father, You want me to succeed. I believe that You will assign angels to escort me through any crisis or trial. Thank You for the gift of the Holy Spirit, my Mentor, Who will reveal to me step by step how to become an overcomer. In Jesus' name. Amen."

Passion Is
A Sign Post
To The Season
You Are Entering.

-MIKE MURDOCK

36

PASSION

—————➤◦◄—————

Passion Is The Difference Between Humans.

9 Facts About Your Passion

1. Passion Is An Excessive And Uncommon Desire. It includes the desire to change, serve or achieve a goal.

Men who succeed greatly possess great passion for their Assignment. They are consumed and obsessed. It burns within them like fire. Nothing else matters to them but the completion of the instructions of God in their lives.

2. Passion Is Power. You will never have significant success with anything *until it becomes an obsession with you.* An obsession is when something consumes your thoughts and time.

You will only be remembered in your life for your obsession. Henry Ford, the automobile. Thomas Edison, inventions. Billy Graham, evangelism. Oral Roberts, healing. The Wright brothers, the airplane.

Jesus had a passion for His mission and goal in life. "For the Son of Man is come to seek and to save that which was lost" (Luke 19:10). "How God anointed Jesus of Nazareth with the Holy Ghost and with power: Who went about doing good, and healing all that were oppressed of the devil; for God was with Him" (Acts 10:38).

3. Passion Is Magnetic. What do you love to *discuss?* What do you love to *hear about?* What *excites* you? These are clues to your Assignment. These are clues to your abilities. *You will always have Wisdom toward whatever you love.*

If you love children, you will probably possess an innate and obvious Wisdom toward *children.*

If you love computers, you will discover a natural inclination to understand this *computer age.* If you love to work on cars, you will have a natural Wisdom toward *mechanical things.*

Great singers do not normally say, "I really hate singing. I would rather sell cars. God is making me sing." Of course not. They *love* to sing.

You will never hear a great pianist say, "I hate playing the piano. It is something I *have* to do. God is *making* me do it. I would much rather be building houses."

What you love is a clue to your Assignment.

4. Uncommon Men Of God Have Uncommon Passion. *Isaiah was passionate.* "For the Lord God will help me; therefore shall I not be confounded: therefore have I set my face like a flint, and I know that I shall not be ashamed" (Isaiah 50:7).

The Apostle Paul was passionate. "Brethren, I count not myself to have apprehended: but this one thing I do, forgetting those things which are behind, and reaching forth unto those things which are before, I press toward the mark for the prize of the high calling of God in Christ Jesus" (Philippians 3:13,14).

Jesus was passionate about completing and finishing His Assignment on earth. "Looking unto Jesus the Author and Finisher of our faith; Who for the joy that was set before Him endured the cross, despising the shame, and is set down at the right hand of the throne of God. For consider Him that endured such contradiction of sinners against Himself, lest ye be wearied and faint in your minds" (Hebrews 12:2,3).

5. You Are Instructed To Develop A Passion For The Word Of God. The Lord spoke to Joshua about the Law and instructed him to "...turn not from it to the right hand or to the left, that thou mayest prosper whithersoever thou goest. This book of the law shall not depart out of thy mouth; but thou shalt meditate therein day and night, that thou mayest observe to do according to all that is written therein: for then thou shalt make thy way prosperous, and then thou shalt have good success" (Joshua 1;7,8).

So move toward His presence today. Habitually schedule time in The Secret Place. "He that dwelleth in the secret place of the most High shall abide under the shadow of the Almighty" (Psalm 91:1). In His presence your passion for Him will grow from a tiny acorn to a huge oak within you.

6. Wrong Relationships Will Weaken Your Passion For Your Assignment For God. Recently, I went to dinner with several friends after a service. Within one hour, the discussion had become filled with the problems with people, financial difficulties and complaining attitudes. I was shocked at what began to grow within me. Though I had left the service with great joy, something began to die within me. As others discussed the difficult situations in their lives or how difficult it was to reach their goals, I felt my own fire begin to go out. Paul warned of such associations. "Be not deceived: evil communications corrupt good manners" (1 Corinthians 15:33).

7. It Is Your Responsibility To Protect The Gift Of Passion Within You. Guard your focus every hour. Be ruthless with distractions.

Feed the picture of your goal continually. Watch for the Four Enemies of Passion: fatigue, busyness, over-scheduling and putting God last on your daily schedule.

8. Passion Is Unforgettable. Jesus focused on doing the exact instructions of His Heavenly Father. He healed the sick. He noticed the lonely. He came to make people successful, to restore and repair their life to full fellowship with His Father.

You Will Only Have Significant Success With Something That Is An Obsession.

9. Your Passion May Cost You Everything. The obsession of Jesus took Him to the cross. It took Him to the crucifixion. Eight inches of thorns were crushed into His brow. A spear punctured His side. Spikes were driven into His hands. Thirty-nine stripes of a whip tore His back to shreds. Four hundred soldiers spit on His body. His beard was ripped off His face. But *He was obsessed with the salvation of mankind.*

And He succeeded.

You may start small. You may start with very little. But, if what you love begins to consume your mind, your thoughts, your conversation, your schedule, look for extraordinary success.

Do you dread going to work every morning? Do you anxiously look at the clock toward closing time each afternoon? Is your mind wandering throughout the day toward other places or things you would love to be doing? Then you will probably not have much success at what you are doing.

Find something that consumes you. Something that is worthy of building your entire life around. Consider it.

An Uncommon Assignment Will Require Uncommon Passion.

Treasure And Protect Your Flow Of Passion.

This is one of the Secrets of Champions.

RECOMMENDED BOOKS AND TAPES:
TS-06 Secrets Of The Greatest Achievers Who Ever Lived, Vol. 1 (6 tapes/$30)
TS-07 Secrets Of Uncommon Achievers, Vol. 2 (6 tapes/$30)
B-99 Secrets Of The Richest Man Who Ever Lived (180 pages/$10)
B-118 Seeds Of Wisdom On Problem-Solving (32 pages/$5)

Peace Is Not The Absence
Of Adversity,
It Is The Absence
Of Inner Conflict.

-MIKE MURDOCK

⇚ 37 ⇛

PEACE

Peace Is The Absence Of Inner Conflict.

Inner battle is devastating. Sometimes, our conscience is at war against *things* we have done. Our focus on things greatly influences our emotions. If you analyze, evaluate and continually think about injustices done to you, your heart will become chaotic. Your mind will become fragmented. Your attitude will become critical.

The Holy Spirit solves every inner turmoil.

6 Facts About Peace

1. The Fruit Of The Holy Spirit Is Peace. "But the fruit of the Spirit is love, joy, peace, longsuffering, gentleness, goodness, faith, Meekness, temperance: against such there is no law" (Galatians 5:22,23).

You see, *His presence brings peace.* When you obey His instructions, a calmness will enter your spirit. The greatest warfare of your life is the Holy Spirit versus your flesh and self. "For the flesh lusteth against the Spirit, and the Spirit against the flesh: and these are contrary the one to the other: so that ye cannot do the things that ye would" (Galatians 5:17).

When you permit the leadership of the Holy Spirit in your life, you will enter the most remarkable and unforgettable season of calm and inner peace you could imagine.

2. Divine Peace Is Much Different Than A Passive Acceptance Of Life.

▶ *Man* cannot give this peace.

▶ *Popularity* does not create this kind of peace.

▶ *Wealth* cannot produce this peace.

▶ *Counselors* cannot produce this kind of peace.

▶ A *loving mate* does not produce this kind of peace.

3. Uncommon Peace Is A Gift From An Uncommon God. "And the peace of God, which passeth all understanding, shall keep your hearts and minds through Christ Jesus" (Philippians 4:7).

4. When You Focus On The Holy Spirit, Your Mind Begins To Grow And Become The Mind Of Christ. "For to be carnally minded is death; but to be spiritually minded is life and peace" (Romans 8:6).

5. When The Holy Spirit Becomes Your Focus, The Storm Begins To Settle In Your Mind. You enter the rest He promised. "This is the rest wherewith ye may cause the weary to rest; and this is the refreshing: yet they would not hear" (Isaiah 28:12).

6. The Holy Spirit Must Become Your Focus Before You Ever Experience Total And Continuous Peace. "Thou wilt keep him in perfect peace, whose mind is stayed on Thee: because he trusteth in Thee" (Isaiah 26:3).

3 Ways The Holy Spirit Affects Your Peace

1. The Holy Spirit Will Give You Discernment Regarding Your Friendships. Some are contentious. Their faultfinding words create a climate of conflict, anger and cynicism. "...from such turn away" (2 Timothy 3:5). Mark people who carry a spirit of debate and strife. When the Holy Spirit is in leadership, you will discern such people quickly (see 2 Timothy 2:23).

2. The Holy Spirit Increases Your Patience Which Always Brings Peace In A Social Setting As Well. "And the servant of the Lord must not strive; but be gentle unto all men, apt to teach, patient" (2 Timothy 2:24). *Unfortunately, most of us blame everyone around us for the climate of battle.* However, battle requires two or more. If you refuse to fight, the war cannot continue. "Where no wood is, there the fire goeth out: so where there is no talebearer, the strife ceaseth. As coals are to burning coals, and wood to fire; so is a contentious man to kindle strife" (Proverbs 26:20,21).

3. The Holy Spirit Will Give You The Courage And Strength To Withdraw From The Company Of Foolish People. This increases your peace. "Go from the presence of a foolish man, when thou perceivest not in him the lips of knowledge" (Proverbs 14:7).

After a service one night, I was so happy. Many had come to Christ. A good number had been healed. Everything was so peaceful. When several of us arrived at the restaurant, a staff person from the local church began to complain to the waitress. A spot or something was on their glass. Within a few moments everyone circulated their experiences of "roaches in food" and other unhappy and unfortunate experiences with restaurants during their lifetime. In less than thirty minutes, we went from a glorious move of the Holy Spirit, to pessimism and despondency.

It came through one person.

You are a Door or a Wall. You can become a Wall against discouragement, cynicism and pessimism. Or, you can be a Door for others to walk through and continue in the presence of God.

Sometimes, it is wonderful to be a Door that the presence of God can walk through.

But it is sometimes necessary to become a Wall against things that are unholy, unrighteous and that bring unhappiness.

The Word of God is the instrument of peace for the Holy Spirit to use. "Great peace have they which love thy law: and nothing shall offend them" (Psalm 119:165).

When the Word of God is sown continuously in your heart, it grows a Harvest of peace.

When someone approaches me in great emotional havoc and disturbance, I know that the Word of God is not dominating their life. They discuss their battles instead of the One Who is fighting for them.

They discuss their warfare, instead of the promise of victory.

They discuss their doubts, instead of their faith in God.

Their focus is their enemy, instead of their Comforter.

When the Word of God dominates your mouth, it dominates your mind.

When the Word of God dominates your mind, it controls your conduct and behavior.

You must embrace the Word of God as the most effective instrument for change. That is why Paul wrote Timothy, "All scripture is given by inspiration of God, and is profitable for doctrine, for reproof, for correction, for instruction in righteousness: That the man of God may be perfect, thoroughly furnished unto all good works" (2 Timothy 3:16,17).

The Holy Spirit inspired the Scriptures.

The Holy Spirit affects your words.

The Holy Spirit uses the Word of God to bring peace into your heart. Do not throw it away. Do not treat it lightly.

4 Keys To Creating A Peaceful Climate

1. Recognize That Conflict Is The Trap Of Distraction. Satan uses conflict to break your focus on your Assignment. Have you ever wondered after an argument with someone, why they have focused on such trivia? It did not make sense, any sense at all. Some have forfeited a twenty year friendship or marriage, because of one sentence spoken in a day. That is demonic. It is satanic. It is not even logical. The purpose was to break your focus on things that are good.

That is why the Apostle Paul wrote to the church at Philippi, "And the peace of God, which passeth all understanding, shall keep your hearts and minds through Christ Jesus. Finally, brethren, whatsoever things are true, whatsoever things are honest, whatsoever things are just, whatsoever things are pure, whatsoever things are lovely, whatsoever things are of good report; if there be any virtue, and if there be any praise, think on these things" (Philippians 4:7,8).

2. **You Determine Your Own Focus.** Nobody else can. You can complain. You can blame others. But, you are responsible for what you give your attention to.

3. **Your Focus Is Creating Your Feelings.** Whatever you are feeling is produced by your focus. Your focus is your personal decision. Stop, take time to change your focus.

4. **Pay Any Price To Protect Your Focus And Keep It On Right Things.** "And if thy hand offend thee, cut it off: it is better for thee to enter into life maimed, than having two hands to go into hell, into the fire that never shall be quenched: And if thine eye offend thee, pluck it out: it is better for thee to enter into the kingdom of God with one eye, than having two eyes to be cast into hell fire:" (Mark 9:43,47). "Thou wilt keep him in perfect peace, whose mind is stayed on Thee: because he trusteth in Thee" (Isaiah 26:3).

Always remember, the Holy Spirit is your only Source of true peace.

Our Prayer Together...

"Father, thank You for the promise of peace. The world is in battle. Every day is an emotional war. Everything around me seems designed to break my focus and create distraction. But, Your Word is a lamp unto my feet and a light unto my path. Because I love Thy Word, my peace is great. Holy Spirit, You are the true Source of peace. You are the Spirit of peace, and I embrace You today. Your words matter to me. Thank You for the Word of God, the Instrument of Peace, that You have given to me. It drives out darkness and brings me into a place of rest. In Jesus' name. Amen."

RECOMMENDED BOOKS AND TAPES:
B-80 The Greatest Success Habit On Earth (32 pages/$5)
B-115 Seeds Of Wisdom On The Secret Place (32 pages/$5)

～ 38 ～

PLANNING

Champions Plan.

Planning is the starting point for any dream or goal that you possess.

11 Facts About Planning

1.   A Plan Is A Written List Of Arranged Actions Necessary To Achieve Your Desired Goal.   "...Write the vision, and make it plain upon tables, that he may run that readeth it" (Habakkuk 2:2).

2.   An Uncommon Life Will Require An Uncommon Plan. The command is not the plan. The command can take a *moment.* The plan can involve your *lifetime.*   In a moment, God gave Noah an instruction to build the ark, but the instructions were specific and required precision.

Recently I read where the Chief Executive Officer of 200 corporations invested the first hour of each day in meticulous planning of that 24-hour day. I have never known anyone personally who has spent that kind of time carefully *planning a day.* This man writes out his plans in detail on paper.

Lee Iacocca, the legendary former head of Chrysler, said that one of his greatest mentors insisted that any ideas he had be written out in detail on paper before he would consider them.

The heavyweight boxing champions plan many weeks *before* they will fight. *They prepare.* They know it is the only difference between winning and losing. I have often said that champions do not *become* champions in the ring. They are recognized in the ring. *Their becoming champions occurred in their daily routine.*

3.   Jesus Planned Your Future. "In My Father's house are many mansions: if it were not so, I would have told you. I go to prepare a place for you" (John 14:2).

Think for a moment. God scheduled the birth, the crucifixion and the resurrection of His Son before the foundation of the earth. "And all that dwell upon the earth shall worship Him, whose names are not written in the book of life of the Lamb slain from the foundation of the world" (Revelation 13:8).

I think it is quite fascinating that God would schedule a meal, the marriage supper, six thousand years ahead of time!   "Blessed are they which are called unto the marriage supper of the Lamb" (Revelation 19:9).

4.   God Always Honored Men Who Planned. Noah *planned* the building of the ark. Solomon, the wisest man who ever lived on earth, *took time to plan* the building of the temple. Moses, the great deliverer who brought the Israelites out of Egypt, *took time to plan* the tabernacle.

5.   Your Bible Is The Plan Of God For You, The World And Eternity. It is the undeniable proof that God thinks ahead. Most of the Bible is prophecy, a description of the future before it ever occurs.

Jesus taught, "For which of you, intending to build a tower, sitteth not down first, and counteth the cost, whether he have sufficient to finish it? Lest haply, after he hath laid the foundation, and is not able to finish it, all that behold it begin to mock him, Saying, This man began to build, and was not able to finish. Or what king, going to make war against another king, sitteth not down first, and consulteth whether he be able with ten thousand to meet him that cometh against him with twenty thousand?" (Luke 14:28-31).

6.   Make A List Of Things To Do Every Day Of Your Life. Write six things you want to accomplish that day. Focus your total attention on each task. Assign each task to a specific time. (If you cannot plan events for twenty-four hours in your life, what makes you think you will accomplish your desires for the next twenty-four years?)

Think of each hour as an employee. *Delegate a specific Assignment to each hour.* What do you want to accomplish between 7:00 a.m. and 8:00 a.m.? Who should you telephone today?

7.   Write Out Your Plan Clearly On A Sheet Of Paper. *Successes are usually scheduled events.* Failures are not.

Planing is laborious. It is tedious. It is meticulous. It is grilling, demanding and exhausting. In my personal opinion, detailed planning is really never fun. *But, sometimes you have to do something you hate to create something you love.*

8.   Your Planning Should Involve The Constant Consulting Of Your Lifetime Mentor, The Holy Spirit. "But the Comforter, which is the Holy Ghost, Whom the Father will send in My name, He shall teach you all things, and bring all things to your remembrance, whatsoever I have said unto you" (John 14:26).

9. Your Plan Should Prioritize Your Time In The Secret Place. "He that dwelleth in the secret place of the most High shall abide under the shadow of the Almighty" (Psalm 91:1).

Your Time In The Secret Place Determines Your Strength In The Public Place. "But they that wait upon the Lord shall renew their strength; they shall mount up with wings as eagles; they shall run, and not be weary; and they shall walk, and not faint" (Isaiah 40:31).

10. The Secret Of Your Future Is Hidden In Your Daily Routine. Even ants think ahead. "Go to the ant, thou sluggard; consider her ways, and be wise: Which having no guide, overseer, or ruler, Provideth her meat in the summer, and gathereth her food in the harvest" (Proverbs 6:6-8).

11. Your Planning Should Involve Your Circle Of Counsel. "Two are better than one; because they have a good reward for their labour" (Ecclesiastes 4:9).

Worthy advisors keep you safe from mistakes. "Where no counsel is, the people fall: but in the multitude of counsellors there is safety" (Proverbs 11:14).

"And of the children of Issachar, which were men that had understanding of the times, to know what Israel ought to do; the heads of them were two hundred; and all their brethren were at their commandment" (1 Chronicles 12:32).

5 Important Principles That Have Helped Me Greatly

1. Praying Does Not Replace Planning.

2. Planning Cannot Replace Praying. Let me illustrate. Study Joshua and the two battles of Ai in Joshua 7. Joshua did not consult the Lord and lost the first battle of Ai. It devastated him. "And Joshua rent his clothes, and fell to the earth upon his face before the ark of the Lord until the eventide, he and the elders of Israel, and put dust upon their heads" (Joshua 7:6).

Prayer Is Your Key To Power. Read fully this unforgettable passage in Acts 12.

"Peter therefore was kept in prison: but prayer was made without ceasing of the church unto God for him. And when Herod would have brought him forth, the same night Peter was sleeping between two soldiers, bound with two chains: and the keepers before the door kept the prison. And, behold, the angel of the Lord came upon him, and a light shined in the prison: and he smote Peter on the side, and raised him up, saying, Arise up quickly. And his chains fell off from his hands" (Acts 12:5-7).

Prayer gives you, the believer, *authority* over satan.

3. Prayer Changes Your "Inner World." The peace and presence of God fills you. It also changes your *external* circumstances. The hand of God moves people around you and miracles begin to happen.

4. Prayer Pleasures The Heart Of God. "And there I will meet with thee, and I will commune with thee from above the mercy seat, from between the two cherubims which are upon the ark of the testimony, of all things which I will give thee in commandment unto the children of Israel" (Exodus 25:22).

God enjoys your companionship.

He seeks communion with you.

5. Prayer Pleasures You. "Come unto Me, all ye that labour and are heavy laden, and I will give you rest" (Matthew 11:28). When you pray, your spirit is fed the essential "bread of life." Prayer is as necessary for your spirit as food is for your body.

Why do people avoid planning? Some avoid it because it is time consuming. They are so busy "mopping up the water" that they do not take the time to "turn off the faucet!"

Jesus had a plan.

Jesus took time to plan...this was one of the Leadership Secrets of Jesus.

Our Prayer Together...

"Father, I thank You for giving me the ability to plan. I ask that You give me Wisdom in ordering my daily routine so that it allows me to get the most out of every hour. In Jesus' name I pray. Amen."

RECOMMENDED BOOKS AND TAPES:

B-91 The Leadership Secrets Of Jesus (197 pages/$10)
B-99 Secrets Of The Richest Man Who Ever Lived (180pages/$10)
B-127 Seeds Of Wisdom On Goal-Setting (32 pages/$5)

⇜ 39 ⇝

PRAYER LANGUAGE

Your Prayer Language Is A Precious And Important Gift.

While millions have never understood this wonderful and glorious experience, thousands of others are tasting this incredible phenomenon—"praying in the heavenly language." It is quite simple, really.

The Holy Spirit is a Communicator. He even provided animals with sounds to communicate between themselves. The wildest animals on earth communicate to each other!

Relationship is essential in this incredible world of our Creator, the Holy Spirit. He provided every nationality a language of its own. The Spanish have their language. The French have their language. The Germans have their language. The English have their language. The Holy Spirit has a language.

15 Keys You Should Know About Tongues And Your Prayer Language

1. The One Who Gives Languages On Earth Simply Has One Of His Own. Most of us call it The Heavenly Language. "For he that speaketh in an unknown tongue speaketh not unto men, but unto God: for no man understandeth him;" (1 Corinthians 14:2).

2. There Are Many Qualities Of This Unknown Tongue That Are Varied, Rewarding And Apply To Different Situations. For example, when the Holy Spirit came on the Day of Pentecost, He provided a language that was unknown only to those who were speaking it! Others *around them* understood because the Holy Spirit was providing an opportunity for the gospel to be heard *in other dialects.* "...the multitude came together, and were confounded, because that every man heard them speak in his own language. And they were all amazed and marvelled, saying one to another, Behold are not all these which speak Galilaeans? And how hear we every man in our own tongue, wherein we were born?" (Acts 2:6-8).

Yet, Peter and the others who were speaking "in tongues," did not understand what they were saying. This was *not* the heavenly language, but rather the Holy Spirit using another language or dialect to confirm His presence among them.

3. The Holy Spirit Often Uses Varying Ways To Use "Unknown Tongues" To Impress Unbelievers About A Supernatural God. "Wherefore tongues are for a sign, not to them that believe, but to them that believe not:" (1 Corinthians 14:22).

4. The Holy Spirit Is Meticulous And Orderly In How And When Tongues Are Used. Sometimes, when followed by an interpretation, Tongues are used to bless the entire church so the people can be edified and blessed. "Wherefore let him that speaketh in an unknown tongue pray that he may interpret" (1 Corinthians 14:13).

5. The Holy Spirit Delights When You Enter Into A Private Time Of Intercession "Through Tongues" For Others. "Likewise the Spirit also helpeth our infirmities: for we know not what we should pray for as we ought: but the Spirit itself [Himself] maketh intercession for us with groanings which cannot be uttered. And He that searcheth the hearts knoweth what is the mind of the Spirit, because He maketh intercession for the saints according to the will of God" (Romans 8:26,27).

6. When You Pray "In Tongues," You Are Building Up Yourself, Your Personal Faith And Confidence In God. Something supernatural occurs. It is indescribable, unexplainable and undeniable. "But ye, beloved, building up yourselves on your most holy faith, praying in the Holy Ghost, Keep yourselves in the love of God, looking for the mercy of our Lord Jesus Christ unto eternal life" (Jude 20,21). This is essential for overcomers. You see, *your victories depend on your faith.* Faith is confidence in God. It is *the only way* to bring pleasure to God. "But without faith it is impossible to please Him: for he that cometh to God must believe that He is, and that He is a rewarder of them that diligently seek Him" (Hebrews 11:6).

7. Recognize That Many Times You Do Not Really Know What To Pray About, So It Is Important To Permit The Holy Spirit To Pray Through You.

8. Trust The Holy Spirit That He Will Not Fail You Or Lead You Into Error. Remember, He is the Spirit of truth (see John 16:13).

9. When You Pray In The Holy Spirit, Trust Him Enough To Avoid Logic And The Temptation To Understand Everything He Is Doing. He is at work.

I have had unforgettable experiences with my prayer language. I experienced the baptism of the Holy Spirit and "speaking in tongues" at the age of ten. My second dramatic encounter was about the age of fifteen in Beaumont, Texas.

I have always prayed in the Holy Spirit. But, I have never

understood the practice of interpreting back in English, my own language, what the Holy Spirit had spoken through me to the Father. One of my beloved mentors, Oral Roberts brought me into a special understanding of this.

I was in a huge conference at the Mabee Center in Tulsa, Oklahoma. After the service one day, Oral Roberts walked over to me and asked me to go with him to one of his offices. There, he began to tell me the secrets behind the remarkable blessings of God on his ministry and work.

"The two keys to everything I have accomplished for God have been Seed-Faith and praying in the Spirit," he explained.

"Mike, God has shown you more about the principle of Seed-Faith than any man I've ever known in my life, but I'd like to tell you about *praying in the Spirit and interpreting back in English.*"

Well, this seemed a little strange to me. But, I knew that the hand of God was strong in his life. He has been a remarkable mentor in my life that I value and celebrate. I listened.

Uncommon Experiences Create Uncommon Men.

He explained that after praying in the Spirit (in tongues), if I would ask the Holy Spirit and be willing to trust Him, He would provide me the interpretation in my own language, English. Then, I could plan and prepare my life according to what the Holy Spirit had been praying through me.

"But," I protested, "what if something comes out of my mouth that is crazy, illogical and ridiculous?"

"Trust the Holy Spirit," he said gently.

The next morning, I arose at 5:30, my prayer time. I was scheduled to meet with a realtor at 9:30 and purchase an office building in Tulsa. Someone was giving me a ride at 9:00 to the appointment. My manager had been selected and several houses were being purchased for my staff. As I began to pray in the Spirit, suddenly, I began to pray in English. It burst out of my mouth suddenly and unexpectedly: *"This day will not go as you have planned. But, do not fear— for it is My Will."*

I felt odd, a little peculiar, but aware that I was moving into a different realm than normal.

At 9:00, my ride appeared. Within 30 minutes, some unexpected things occurred. Statements were made and things happened beyond my control. The purchase of the building was cancelled. The peace of God came to me to stay in Dallas instead of moving to Tulsa. It was shocking. Yet, as I mentally replayed my prayer time at 5:30 that morning, the Holy Spirit had told me in English that the day "would not go" as I had planned. What is it then? "I will pray with the Spirit, and

I will pray with the understanding also:" (1 Corinthians 14:15).

It is important for you to keep your prayer language alive and vibrant. "I thank my God, I speak with tongues more than ye all:" (1 Corinthians 14:18).

I had two other unusual encounters with my prayer language in my Secret Place at home. As I was praying fervently in tongues, suddenly I burst out in English these words:

"Expose fraudulent people in my life! Holy Spirit, expose fraudulent people in my life!"

I could hardly believe what was coming from my mouth. Fraudulent people? I did not know any fraudulent people around my life. I trusted everyone close to me explicitly. I have always felt very discerning and that I could "pick up anything wrong." But, the Holy Spirit knew something I did not know. *He knows the hearts of others years before you do.*

I had turned my personal finances over to a long-time friend. I trusted this friend more than any human on earth. Yet, within seven days I discovered this friend had written checks for thousands of dollars unauthorized and without my permission. It was shocking, unsettling and disheartening. But, the Holy Spirit had helped prepare my heart. He was talking to the Father *in my behalf.* When I interpreted in English what He was praying through me (in tongues), it became a spiritual milestone in my memory.

Since then, I have trusted the Holy Spirit to pray anything He desires...knowing that *He wants only that which is good for me.* "...no good thing will He withhold from them that walk uprightly" (Psalm 84:11).

A few days later, another uncommon event occurred. As I was praying in the Spirit, suddenly these words burst from my lips:

"Purge my ministry! Holy Spirit, please purge my ministry!"

Purge my ministry? I had no idea what the Holy Spirit was trying to communicate to the Father. But, I trusted Him. Within seven days or so, someone that I really trusted in my ministry was caught in a sad, terrible and tragic sin. It had been going on periodically for some time. I was too focused on my ministry to notice their erratic behavior. But, the Holy Spirit protected me. He was praying *through me to the Father* that anything unlike Him would be stripped away from our work for God.

Millions have never tapped into this supernatural power. Yet, those who are moving toward a life of total addiction to the Holy Spirit are birthing the most uncommon events of their lifetime.

Before you feed your doubts and misgivings think about this:

▶ You have not been *everywhere...*yet everywhere *continues to* *exist* without your knowledge.

▶ You do not know *everybody*...yet millions continue to live each day *without your acquaintance.*

▶ You do not know *every* operation of the Holy Spirit...yet millions are tasting the supernatural and uncommon events in their communication with Him...*every day of their life!* You can, too!

10. Acknowledge That You Do Not Know Everything Or Know How To Pray Effectively Through Your Own Logic And Mind.

11. Recognize The Holy Spirit As Your Earthly Intercessor And Jesus As Your Heavenly Intercessor. Permit them to work through your life.

12. Ask For The Prayer Language. "...ye have not, because ye ask not" (James 4:2). Anything you ask in His name, you will receive it according to His will.

13. Be Willing To Grow Into The Relationship. It may not happen immediately or overnight. Step by step, line upon line, you can begin to build your relationship with the Holy Spirit.

14. Ask The Holy Spirit To Draw You Toward Him. My father told me this is the greatest and most important prayer someone could ever pray in his whole lifetime. When you get in His presence, you will change. You will behold and see truths you have never seen in your lifetime.

15. Recognize And Treasure Any Mentors He Brings Across Your Path To Provide More Revelation About Him. Walk in the present light you have, and more will be provided by the One Who created you, the Holy Spirit.

Always remember, the Holy Spirit can provide you a prayer language that nobody understands but God.

Our Prayer Together...

"Precious Holy Spirit, You gave languages to the whole earth to communicate, connect and strengthen relationships. Animals have *sounds*. Humans have *words*. Holy Spirit, You have a special *prayer language* for me to use in my personal prayer life. Teach me, step by step, how to enter into the supernatural prayer life. You are my Intercessor on earth. I celebrate and value each moment in Your presence today. I am willing to be *changed*. I am willing to make new discoveries. Please help me to overcome any erroneous teaching received in my childhood, any prejudices that have come to me through any false teaching. I will pursue You because You are Truth, the Spirit of Truth. In Jesus' name. Amen."

When God Wants To Bless You,
He Puts A Person In Your Life.
When Satan Wants To Destroy You,
He Puts A Person In Your Life.

-MIKE MURDOCK

❧ 40 ❧

RELATIONSHIPS

Intimacy Can Destroy.
Intimacy with one wrong person can destroy you forever.
When God Wants To Bless You, He Puts A Person In Your Life.
When Satan Wants To Destroy You, He Puts A Person In Your Life.

4 Questions That Qualify People For Intimacy

▶ *Have They Taken The Time To Pray Privately About Your Visions And Goals?*
▶ *Have They Questioned You At Length To Develop A Full Understanding Of Your Assignment?*
▶ *How Many Hours Have You Really Spent With Them?*
▶ *Are They Willing To Pray With You And Walk Side By Side With You Concerning Your Assignment?*

There Are 4 Kinds Of People Satan Will Use To Distract You, Demoralize You And Discourage You

1. Those Who Do Not Really Accept Your Assignment. They do not really know you. They have not spent time with God, *fasting and praying for you.* Usually, they look on the outward appearance of you and your circumstances. They laugh at your dreams and goals.

I have a precious friend who is well along in years. He is a white-haired fireball of energy. When God spoke to him to birth a church in a new city, some folks laughed. He had been a businessman. *But, he knew the voice of God.* Those who refused to accept his Assignment as from the Lord *refused to participate.* Now, he is a very successful pastor and is doing a great work for God. Had he listened to those who had never consulted the Holy Spirit in the first place, he might have been a total failure today.

2. Those Who Do Not Truly Respect Your Assignment. I must tell you this personal illustration. I really believe every person should have a life product, a life legacy. For example, furniture companies produce furniture. Piano companies produce pianos. Sign companies produce signs. An automobile company produces automobiles. You should know *the legacy God has designed for you to leave upon earth*—your Assignment.

So, I asked my precious mother, "Mother, what is your life product?"

"Oh son, I do not have any life product. I am just trying to get you seven kids to Heaven."

Now, that truly is a life product—the salvation and redemption of your seven children!

Some people have criticized my mother because she had dedicated her entire life to being a wife to my father, and a full-time mother at home. I have heard many words over the years as people said, "You need to get out of this house and away from these kids and get yourself a job!"

Those people have little respect for mothers, housewives and those who are called alongside their husbands. How I thank God that my mother refused their influence! My memories of home are of constant and total access to my mother and father. They had family altar times twice a day, morning and night. Mother enforced memorization of one scripture each morning. I believe that my own Assignment became defined, refined and confined because of a mother who respected her own Assignment.

Recently, a pastor of a large well-known church asked me, "Mike, I wish you would not hold crusades at these small little churches around town here. My people like to feel that our church is so successful that we can attract international ministries others cannot schedule. It would mean a lot to me if you would come to just my church when you come to this city." He had little respect for ministers with small congregations. This kind of attitude is sad.

Mark Those Who Have Little Respect For Your Assignment. They may love you, but they do not respect your Assignment. Let me explain. I host a major World Wisdom Conference each year. It costs thousands of dollars for me to sponsor it. I fly in some of the most effective ministers who have ever spoken. It is first-class all the way. Yet, some people live within 30 minutes and will not even drive over to the conference for one day. I have relatives and close family members who will not come for just one day. It is the focus of my entire year, but they have little respect for Wisdom, the anointing or my ministry. Now, I cannot say they do not love me. But, they do not respect the mantle, the calling, the Assignment.

Love Is Finding Someone Desirable.

Respect Is Finding Someone Necessary.

Never Linger In The Presence Of Those Who Do Not Respect Your

Assignment. People will never protect what they do not respect.

3. Those Who Will Not Protect Your Assignment. *What You Respect, You Will Protect.* I have known hundreds of men of God during my 57 years on earth. Some are well known, effective and have done an incredible work for God. Yes, I have observed their weaknesses, flaws and human traits. It has endeared me to them, not alienated me from them. *I have refused to discuss those flaws with anyone.* Why? It is the right thing to do in the eyes of God.

Have you ever read the complete story of David and how he protected the position and calling of Saul? He refused to damage and destroy the influence of Saul, though Saul's actions were foolish and devastating. He even tried to kill David and his own son, Jonathan (David's closest friend).

Yet, the discretion and loyalty of David became legendary. An entire nation saw a man of integrity, honor, graciousness and dignity. He was not condoning the behavior and conduct of a fool. Rather, *he respected the Assignment of Saul.*

Years later, when David was brokenhearted, his mind was aflame with memories of the water at Bethlehem. He wished for it aloud. One of his thoughts of longing was, "And David longed, and said, Oh that one would give me drink of the water of the well of Bethlehem, which is by the gate!" (2 Samuel 23:15). His three strongest leaders broke through the host of the Philistines and brought him back water. He refused to drink it because it involved the life of his own men that he loved. That kind of loyalty was inspired because David protected the anointing, the mantle and the Assignment of *another.* In time, his own men had *developed a protection* for his Assignment.

One of my close friends had a drug problem. It concerned me deeply. Even though he refused to face it honestly, I refused to advertise his problem. Why? I want to protect his Assignment. His life is not over. His future is not ended. God *still* has his hand on his life. As I protect that Assignment within him, God will honor and bless my own ministry for it.

Move Away From Wrong People Who Will Not Protect Your Name, Your Focus And Your Calling. Look at Samson. Watch the conniving, scheming and manipulation of Delilah as she sought to probe for his area of weakness.

Wrong People Breathe Life Into Your Weakness.

Right People Starve Your Weakness.

4. Those Who Do Not Expect You To Really Achieve Your Assignment. They have little faith in you. Remember Eliab, the oldest brother of David who acted angrily when David discussed killing the lion?

Eliab reacted angrily toward David. "...why camest thou down hither? and with whom hast thou left those few sheep in the wilderness? I know thy pride, and the naughtiness of thine heart; for thou art come down that thou mightest see the battle" (1 Samuel 17:28).

His own family saw him as a little shepherd boy, *unaware of his victories* over the lion and bear. They *expected* him to fail. They could not imagine him on the throne. He was their "baby brother."

Do you have someone in your family who feels the same way about your life and future? *Do not waste your energy* and time attempting to persuade them. God will vindicate you.

Time Will Validate You. "And let us not be weary in well doing: for in due season we shall reap, if we faint not" (Galatians 6:9).

Keep Solving Problems. Stay alive and vibrant. Keep your spirit sweet and permit God to do the *promoting.* "As we have therefore opportunity, let us do good unto all men, especially unto them who are of the household of faith" (Galatians 6:10).

Men Are Merely Channels, They Are Not Your Source. "For promotion cometh neither from the east, nor from the west, nor from the south. But God is not judge: He putteth down one, and setteth up another" (Psalm 75:6,7).

7 Important Reminders For Relationships

1. **Intimacy Should Be Earned, Not Freely Given** (read 1 Thessalonians 5:12,13).

2. **Intimacy Should Be The Reward For Proven Loyalty** (read John 15:13,14).

3. **True Friendship Is A Gift, Never A Demanded Requirement** (read 1 Corinthians 13).

4. **When Wrong People Leave Your Life, Wrong Things Stop Happening** (read Jonah 1:15).

5. **When Right People Enter Your Life, Right Things Begin To Happen** (read John 4:4-30).

6. **If You Fail To Guard Your Own Life, You Are Like A City Without Walls** (read Proverbs 25:28).

7. **Failure Occurs When The Wrong Person Gets Too Close** (read Judges 16:4).

There Are 3 Kinds Of People You Permit In Your Life

Yesterday, Today And Tomorrow People.
Those that God used yesterday may not have a single place in your

future.

Do not worry about it. Move quickly toward the promises of God. Prepare to enter your future without yesterday people.

You will not make the mistakes of yesterday again. *You have more knowledge today than you have ever had in your whole lifetime.* You have learned from the *pain.* You have learned from your *losses.* You have watched carefully and documented what has happened in other people's lives.

Do not fear that yesterday will crawl behind you like a predator and choke you to death.

It will not happen. "Remember ye not the former things, neither consider the things of old. Behold, I will do a new thing; now it shall spring forth; shall ye not know it? I will even make a way in the wilderness, and rivers in the desert" (Isaiah 43:18,19).

"Forgetting those things which are behind, and reaching forth unto those things which are before, I press toward the mark" (Philippians 3:13,14).

The Holy Spirit Is Your Enabler. "But ye shall receive power, after that the Holy Ghost is come upon you" (Acts 1:8).

The Holy Spirit Is Your Comforter. "But when the Comforter is come, Whom I will send unto you from the Father, even the Spirit of truth" (John 15:26).

The Holy Spirit Is Your Teacher. "He shall teach you all things, and bring all things to your remembrance, whatsoever I have said unto you:" (John 14:26).

The Holy Spirit Is The Revealer Of Those Things Which Are To Come. "Howbeit when He, the Spirit of truth, is come, He will guide you into all truth:" (John 16:13).

3 Reasons You Need The Holy Spirit In Choosing Your Relationships

1. **The Holy Spirit Will Give You Discernment Regarding Your Friendships.** Some are contentious. Their faultfinding words create a climate of conflict, anger and cynicism. "...from such turn away" (2 Timothy 3:5). Mark people who carry a spirit of debate and strife. When the Holy Spirit is in leadership, you will discern them quickly. "But foolish and unlearned questions avoid, knowing that they do gender strifes" (2 Timothy 2:23).

2. **The Holy Spirit Increases Your Patience With Others.** This always brings peace when you interact with those you love. "And

the servant of the Lord must not strive; but be gentle unto all men, apt to teach, patient," (2 Timothy 2:24). Unfortunately, most of us blame everyone around us for the climate of battle. However, battle requires two or more. If you refuse to fight, the war cannot continue. "Where no wood is, there the fire goeth out: so where there is no talebearer, the strife ceaseth. As coals are to burning coals, and wood to fire; so is a contentious man to kindle strife" (Proverbs 26:20,21).

3. The Holy Spirit Will Give You The Courage And Strength To Withdraw From The Company Of Foolish People. This increases your peace. "Go from the presence of a foolish man, when thou perceiveth not in him the lips of knowledge" (Proverbs 14:7).

It fascinates me that Ruth was willing to leave everything comfortable to *pursue her future.* Her kinfolks were in her past. She refused to let her upbringing and her religious background become the noose around her neck that sabotaged her future. She refused to let her past rob her of the potential of tomorrow.

I have said many times that *intolerance of the present creates a future.* As long as you can adapt to the present...you really do not have a future.

Ruth refused to build her future around her past. Some of us remember painful experiences from yesterday. We have built our entire lifestyle around that experience. Our conversations are consumed with occurrences of ten years ago.

This is dangerous.

It is devastating.

When You Discuss Your Past, You Perpetuate It.

Words impart life. When you continually replay painful confrontations and situations of the past, you are giving life to them, you are giving a future to them.

Champions permit yesterday to die.

Ruth did. She did not try to straddle the fence. She refused to become the link between the past and her future.

She totally abandoned the empty relationships of her past.

One of the saddest pictures is in the life of the great patriarch, Abraham. He insisted on bringing Lot, his nephew, with him into the future God had prepared. Lot was a distraction. Most of Abraham's continual problems could be traced to the *presence of Lot.* You see, God had told him to leave his kinfolks and move on to a different territory. *He insisted on bringing someone he was comfortable with—to the detriment of his future.*

Yesterday people will rarely enjoy your future.

It is natural and normal to want to bring everyone close to us into the chapters of our future success. Few will qualify.

Your future must be *earned.*

It is not guaranteed. It is *not* the same for everyone. Your future is a Harvest produced by the Seeds you are willing to sow. Bringing yesterday people into the future is like using old wineskins for the new wine of tomorrow. It simply will not work.

So, prepare to enter your future without yesterday people. God will bring the right associations with you...or He has scheduled outstanding divine connections beyond your greatest and wildest dreams.

Move away from yesterday. You exhausted its benefits. Refuse to waste your energy on repairing it. Rather, rebuild by focusing on your future. Certainly, yesterday can be a reservoir of Wisdom and information. You are not forfeiting loyalty. You are not forgetting the precious lives whom God used mightily for your continual survival and success. But you are refusing to abort your future joys and victories by replaying the memories of yesterday's painful experiences.

Paul refused to wallow in the tears of his past. Few made greater mistakes than he. He caused people to be cast into prison. Christians were murdered because of him. He held the coats of those who stoned the great deacon, Stephen. Yet, he refused to forfeit his future by focusing on his past.

His mistakes were *over.*

His sins were *behind* him.

His name had been *changed.*

Eventually, you will be forced to make a major decision in your life. *It will be the decision to totally abandon your memories, and empty your energy into the palace of your future.*

Your conversation must become more creative. Start using your imagination instead of your memories. Meet new friends. Experience new places.

Ruth knew when she had exhausted the benefits of her present season. This is so powerful and important. Every season in your life contains certain advantages. Whether it is one month of a relationship or 90 days on a job, you must discern the divine purpose of God in *every situation* in your life. You must discern the divine purpose of God in *every relationship.*

Never linger in a conversation with someone when it is over. Would you keep chewing the same mouthful of food for three hours? Of course not.

Would you keep reading the same page of a book for three days? Of course not. Would you leave a broken record on at the same groove replaying the same note over and over again for several hours? Of course not. Would you keep brushing your teeth for 12 hours in a row? Of course not.

When something is finished, it is finished.

Discern it. Recognize it. Look for it. Consistently be intuitive in discerning when a specific season in your life has *concluded.* Then, move *quickly* and *expectantly* to the next season God has arranged for you.

This quality made Ruth unforgettable.

This quality makes champions unforgettable.

Focus Your Energy On Your Future.

Relationships do not always last forever.

So, it is important to exit every Door of Friendship properly. You cannot enter the next season of your life with joy unless you exit your present season *correctly.*

Jesus finished His work on earth. He cried out from the cross, "It is finished!" Salvation was complete. Redemption had taken place. He had paid the price for the sins of man. Three days later, the resurrection would take place. He would return to the Father where He would make intercession for you and me. He finished *properly*—with the approval of the Father.

Solomon finished the temple. It was an incredible feat. Some value his temple today at over $500 billion dollars. He was respected, pursued and celebrated. He *completed* what he started.

Paul finished his race. He fought a good fight, kept his course and finished the race. He was a success in the eyes of God. He made his exit from his earthly ministry with grace, passion and dignity.

Your life is a collection of *Beginnings.*

It is also a collection of *Exits.*

You will not stay in your present job forever.

You will some day leave your present position. Your supervisor today could be another acquaintance in your life next year. Close the relationship with dignity.

8 Keys To Remember When A Relationship Is Ending

1. **Close Every Door Gently.** Do not slam Doors. Do not kick Doors. Do not yell at Doors. They are Doors *through which you may need to return again* in the future. The attitude of *your exit* determines

if you can ever walk back through that Door again. "A soft answer turneth away wrath: but grievous words stir up anger," (Proverbs 15:1).

2. Close Doors With Forgiveness. Unforgiveness is poisonous. It is the cancer that will destroy you from within. Release others to God. Permit Him to do the penalizing or correcting. Like Joseph, recognize that the ultimate plan of God will bring your promotion (see Romans 8:28).

3. Close Doors With Kindness. If your fiancee leaves you with cutting and bitter words, thank the Holy Spirit for salvaging you. Perhaps she was not your *Proverbs 31 Woman* after all. "...in her tongue is the law of kindness" (Proverbs 31:26).

4. Close Every Door With Promises Fulfilled. Do not leave your job until you have finished *what you promised*. Complete every vow. *Whatever* the cost. Integrity is easy to test. Simply ask yourself: did I fulfill my promise? (See Ecclesiastes 5:4,5).

When people lose you in the Forest of Words, apply this Principle of Vow Fulfillment. Forget the blaming, complaining and accusations. This principle reveals everything you need to know about another.

5. Close Every Door With Integrity. Few will do it. *People are rarely angry for the reason they tell you.* Much is never discussed. The trap of deception is deadly. It begins when you deceive *yourself,* then, those around you. Always be honest to others about *the reason* for the Doors closing. It is not necessary to give *every* detail. But it is important that the details you give are *accurate.*

6. Close Every Door With Courage. It is not always easy to close a Door that the Holy Spirit requires. So, closing that Door requires uncommon courage to face the future without that person. Remember the precious Holy Spirit will never leave you nor forsake you (see John 14:16). He opens Doors. He closes Doors. He is the Bridge to every person in your future.

7. Close Every Door With Expectation Of Promotion. "For promotion cometh neither from the east, nor from the west, nor from the south. But God is the judge: He putteth down one, and setteth up another" (Psalm 75:6,7).

8. Close Every Door By The Timing Of The Holy Spirit. Do not close it in a fit of anger. Do not close the Door because of a misunderstanding that erupts. Do not close it just because someone *recommends* that you exit. Know the timing of God (see Ecclesiastes 3:1-8).

A young man sat in my kitchen a few weeks ago. I was quite concerned. He wanted a position in my ministry. I asked him about his relationship with his previous boss, my pastor friend. He avoided the issue continually. In fact, I had to ask him the question four or five times before I got a partial answer. At the end of the conversation, he explained his financial dilemma. He had left a job before ever securing another one. I explained to him how foolish this was. If God were moving him, He would tell him the place he was to go.

When God told Elijah to leave the brook, Zarephath was scheduled (see 1 Kings 17).

When the Israelites left Egypt, Canaan was their determined destination (see Exodus 13).

God always brings you out of a place to bring you into another place. So, close every Door with God's timing. When you close Doors gently, news will travel, and it will be good news.

31 Keys In Protecting A Worthy Relationship

1. **Send Someone A Signal That They Matter.**
   ▶ Everyone needs reassurance of their worth.
   ▶ Remind yourself throughout today that each person you meet has encountered waves of criticism, condemnation and inferiority...which you can change.
   ▶ Your words of reassurance can be like water on their Seeds of Hope.
2. **Salvage Someone.**
   ▶ You are not the only person who is struggling today. Others around you are hurting too.
   ▶ *Be extremely attentive to the silent cries* of someone close to you who may be drowning in the Ocean of Helplessness.
   ▶ Permit God to make you their life jacket.
3. **Become Someone's Bridge.**
   ▶ Someone may open up and share the dream of his heart to you...*Listen.*
   ▶ Someone close to you may ache to hear an approving encouraging word from you...*Say it.*
   ▶ Someone may make a simple request that could unlock an important door for him...*Do it.*
4. **Quench The Urge To Judge.**
   ▶ You cannot draw conclusions as long as there is missing

information.

▶ Things are never as they first appear. Reserve judgment.

▶ Never attempt to explain...or penalize someone for actions you do not fully understand.

5. **Abandon Abusive Friendships.**

▶ There are four kinds of people in your life: Those who add, subtract, divide or multiply.

▶ Those Who Do Not Increase You, Inevitably Will Decrease You.

▶ It is the responsibility of others to discern your worth.

6. **Make Anger Work For You.**

▶ Anger is energy. *Harness it.*

▶ Some anger can be devastating to your family, your career or your life. You can *master* it through prayer or channel it in a worthwhile project.

▶ *Direct* your anger towards your true adversary, satan, instead of those you love.

7. **Skip Warfare Today.**

▶ Make today a peaceable day.

▶ Do not feed an argumentative spirit in those around you. Insist on praying together with those who pursue points of disagreement.

▶ God is well-known for *honoring* peacemakers.

8. **Talk It Out.**

▶ Friendships die through *neglect.*

▶ Do not expect others to read your mind. *Voice your concerns* over any offense and *express your desire* to make things right.

▶ Silence often waters the Root of Bitterness. Talk it out.

9. **Reprove With Sensitivity.**

▶ Criticism *hurts.* Even when you give it in love.

▶ Yet, it is your personal responsibility to provide caution, correction and warnings when someone you love is on the brink of disaster.

▶ Your instruction is their opportunity for *promotion* from God.

10. **Fertilize Friendships.**

▶ Do not permit the name of a friend to be maligned in your presence.

▶ Do not absorb a slanderous report about a friend, unless he is present to defend himself.

▶ A good friend is worth any *price,* any *effort,* any *defense.*

11. Keep Your Word.

▶ Carefully review and fulfill any vows, promises or pledges you have made to anyone.

▶ *Never promise what you cannot produce.*

▶ Make things right with anyone you have wronged in the past.

12. Sow Affection Generously.

▶ Hospital tests have proven that even babies will die if they do not receive touching and loving affection.

▶ *You are not an exception.*

▶ Reach out to someone today. *Touch...hug.*

13. Develop The Gift Of Romance.

▶ Romance is when you deliberately *create a special moment or memorable event* in someone's life.

▶ Do not wait for your mate to create a perfect occasion. Aggressively, creatively and with spontaneity start scheduling unique moments and methods to express your love.

▶ To be unforgotten, do something *unforgettable* TODAY.

14. Interview Your Children.

▶ Your child is worth knowing. *Really* knowing.

▶ Talk. Exchange. Observe. Carefully collect any piece of information that paints a portrait of this "heritage of the Lord."

▶ Communicate with the intent to *learn,* not condemn.

▶ Give your child what he cannot find anywhere else—*non-judgmental conversation*—and he will keep coming back.

15. Learn Something "New" About Someone You Love.

▶ *Knowledge increases confidence.* The more knowledgeable you become about someone the more capable you become at anticipating their needs.

▶ Develop a Personal Portfolio of their particular preferences, such as favorite car, food, colors, songs, books and secret ambitions.

▶ Our Heavenly Father created uniqueness to be discovered, appreciated and *celebrated.*

▶ Greatness will unfold with each discovery.

16. Make Smile Your Style.

▶ Your face *telegraphs* your attitude...toward *life*...toward

*others...*about *yourself.*
▶ Your countenance *creates a climate that attracts* people toward you or causes them to move away from you.
▶ When you smile *first,* you have decided the direction the relationship will go.

17. Learn Love-Talk.
▶ Love-Talk breathes excitement into every relationship.
▶ Love-Talk is letting another know how much you care...through your words, a gesture or giving of a gift.
▶ Say "I love you" today! Whisper it! Shout it! Write it in a note...or with a flower—*just say it* to the one you love!

18. Furnish Gentleness.
▶ Gentleness is like heat in a cold world.
▶ Those around you bear the wounds of rivalry, jealousy and inferiority.
▶ *Pour the Oil of Gentleness* and you will become their greatest memory of the day.

19. Compliment Someone Today.
▶ A popular, but inaccurate statement is, "words are cheap." Nothing could be farther from the truth.
▶ Words cause wars. Words *settle* wars. Words *create* the waves of emotion that control our world.
▶ Your words of kindness today could easily create the Wave that carries someone to his dream.

20. Celebrate Those Who Celebrate You.
▶ Those who discern your worth deserve special recognition.
▶ Even Jesus instructed His disciples to respect those who received them and disconnect from those who rejected them.
▶ *Go where your contribution is celebrated.* Jesus did.

21. Triumph Over Trivia.
▶ Think of each friendship as a beautiful flower in the Garden of *your* life.
▶ That Garden must be nurtured, fertilized and watered *regularly.*
▶ Do not let petty and insignificant differences—Trivia—sap the beauty of those flowers.

22. Confide In Few.
▶ Someone has said that even a fish would not get caught if it kept its mouth *shut!*
▶ Confidentiality is a *gift* to be shared in the privacy of prayer

or with an intercessor God has assigned to your life.

▶ Never share your troubles with someone *unqualified* to help you.

23. Never Complain About What You Permit.

▶ Your circumstances are not permanent.

▶ You have permitted your present circumstances or they would not exist.

▶ What you tolerate, you authorize to exist.

▶ Either accept the present without complaint or make a decision *to use your faith* and *attract a miracle* from God.

24. Insist On Integrity.

▶ Integrity is *truthfulness.* It is doing what you say you will do.

▶ *Demand* it from yourself and *reward* it in others.

▶ Do right by others and God will do right by you.

25. Recognize That Others Increase Your Worth.

▶ Your *best* qualities will surface in the presence of good people.

▶ Treasure any friend who generates *energy* and *enthusiasm* toward your dreams or goals.

▶ Go the extra mile to nurture and protect any God-given relationship.

26. Withdraw From Contentious People.

▶ A contentious person is a trouble-maker. He spreads discontent, frustration and distrust.

▶ He gossips. He slanders. He promotes strife.

▶ Do not feed a relationship with such a person.

27. Nullify Satanic Attacks Against Your Friends.

▶ Your prayers can *cancel* satan's Assignment against your family and friends.

▶ *Call their name* boldly before the throne of God today and *make your request known* in their behalf.

▶ *Expect* your prayer of agreement *to produce* miraculous results as He promised in His Word.

28. Resurrect Hope In Someone Today.

▶ Hope is the expectation of *favorable changes.*

▶ Do not permit someone in your life to remain depressed and devastated by their present circumstances.

▶ Remind them that Jesus Christ is still the Healer and Miracle Worker in *every* circumstance of life.

29. Interrogate Your Friends.

▶ Everyone is a Well of Information. *Draw from it.* Drop your bucket regularly into that well.

▶ Schedule an appointment this week with your three most successful friends.

▶ Bring your list of most important questions and *get the answers you need.*

30. Value The Opinions Of Others.

▶ One of the greatest gifts you will ever give anyone is...the Gift of Recognition.

▶ Every husband...wife...and child...is authorized by the Creator to have a viewpoint, and an opportunity to express it.

▶ Honor their right to be heard.

31. Generate Energy.

▶ *God energizes.* In Genesis 1, He created...moved...spoke... divided..called...and so forth.

▶ *You are His offspring. You were created for movement.* Your tongue speaks. Your eyes see. Your ears hear. Your hands grasp. Your feet walk. Even your mind creates thoughts, *each containing a different measure of energy.*

▶ *You are a Living Current, carrying others into your future.* Use your life today to excite others about the God you serve and the *future made possible* through a commitment to Jesus Christ.

RECOMMENDED BOOKS AND TAPES:

B-136 The Wisdom Commentary, Vol. 1 (256 pages/$20)
B-144 The Wisdom Library Of Mike Murdock, Vol. 1 (268 pages/$30)
B-175 The Wisdom Library Of Mike Murdock, Vol. 2 (240 pages/$30)

Whatever You Are Missing
In Your Life
Is Something You Do Not
Yet Value Greatly.

-MIKE MURDOCK

⇜ 41 ⇝

RESPECT

What You Respect You Will Attract.

Respect is different than love. To love somebody is to find them valuable. There are people that I respect that I cannot love. They are not desirable, but they are valuable. There are people that I love that I cannot respect. I find them desirable, but not valuable. Delilah was desirable, not valuable. The Law of Respect is to find something necessary, important, a treasure, a valuable thing.

Do you want *friends?* Then begin showing respect for people. Do you desire *good health?* You must begin respecting your body. Then, establish the habits that reflect your respect for your body. Do you want *money* to flow into your life? Then use wisely what God has already given you.

There is a number of things you have to respect to succeed, and if you do not, you will fail.

12 Things You Must Respect In Order To Succeed

1. Respect What You Have Already Been Given. Jesus taught that those who respected and appreciated what they were given would receive even more.

"His lord said unto him, Well done, thou good and faithful servant: thou hast been faithful over a few things, I will make thee ruler over many things: enter thou into the joy of thy lord" (Matthew 25:21).

2. Respect What You Want To Come Toward You. What you do not really appreciate, you will eventually lose. It may be your teenage son, your health or your job. When you do not respect a family member, he will probably withdraw from you. When you lack respect for your body, your health deteriorates. When you become careless toward your job, you risk losing it.

This reminds me of a young man who once worked for me. I liked him immensely and really felt he would always be a part of my ministry. He loved to laugh and truly seemed to enjoy his responsibilities.

But, after some months, his work became sloppy. It became

obvious that he did not take my deadlines seriously. He became too comfortable with his position.

One day, when his parents were visiting town, he took the liberty of leaving the office at midday, taking the remainder of the day off to be with his parents. He did the same thing the next day—both times without the consent of his supervisor.

My office manager called me long distance. "What should I do?" she asked, frustrated.

"Well, it is evident he does not really take his job seriously," I replied. "So, let him go if you feel that it is necessary."

We hated to fire him, but his lack of caring would eventually affect the morale of our entire office and ministry. *What this young man failed to respect, he lost.*

What you respect will inevitably come toward you.

Favor.

Finances.

Friends.

Zacchaeus of the New Testament is an example. His respect for Christ motivated him to climb a tree just to catch a glimpse of Jesus. It was that respect and love which then motivated Jesus to visit Zacchaeus' house for a meal.

3. Respect Uncommon Friendships Or Relationships. Think about your own life for a moment. Those who respect you are the people you love to spend time with. They are the ones who receive your attention, your time, your love. On the other hand, you probably withdraw from those who have shown you disrespect in some way.

"Hello, Dr. Murdock. So good to see you again!"

With these words I am always greeted at one of my favorite restaurants in Dallas. The owner always makes me feel special and respected. Naturally, I love it. His kindness is part of a magnetism that draws me back.

However, I have visited restaurants where I was treated as a nuisance, an interruption in their day. When I asked for A-1 Sauce to flavor my steak, they made me feel as though I had committed the unpardonable sin! Needless to say, I rarely return to those places.

4. Respect Miracles And Blessings. I heard a television host one night make sarcastic remarks about preachers who pray for the sick and believe in miracles. He sneered as he labeled them "faith healers."

Defiantly, he remarked, "I've never had a miracle or healing in *my* life."

He displayed complete disrespect for ministers of God who believed in miracles. I could not help but think of this principle of respect. It possibly explained why this man had not experienced miracles. *How could he attract miracles when he had no regard for them?*

As my friend Richard Roberts says, "He will start believing in miracles when he truly needs one!"

Do you *appreciate* blessings from God? If so, you will respect *men of God.* They are God's *gifts* to the world to help unlock our faith for miracles. This is one of the reasons I support a number of ministries every month. It is my way of showing God that I respect them and His ministry through them.

So predictably, people who slander and criticize faith ministries may experience fewer miracles and blessings in their own lives.

5. Respect Your Health. If you are like me, you can think of many things you would rather do than follow a daily regimen of physical exercise.

Perhaps no one has ever motivated you to eat properly and exercise consistently. You simply have not learned the importance of maintaining good health. Consequently, when you face a sickness, you may find it difficult to use your faith because good health has never been a priority to you.

God began to show me this in my own life. I could not abuse my body and expect to keep functioning properly. If I *really* wanted good health, I had to begin respecting my body. It deserved my time and effort when I was well as much as when I was sick!

It was not an easy task for me. I knew I should begin walking or jogging daily and develop a routine of exercise. But something within me kept rebelling. I became puzzled and frustrated at myself.

Then one day it dawned on me. Back in high school days, the coach used extra laps and extra push-ups as *punishment* for us. *So I subconsciously equated exercise as punishment.* This stirred up the resentment I had known as a teenager.

I had to change my opinion and *create a new respect* for physical fitness. I had to see exercise as a stepping stone to happiness instead of a punishment to my body. I had to rebuild my respect for a healthy body.

Maybe you are having a similar problem. Perhaps a sickness, a weakness or even an overweight condition has haunted you throughout your life. It may require a little additional effort on your part to build a healthy respect for God's "Temple," your body, but it is worth your time and effort to be whole, healthy and fully alive again.

6. Respect Money And Those Who Unlock It Into Your Life. I received a letter recently that was rather startling.

"When we saw you several months ago on television you were

teaching on prosperity. Frankly, my husband and I were turned off. We refused to watch your program until you started speaking on another subject. We have really been blessed this month through your teaching on the hurt and healing of divorce."

The letter continued, "I wish we had enough money to buy your book. But we don't have anything left after our bills are paid. Here is our best offering we can afford at this time."

Taped to this letter was a quarter.

Here is what disturbed me. The woman who wrote said she and her husband were so poor they could scarcely pay their bills. They were unable to give more than 25 cents to the work of God! *Yet, they became upset at me for teaching the laws of supply and blessing!*

Such reasoning amazed me. Here I was trying to help them *use their faith for finances* and it angered them. But this is often typical of those who struggle in the throes of misfortune. Feeling inferior and intimidated because of their lack, people often become critical and disrespectful toward the very message they need and toward ministers God has sent to them.

You must respect the things in life that you want to attract.

When I was young, I remember taking drives with friends through wealthy neighborhoods of our town. Often, someone would say, "See that nice home? The people who live there are probably miserable."

Envy usually creates resentment. For that reason the poor sometimes feel hostile toward the wealthy, rather than learn from them.

Sometimes our background teaching has programmed us to feel guilty about desiring money and nice things, so we fail to attract them.

I know this has been controversial in some circles, but revolutionary principles are not always easily understood at first.

The bottom line is the Word of God, not the opinions of uninformed men. And, the Scriptures teach that wealth and riches come from the hand of God.

"But thou shalt remember the Lord thy God: for it is He that giveth thee power to get wealth, that He may establish His covenant which He sware unto thy fathers, as it is this day" (Deuteronomy 8:18).

7. Respect For Your Mother And Father. The first thing we are taught to respect with the promise of a benefit is the Fifth Commandment. "Honor your mother and father that your days will be long on the earth and it will go well with you." (see Exodus 20:12).

Recently, teaching in a Bible college, I told young preachers, "Don't marry a girl who can't get along with her parents. You're marrying a tragedy." If a person cannot get along with the people who have paid their bills for a quarter of a century, nobody else has a chance with them. All I have to do is listen to a person talk about their mom and dad and I can predict their level of success. He did not say honor a good mom and dad. Honor your parents that it may go well with you. Why? It is obvious from Jeremiah 1:4-8 that in your mother's womb, God selected not only your Assignment, but He selected who would parent you. He selected your mom. The Holy Spirit selected your dad.

8. Respect For The Word Of God. The Law of Respect applies also to respecting His Word. If I do not read this Bible for days, that is proof of disrespect—I have documented my disrespect. I want to respect the Word of God, that is why I read 40 chapters a day in this Bible once a month. Not words. Anybody can say words. I have hidden this Law in my heart that I might not sin against God.

I asked the Lord some months ago what was the most important thing that I can do for others while I am on the earth. I have concluded that the most important thing you can do for someone is to birth a passion for His Word. If I can birth a passion for His Word in you, it will solve every problem in your life.

If I can birth a passion for His Word in you it will solve your mind problems, and every problem begins as a mind problem. The Bible said his mind is kept in perfect peace whose mind is stayed on Him.

It will solve your *financial problems.* Psalm 112:1-3 says a man that loves this law, wealth and riches will be in his house.

It will solve your *depression problems.* Jesus said in John, "I've spoken these words to you that my joy might remain in you and be full."

It will solve your *sex problems.* Psalm 119:9 says, "Wherewithal shall a young man cleanse his way? by taking heed to Thy word."

It will solve your *emotional problems.* "Great peace have they that love Thy law and nothing shall offend them."

It will solve your *health problems.* Exodus says, "A man that obeys this law, sickness and disease will be removed from him."

If I can get you to have a passion for this Book, I can solve every battle you are involved in.

9. Respect For Your Boss. Ephesians speaks of respecting your boss, your employer, the person who signs your check, who gave you the gift of access; the first important gift anybody can give you. The most important gift you will ever receive from another human is the gift of access. And your boss gave you the gift of access and believed in your gift and your potential and believed in you enough to say, "I will commit this money to you." And even when you walk down the hall and you were doing nothing and not solving a problem, and even when you go to the bathroom and you are there for ten minutes, he is still paying you. That is incredible. That is remarkable. And it says if you will respect him as if you were working for God, God will bless you ten-fold.

Not the boss, God would reward you.

If your boss has to tell you something twice, you ought to be getting half your salary.

When you refuse to follow an instruction from your boss, it is proven disrespect.

10. Respect For The Anointing Of The Spirit Of Men And Women Of God. Who will make fun and belittle a man of God because they do not understand the anointing that moves through him? I fear for the so-called Christians, not the unsaved, the unbeliever or the wicked who do not have the Spirit of God to discern right and wrong. I fear for the church world which belittles the preachers of prosperity, and sneers at a man of God talking to them about a Jehovah-jireh who wants to get them debt-free. I fear for the people that have no respect for the uniqueness of that anointing. I fear for people who make fun of healing ministries and act like they are all con artists making up people who are sick.

Respect the anointing that God allows to cross your path. Under this ministry, they cry. Under this ministry...I do not understand the different anointings of the Holy Spirit, but if I do not respect the way God uses somebody, I will forfeit every benefit God puts across my path.

How beautiful are the feet of those who preach the gospel.

Give honor to whom honor is due.

11. Respect For The Presence Of God. I entered my Secret Place as I do every morning from 9:00 to 10:00. (I have a room at my house. It is not my office. No fax machines. No telephones. Not a bunch of books. That is my next room, my Wisdom Room, my library. But I have a place sanctified exclusively for the Holy Spirit. He is my obsession.) Suddenly I felt funny. I said, "What's wrong?" I was there in shorts, a T-shirt and tennis shoes. I said, "I'm sorry." I went back over to my main house, changed clothes and came back into His presence. I never dreamed that it really mattered to Him. Protocol matters to the Spirit. You come into His presence right or you never enter His presence.

Respecting His presence. I have gone into churches with teenagers talking. I have removed entire rows of teenagers talking in the middle of a service. You will not disrespect the presence of God, because what you do not respect will move away from you. And you cannot live without His presence.

12. Respect Authority And Government. *Authority creates order.*

Imagine a nation without a leader. A workplace without a boss. An army without a general. Authority creates order, *the accurate arrangement of things.* That is why you do not park your car in the bathroom! You do not eat your meals in the garage! There is a place and a time for everything.

Respect those in authority over you. Your success is affected by it. Honor those who have lived before you. They possess a wealth of knowledge. Listen. Learn. Observe them.

Mentorship is the Master Key to extraordinary success.

Jesus understood this. He was the Son of God. He knew more than any other human on earth, yet He honored the authority of His own government. When people came to Him questioning His opinion on paying taxes to Caesar, He answered, "Render to Caesar the things that are Caesar's and to God the things that are God's" (Mark 12:17).

Are you speaking words of doubt about your own business? Are you belittling or criticizing your up-line? Stop it now. True, those in authority may not be perfect. They make mistakes.

What you respect will come toward you. I do not care if it is money or a dog or God. What you do not respect will move away from you. The Pharisees did not respect Jesus and He did not have a meal with them. But when Zacchaeus, the ungodly tax collector, put forth the effort to climb a tree to make certain he could see Jesus, then Jesus made time to have a meal with him.

RECOMMENDED BOOKS AND TAPES:

TS-41 School Of Wisdom, Vol. 1: The Uncommon Life (6 tapes/$30)

TS-42 School Of Wisdom, Vol. 2: 101 Wisdom Keys That Have Most Changed My Life (6 tapes/$30)

TS-43 School Of Wisdom, Vol. 3: What I'd Do Differently If I Could Begin My Life Over (6 tapes/$30)

TS-44 School Of Wisdom, Vol. 4: Unleashing Uncommon Favor (6 tapes/$30)

What You Believe Decides What You Receive.

-MIKE MURDOCK

～ 42 ～

SALVATION

My Greatest Mind Battle Was Over The Word.

When I entered my late teens, intense warfare emerged in my mind. It seemed that contradictions in the Scriptures existed. Then, I began to doubt the validity of the Bible when I saw hypocrisy in believers, inconsistencies in ministers and my own difficulty to live "the Biblical standard."

Two years of erratic and emotional turmoil occurred. I loved the presence of God and *received* from the Word of God. However, it seemed that the *logic* of my mind and the *faith* in my heart were in constant opposition. One day in honest desperation I asked the Lord to provide confidence and inner peace that the Bible was truly His infallible Word, not merely the compilation of human thoughts and ideas.

3 Powerful Truths Emerged

1. No Human Would Have Written A Standard As High As The Scriptures Teach. No husband would have written to treat your wife like Christ treats the church. No wife would have written to obey your husband. No teenager would have written that foolishness is bound in the heart of a child, but the rod of correction will drive it far from him. No rich man would have admitted that he that trusts in his riches will fail.

2. The Changes That Occur In Those Who Embrace The Word Of God Are Supernatural. Drug addiction has been broken. Alcoholics have been set free and delivered. Those who are violent have become meek and submissive.

3. The Very Presence Of A Bible Often Produces An Aura And Change In The Atmosphere. I have been on planes and noted an entire group of people become instantly silent when I pulled out my Bible. No novel of fiction affects men like this. Encyclopedias do not affect men like this. Lay a dictionary on a restaurant table. Nobody looks at you twice. But, lay a Bible on a restaurant table in visible view, and they will stare at you the entire meal. The magnetism of the Word of God is indescribable, irrefutable and unforgettable.

The Evidence Of God's Existence Far Outweighs The Proof Of His Absence.

Sometimes we make unfortunate mistakes.

Sometimes we make unwise decisions.

Sometimes we take devastating wrong turns in life. We become damaged. Severely damaged. Suicidal thoughts dance across the stage of our mind, mocking, sneering and defying us. Self-destruction seems a magnetic, compelling...an even desirable option to our present mess we have created. We need a New Beginning. A Second Chance. That is why I have stayed in love with Jesus. He gives you a Second Chance.

Then Bible says, "That if thou shalt confess with thy mouth the Lord Jesus, and shall believe in thine heart that God hath raised Him from the dead, thou shalt be saved. For with the heart man believeth unto righteousness; and with the mouth confession is made unto salvation" (Romans 10:9,10).

To receive Jesus Christ as Lord and Savior of your life please pray this prayer from your heart today!

Our Prayer Together...

"Dear Jesus, I believe that You died for me and rose again on the third day. I confess to You that I am a sinner. I need Your love and forgiveness. Come into my life, forgive my sins and give me eternal life. I confess You now as my Lord. Thank You for my salvation! I walk in Your peace and joy from this day forward. Amen."

I urge you to confront and resist the spirit of unbelief that assaults you today. And in Jesus' name, start using your God-given faith to move the mountains in your life.

"My precious Father, I come boldly to You today in the name of Jesus. I come in behalf of my friend in desperate need of You in his life.

"I *bind* the spirit of unbelief and doubt that has invaded the *mind, home* and *heart*. I *command* every demon spirit to come out and depart from his life. I loose him and set him free in the name of Jesus of Nazareth. I *forbid* those spirits to ever return into his life again."

Now, my friend, I *release* the presence of Jesus *into your life.* Receive the forgiveness and healing power of Jesus Christ *into your mind,* your *heart,* your *body* and your *soul.*

Be healed in your *mind.*

Be healed in your *emotions.*

Be healed in your *memories.*

Be healed in your *body.*

Be healed in your *marriage.*

Be healed in your *finances.*

Be healed in your *broken heart.*

Be healed in your *alcoholism.*

Be healed in your *drug addiction.*

Be healed in your *inferiority complex.*
Be healed in your *sense of unworthiness.*
Be healed in your *lack of confidence.*

"I pray this today in the powerful and precious name of Jesus of Nazareth, Who loves you and gave His life for your *complete deliverance* and *total freedom.* In Jesus' name, *It is done.* Amen."

31 Keys For New Believers

1. Despise Your Present Chains. You are a child of the Most High God. Captivity is unnatural for you. Learn to hate the chains of any habit that enslaves you.

While drug addicts and alcoholics may want the taste of sin, they certainly do not want the torment. But they will never be free until they learn to despise those chains.

Habit is hell's greatest weapon in destroying your life. Let God break your chains.

What You Can Tolerate, You Cannot Change.

So, do not complain about the things you are permitting to go on in your life.

"The Spirit of the Lord God is upon me; because the Lord hath anointed me to preach good tidings unto the meek; He hath sent me to bind up the brokenhearted, to proclaim liberty to the captives, and the opening of the prison to them that are bound;" (Isaiah 61:1).

"If the Son therefore shall make you free, ye shall be free indeed" (John 8:36).

2. Confess All Sin. *Guilt is the thief of faith.*

When you permit sin in your life, you become uncomfortable in the presence of God. It is difficult to expect a miracle from a God you resent. Confess your failure. He forgives. Your mistakes and sins have not shocked God. He anticipated your need for mercy. The Master Key to recovery is repentance. Do not justify yourself. Quit blaming others for the decisions you have made. Repent. Immediately.

"If I regard iniquity in my heart, the Lord will not hear me:" (Psalm 66:18).

3. Consider The Consequences Of Rebellion To God. Rebellion is punished. Always. It may not happen today, but it is inevitable. Each Seed of Disobedience is like a magnet attracting tragedies into your life.

God Will Never Advance You Beyond Your Last Act Of Disobedience. Joshua learned this at the Battle of Ai, when Achan attempted a coverup of his sin. The Israelites lost the battle.

God is not stupid. He is not blind. He sees everything. Sooner or later...He reacts to it. You cannot afford the losses your rebellion will create. When you see an alcoholic or drug addict, you see someone who has lost the most precious things in—his health, loving relationships and self-confidence. God promises gain to the obedient. He guarantees loss to the disobedient. Every loser can be a lesson to us. *Learn.*

"For that they hated knowledge, and did not choose the fear of the Lord: Therefore shall they eat of the fruit of their own way, and be filled with their own devices" (Proverbs 1:29,31).

4. Risk Everything To Become An Overcomer. Overcomers are the Rewarded. In fact, they are the only ones who are rewarded through eternity.

Even the Apostle Paul counted everything as a loss except his position with Christ. Each victory authorizes God to promote you.

In the World System, birth may decide rank. In the Kingdom System, battle decides rank. Every satanic attack upon you is simply another opportunity for promotion.

Refuse to quit.

The Secret of Champions is their refusal to quit trying.

Futility is merely a feeling. Conquer it and keep heading toward your goals.

Create small successes when the large ones seem impossible.

Even skyscrapers are built a brick at a time.

"I have fought a good fight, I have finished my course, I have kept the faith: Henceforth there is laid up for me a crown of righteousness, which the Lord, the righteous Judge, shall give me at that day: and not to me only, but unto all them also that love His appearing" (2 Timothy 4:7,8).

5. Allow Yourself Time To Change. Do not be too hard on yourself. Little-by-little and day-by-day, you will start tasting the rewards of change.

Look at the patience of God with Israel. He "knew they were but flesh." He took many years to even train their leader, Moses. You are not an exception.

Every man fails. Champions simply get back up...and begin again.

Give God time to work.

Sometimes those things you desire the most may take longer to achieve. It takes longer to make a Rolls Royce automobile than a bicycle.

Millions of Miracles have been dashed on the Rocks of Impatience. Give God time.

Something good is happening that you do not see. Wait joyfully with great expectations.

"The Lord upholdeth all that fall, and raiseth up all those that be bowed down" (Psalm 145:14).

"And let us not be weary in well doing: for in due season we shall reap, if we faint not" (Galatians 6:9).

6. Do Not Attempt To Cover Up Your Mistakes. *Everyone has sinned against God.* Publicly or privately.

You are instructed in the Word to confess that sin and turn away from it. Do it now. Obey Him.

Only a fool would attempt to deceive God. Your confession will unlock His mercy.

Your weaknesses do not worry Him. He is not confused and bewildered about your deliverance.

He is waiting for you.

He knows the futility of sin. He is well acquainted with the empty promises of satan.

"For all have sinned, and come short of the glory of God;" (Romans 3:23).

"For the wages of sin is death; but the gift of God is eternal life through Jesus Christ our Lord" (Romans 6:23).

"He that covereth his sins shall not prosper: but whoso confesseth and forsaketh them shall have mercy" (Proverbs 28:13).

7. Begin The Bible Habit. Pick a time...preferably, the morning. Call it your "Wisdom Hour." Read the Bible aloud.

Do not get bogged down in theology, or the Greek and Hebrew translations. Just meditate on His Word.

His Word is life. His Word creates faith. His Word will change the course of your life.

Pour the Word over your mind daily.

Your mind gathers the dirt, grime and dust of human opinion every day.

Renew your mind to the *Truth*—God's Word. Schedule an appointment with the Bible daily. The renewing of your mind is the key to changes within you.

The Words of God are like waterfalls...washing and purifying your mind.

"Study to shew thyself approved unto God, a workman that needeth not to be ashamed, rightly dividing the word of truth. But shun profane and vain babblings: for they will increase unto more ungodliness" (2 Timothy 2:15,16).

8. Celebrate Being In The Book Of Life. God keeps a daily journal. He records the names and victories of every one of His children.

Overcomers will never be blotted out of His Book. The name of every overcomer will echo through the Chambers of Heaven. Angels will hear it.

Get excited today about overcoming. You are stepping into the

Arena of Champions. Your name is becoming familiar in Heaven these days.

"He that overcometh...I will not blot out his name out of the book of life," (Revelation 3:5).

9. Make Prayer Time An Appointment. Two unforgettable disciples, Peter and John, kept their prayer appointment with God.

Daniel prayed three times daily. The psalmist prayed seven times daily. Great men have great habits.

You make appointments with lawyers, doctors and friends. Start making appointments with God.

Enjoy His presence.

When You Get Into The Presence Of God, Something Happens That Does Not Happen Anywhere Else.

Bring to Him your fears, worries, doubts and tears. You greatly matter to Him today.

So, enjoy Him. He certainly enjoys you.

"If ye abide in Me, and My words abide in you, ye shall ask what ye will, and it shall be done unto you" (John 15:7).

"Thou wilt shew me the path of life: in Thy presence is fulness of joy; at Thy right hand there are pleasures for evermore" (Psalm 16:11).

10. Feed Your Faith Daily. *Faith is your confidence in God.* Sometimes it is weak or may even seem nonexistent. At other times, it may be powerful and incredibly strong. It depends on the food you feed it.

Faith is a Tool...a Key...a Weapon. A Tool to create a future; a Key to unlock God's Storehouse of Blessing; and the Weapon that defeats satan.

Faith Comes When You Hear God Talk. Listen today to His Spirit, His servants, His Scriptures.

Absorb the promises of God.

Study the covenant God established with those who walk in obedience to Him.

You can only operate in faith according to your knowledge of His will or desire for your life. For example, if you do not know that God has already provided for your healing, how can you believe Him for a miracle in your health.

You must have a clear photograph of the will of God so your faith can implement it.

"So then faith cometh by hearing, and hearing by the word of God" (Romans 10:17).

"He that cometh to God must believe that He is, and that He is a rewarder of them that diligently seek Him" (Hebrews 11:6).

11. Start Pursuing The Wisdom Of God. *Wisdom is simply doing what God would do in a given situation.*

Jesus is made unto us the Wisdom of God. Whatever you face today, just do what you know Jesus would do.

Jesus said you have received two gifts from God: 1) Your mouth and 2) His Wisdom.

Unexpected things may happen today. Do not worry. The Holy Spirit within you will rise to the occasion and speak through you.

Relax. Someone greater than you is within you. Depend on Him.

"Get wisdom, get understanding: forget it not; neither decline from the words of My mouth" (Proverbs 4:5).

"Length of days is in her right hand; and in her left hand riches and honour" (Proverbs 3:16).

12. Pursue Your Assignment. *You Will Never Possess What You Are Unwilling To Pursue.*

Race horses never win races while they are in stalls.

God rewards reachers. Your enthusiasm will attract the right people in your life.

"The steps of a good man are ordered by the Lord: and He delighteth in his way" (Psalm 37:23).

13. Insist On Attending Church Faithfully. *Get into the presence of God.* Regularly. Your best will come out of you in His presence.

Sit under the teaching of a man of God you respect. Put your time, influence and finances there, faithfully. Even Jesus attended church regularly. There is no substitute for the Golden Link of Godly relationships. Network with others. Remember, one cannot multiply. Develop people skills. Listen, learn and absorb from others. Ask questions and document answers.

Success is a collection of relationships. Whatever you are willing to settle for, determines the quality of your future.

"Not forsaking the assembling of ourselves together, as the manner of some is;" (Hebrews 10:25).

"As His custom was, He went into the synagogue on the sabbath day," (Luke 4:16).

"Two are better than one; because they have a good reward for their labour. For if they fall, the one will lift up his fellow: but woe to him that is alone when he falleth; for he hath not another to help him up" (Ecclesiastes 4:9,10).

14. Tithe And Give Offerings With An Expectation Of A Harvest. Tithe means "tenth." Abraham brought ten percent of his income back to God in thanksgiving for the blessing of God.

This tithe is "Holy Seed."

As you bring your tithe to God this week, wrap your faith and expectation around it and look for the promised Harvest. Tithing is the

Biblical practice of returning ten percent of your income back to God after you have earned it. In the Old Testament, Abraham tithed. In the New Testament, even the Pharisees' tithing was noted by Jesus.

Make God your financial partner. Make every payday a Seed-sowing day. Results are guaranteed.

"Bring ye all the tithes into the storehouse, that there may be meat in Mine house, and prove Me now herewith, saith the Lord of hosts, if I will not open you the windows of heaven, and pour you out a blessing, that there shall not be room enough to receive it. And I will rebuke the devourer for your sakes, and he shall not destroy the fruits of your ground;" (Malachi 3:10,11).

15. Recognize Your Deliverers. God assigns Deliverers. Moses was assigned to lead the Israelites out of Egypt. Elijah was sent to the widow of Zarephath to help her use her faith.

If you are sick, look for the man of God who believes in healing. No one fails alone. If you fail, it will be because you chose to ignore those God assigned to help you. *Recognize messengers from God.* When satan wants to destroy you, he sends a person. *When God wants to bless you, He sends a person.* Recognize them. Whether they are packaged like a John the Baptist in a loincloth of camel's hair, or the silk robes of King Solomon.

Your reaction to a man or woman of God is carefully documented by God. When God talks to you, it is often through the spiritual leaders in your life. Do not ignore them.

"He that receiveth a prophet in the name of a prophet shall receive a prophet's reward; and he that receiveth a righteous man in the name of a righteous man shall receive a righteous man's reward" (Matthew 10:41).

16. Withdraw From Contentious People And Abandon Abusive Friendships. There are four kinds of people in your life: Those who add, subtract, divide and multiply.

Those Who Do Not Increase You, Will Inevitably Decrease You.

It is the responsibility of others to discern your worth.

A contentious person is a trouble-maker. He spreads discontent, frustration and distrust.

He gossips. He slanders. He promotes strife.

Do not feed a relationship with such a person.

"Make no friendship with an angry man; and with a furious man thou shalt not go; Lest thou learn his ways, and get a snare to thy soul" (Proverbs 22:24,25).

"As coals are to burning coals, and wood to fire: so is a contentious man to kindle strife" (Proverbs 26:21).

17. Find The Problem God Created You To Solve. *Everything*

God has made is a solution to a problem.

Your worth and significance are determined by the kind of problems you are solving for someone. If you want to earn $100.00 an hour, you must find a $100.00 an hour problem to solve.

Your significance is not in your similarity to others. It is in your *difference.* Find your point of difference...and solve a problem with it. Prosperity is inevitable.

One of the Master Keys to personal miracles is to get involved with the needs of others. Find your Assignment.

Joseph used his gift of interpreting dreams to calm a tormented Pharaoh. He was promoted from the prison to the palace. Job prayed for his friends during the worst crisis of his life. It released God to reverse the curse.

"Withhold not good from them to whom it is due, when it is in the power of thine hand to do it" (Proverbs 3:27).

18. Keep The Spirit Of A Finisher. Anyone can begin a marathon. Champions finish them. Everyone experiences adversity. It is those who stay strong to the finish who are rewarded. Pace yourself. Determine to "go the distance." Keep aflame the Spirit of a Finisher. Never, never, never give up. Your dreams and goals are worth any fight, any waiting, any pride. Do not give up. Your perseverance demoralizes your enemy. Do not give up.

Patience is a weapon. *Never Give Up.*

"But he that endureth to the end shall be saved" (Matthew 10:22).

19. Listen To Pain. *Pain Is Discomfort Created By Disorder.* It is not really an enemy. It is a signal, a memo, a messenger telling you an enemy exists.

When you were a child, you may have touched a hot iron. It hurt! Pain made you jerk your hand away..make changes...to protect yourself from injury.

If things are going wrong in your life, take it seriously. Pain talks. Initiate any change that may be necessary.

You have already been in your past. It did not satisfy you, or you would have stayed there.

It is time for changes. Big changes.

Get back up. Do not stay down. It is time for a New Beginning.

"Weeping may endure for a night, but joy cometh in the morning" (Psalm 30:5).

"Come now, and let us reason" (Isaiah 1:18).

20. Listen To Mentors. *Your mentor is anyone who consistently teaches you what you want to know.*

Mentorship is accepting perfect knowledge from an imperfect man. Joshua learned under Moses. Timothy learned under Paul. Elisha learned under Elijah. Observe successful lives carefully. Secrets will surface. Reasons for their success will emerge. Treasure your mentors. Pursue and extract the knowledge of the mentors that God has made available to your life.

"A wise man will hear," (Proverbs 1:5).

21. Endure Correction. Wisdom begins with correction. Errors must be exposed. Mistakes must be admitted. Think back over your life. Think of the person who taught you the most. He was probably the one who corrected you the most. Hell is full of people who rejected correction. Heaven is full of people who accepted it. Learn to listen. Somebody knows something you do not know. That information may be invaluable. You have to listen to receive it.

"For whom the Lord loveth He chasteneth," (Hebrews 12:6).

22. Expect A Turn-Around As A Reward To Your Obedience. Today is not permanent. Your worst circumstances today are subject to change.

God is stepping into the Arena of your life. He is turning the tide in your favor.

You Are Never As Far From A Miracle As It First Appears.

Examine the rewards of obedience to God. Obedience is doing whatever God instructs you to do. Each instruction is linked to a miracle in your future.

Each Act Of Obedience Shortens The Distance To Any Miracle You Are Pursuing.

Remember God only feels obligated to the obedient. The obedient always receive answers to their prayers.

"Every valley shall be exalted, and every mountain and hill shall be made low: and the crooked shall be made straight, and the rough places plain: And the glory of the Lord shall be revealed, and all flesh shall see it together: for the mouth of the Lord hath spoken it" (Isaiah 40:4,5).

23. Discern God's Hourly Agenda For You. Your agenda (schedule for today) should be decided in the presence of God. Your daily agenda will create miracles or tragedies depending on whether or not you are lead by the Spirit of God. *Hourly.*

Obedience is an hourly event.

Your inner peace is a signal. Do not make a phone call, an appointment for a decision unless you are at peace in your heart about it.

Remember...success is a daily event.

Success is a daily event...called joy. It happens hourly when you do the Will of God.

Habit is also a daily thing. *Nothing Will Ever Dominate Your Life Unless It Happens Daily.*

Focus on today's priorities. A priority is anything God has commanded you to do today.

"For as many as are led by the Spirit of God, they are the sons of God" (Romans 8:14).

"It is of the Lords' mercies that we are not consumed, because His compassions fail not. They are new every morning: great is Thy faithfulness" (Lamentations 3:22,23).

24. Keep Walking. Picture this. You are in your car. You are driving in a heavy hailstorm. You do not stop...but keep driving knowing you will move out off the storm's range.

Remember Joseph. Remember David. Every day of adversity was simply a stepping stone toward the throne.

Keep walking.

Remember, *seasons change*. Attacks do not last forever. People change. Weather changes. Circumstances change. So do not be discouraged today. Expect supernatural and dramatic changes. Tomorrow is coming. Your future is unlike any yesterday you have ever known. Jesus invested His first 30 years in preparation for His ministry. Moses spent 80 years becoming a great leader. Time is your friend. Do not hurry.

Remember, *Patience Is The Weapon That Forces Deception To Reveal Itself.*

"Weeping may endure for a might, but joy cometh in the morning" (Psalm 30:5).

"When thou passeth through the waters, I will be with thee; and through the rivers, they shall not overflow thee: when thou walkest through the fire, thou shalt not be burned; neither shall the flame kindle upon thee, for I am the Lord thy God" (Isaiah 43:2,3).

25. Tell Someone What Jesus Has Done For You. The first two letters of the word "gospel" spell..."GO."

Christianity is a network of activity. Promote Jesus today. He is the Starting Point of every miracle. Be the bridge that connects Him to somebody in trouble today.

Be bold. *One miracle is worth a thousand sermons.*

You are the creation. He is your Creator. You cannot out-think the One Who made you.

He has delighted in performing the impossible.

He has turned your sickness into health...poverty into prosperity... tears into laughter.

He is the Master of the turn-around.

Jesus has made the difference in your life. Tell someone about it today.

"Go ye into all the world, and preach the gospel to every creature.

And these signs shall follow them that believe; In My name shall they cast out devils; they shall speak with new tongues; They shall take up serpents; and if they drink any deadly thing, it shall not hurt them; they shall lay hands on the sick, and they shall recover" (Mark 16:15,17,18).

26. Make Today The Greatest Event Of Your Whole Lifetime. Do not be passive today. You are alive! Act like it!! Talk like it!! Celebrate yourself!!

Speak a little louder today. Speak a little faster.

Smile bigger...laugh aloud...and exude the joy of Jesus as you spread it generously over every single hour today.

You have accepted Christ as your personal Saviour. "The word is nigh thee, even in thy mouth, and in thy heart: that is, the word of faith, which we preach; That if thou shalt confess with thy mouth the Lord Jesus, and shalt confess with thy mouth the Lord Jesus, and shalt believe in thine heart that God hath raised Him from the dead, thou shalt be saved" (Romans 10:8,9).

"This is the day which the Lord hath made; we will rejoice and be glad in it" (Psalm 118:24).

27. Know Your Opponent. Satan is your real adversary. He is a fallen angel, dispelled from Heaven by a righteous God.

His methods are predictable. He incites the violent nature of men against you. He inflames the normal passions of man into perversion. He introduces thoughts that could ultimately destroy you.

He reacts to the *spoken* Word of God. He is easily demoralized with the Weapon of Praise. He flees when you resist him.

"Who shall separate us from the love of Christ? shall tribulation, or distress, or persecution, or famine, or nakedness, or peril, or sword? Nay, in all these things we are more than conquerors through Him that loved us" (Romans 8:35,37).

"For we wrestle not against flesh and blood, but against principalities, against powers, against the rulers of the darkness of this world, against spiritual wickedness in high places" (Ephesians 6:12).

28. Do Not Be Afraid To Reach For Help During Times Of Trouble. Reaching out for help is not a sign of weakness. So, do it. Only a fool ignores a life jacket when he is drowning.

Overcomers do not do it alone. They conquer their pride. They reject the trap of isolation. They reach. They know the inevitable reward of reaching. Turn to God. Honor those who are qualified to help you. Your future depends on it. Run to the refuge. Cities of refuge existed in Old Testament times. If a man was accused of a crime, he could run into a city of refuge and was guaranteed protection by law. You, too, have a Place of Refuge. When satan the accuser, brings accusations against your life, run to God.

God responds to reachers. Stop looking at where you have been and start looking at where you can be. Run to the Refuge. Do it today.

"When thou art in tribulation...if thou turn to the Lord thy God, and shalt be obedient unto His voice; He will not forsake thee, neither destroy thee," (Deuteronomy 4:30,31).

29. Face Any Problem Honestly. Do not blame others for what you have chosen to do. Do not blame others for the consequences of your choices. Remember...*Never Complain About What You Permit.*

Your life is the result of your choices.

Name your weaknesses. Nobody else can do it. Nobody else will do it. Nobody else should have to do it. Your honesty will determine your victories.

Run toward the mountain you want to see moved, just as David ran toward Goliath when he cut his head off. Your open reach for God sets your new beginning in motion...*today.*

Life is a collection of battles. Subsequently, it is also a collection of *victories.*

Reach down deep inside yourself today and call forth your greatest strength. Today is not a day for weakness. It is time to be tough.

Be tough.

"If thou faint in the day of adversity, thy strength is small" (Proverbs 24:10).

"A wise man is strong; yea, a man of knowledge increaseth strength" (Proverbs 24:5).

30. Do Not Panic When Crisis Occurs. Something may happen today that shocks you. Do not worry about it. God anticipated it.

Remember, satan is merely an ex-employee of Heaven. God knows him quite well. He fired him.

Get alone today in the presence of God. Fear will die and courage will flourish.

Analyze adversity.

There are four ways to respond to a crisis: Maximize it. Minimize it. Advertise it. Analyze it.

Maximizing...is to exaggerate the crisis.

Minimizing...is to understate the crisis.

Advertising...is to tell the whole world about it.

Analyzing...is extracting useful information from it.

Crisis is merely concentrated information. *Adversity Is Simply Your Enemies' Reaction To Your Progress.* Taking the time to analyze it will benefit you.

"Be still, and know that I am God:" (Psalm 46:10).

"In the days of prosperity be joyful, but in the day of adversity consider:" (Ecclesiastes 7:14).

31. Create A Miracle Climate. *Atmosphere Matters.* An atmosphere of praise and worship can unlock your faith for miracles.

When David played his harp for Saul, evil spirits departed from the palace. Anointed music is one of the master keys in creating a miracle-climate.

Keep a cassette player handy. Use it to make a conscious effort today to keep Godly music playing all day long.

Listen to anointed music.

Godly music drives evil spirits away.

When depression enters, and the battle rages...turn on a music cassette that ushers in the Presence of God. Satan reacts to it. He fears it.

"But now bring me a minstrel. And it came to pass, when the minstrel played, that the hand of the Lord came upon him" (2 Kings 3:15).

"And it came to pass, when the evil spirit from God was upon Saul, that David took an harp, and played with his hand: so Saul was refreshed, and was well, and the evil spirit departed from him" (1 Samuel 16:23).

RECOMMENDED BOOKS AND TAPES:

B-91 The Leadership Secrets Of Jesus (197 pages/$10)
B-114 Law Of Recognition (248 pages/$10)
B-118 Seeds Of Wisdom On Problem-Solving (32 pages/$5)
TS-41 School Of Wisdom, Vol. 1: The Uncommon Life (6 tapes/$30)

❦ 43 ❦

SERVANTHOOD

God Has Called You To Serve Someone.

Who are they? Where are they? How can you serve them better? With what kind of attitude and spirit do you serve them?

Serve them with diligence—promotion is guaranteed.

Diligence is immediate attention to an assigned task.

11 Facts About Servanthood

1. Jesus Taught Servanthood. "The disciple is not above his master, nor the servant above his lord" (Matthew 10:24).

2. The Uncommon Servant Uses Everything God Has Given Him. "The slothful man roasteth not that which he took in hunting: but the substance of a diligent man is precious" (Proverbs 12:27).

3. Servanthood Is The Golden Gate To Uncommon Promotion. *There is always a reason for the chain of authority.* There is a reason for obedience.

The purpose of supervision is not restraint, but promotion.

4. Whomever God Has Assigned Over You Is Qualified To Promote You. *That is the purpose of accountability.*

5. You Can Only Be Promoted By Someone Whose Instructions You Have Followed. God established the chain of authority. He was not trying to stop your flexibility or destroy your creativity, but find a person whose authority was the key to your promotion.

6. Uncommon Leaders Have Always Been Uncommon Servants. Examine Joseph. He served Potiphar. When his master's wife falsely accused him, he still served in the prison until he became the head. When released, he was promoted and served Pharaoh as Prime Minister of the nation.

Joshua served Moses.

Esther served the king.

Jonathan served David.

David served Saul.

Elisha served Elijah.

Ruth served Naomi.

7. The Uncommon Servant Will Always Be Pursued By Uncommon Leaders. "Seest thou a man diligent in his business? he shall stand before kings; he shall not stand before mean men" (Proverbs 22:29).

8. The Uncommon Servant Will Always Rise To The Position Of Supervisor. "The hand of the diligent shall bear rule:" (Proverbs 12:24).

9. The Focus Of The Uncommon Servant Is Always To Increase The Success Of His Boss. "The thoughts of the diligent tend only to plenteousness;" (Proverbs 21:5).

Accumulation is the focus.

10. The Uncommon Servant Will Always Prosper. "The soul of the diligent shall be made fat" (Proverbs 13:4).

11. The Uncommon Employee Will Always Increase The Personal Wealth Of His Boss. "The hand of the diligent maketh rich" (Proverbs 10:4).

RECOMMENDED BOOKS AND TAPES:

B-91 The Leadership Secrets Of Jesus (197 pages/$10)
B-114 The Law Of Recognition (248 pages/$10)
B-118 Seeds Of Wisdom On Problem-Solving (32 pages/$5)
TS-41 School Of Wisdom, Vol. 1: The Uncommon Life (6 tapes/$30)

❧ 44 ❧

SINGING

━━━━━━●━━━━━━

34 Facts You Should Know About Singing

1. God Sings. "The Lord Thy God in the midst of thee is mighty; He will save, He will rejoice over thee with joy; He will rest in His love, He will joy over thee with singing" (Zephaniah 3:17).

2. Champions In The Old Testament Sang. "I will sing a new song unto Thee, O God: upon a psaltery and an instrument of ten strings will I sing praises unto Thee. It is He that giveth salvation unto kings: Who delivereth David His servant from the hurtful sword" (Psalm 144:9,10).

3. Moses, The Great Leader, Understood The Heart Of God About Singing. After Israel saw Pharaoh's army destroyed, they sang. "Then sang Moses and the children of Israel this song unto the Lord, and spake, saying, I will sing unto the Lord, for He hath triumphed gloriously: the horse and his rider hath He thrown into the sea" (Exodus 15:1).

4. Champions In The New Testament Sang. "And at midnight Paul and Silas prayed, and sang praises unto God: and the prisoners heard them" (Acts 16:25).

5. Sing When You Enter His Presence. "...come before His presence with singing" (Psalm 100:2).

Sounds are wonderful to the Holy Spirit! Listen to the birds today as they sing out in wonderment! Listen to the sounds of animals, the wind blowing through the trees and even the wonderful love sounds of those family members close to you. Singing is an essential part of this world. That is why the Holy Spirit wants you to be aware of His fervent desire to hear you sing to Him!

6. Sing Together With Other Saints. "Let the word of Christ dwell in you richly in all wisdom; teaching and admonishing one another in psalms and hymns and spiritual songs, singing with grace in your hearts to the Lord" (Colossians 3:16).

7. Sing To The Holy Spirit, Knowing Evil Spirits Will Leave. King Saul discovered this under the anointed music ministry of David. In fact, the music of David refreshed Saul. "And it came to pass, when the evil spirit from God was upon Saul, that David took an harp, and played with his hand: so Saul was refreshed, and was well, and the evil spirit departed from him" (1 Samuel 16:23).

That is why I placed 24 speakers on the trees in my seven-acre yard. I cannot tell you how wonderful it is to walk across my yard, hearing these songs to the Holy Spirit continuously. Words cannot describe the effect it has in your heart and mind. In fact, recently when some of my CD's (compact discs) were damaged, it seemed like death replaced life around my house! *The Holy Spirit comes when He is celebrated.*

Invest in an excellent, quality stereo and make music a major part of every day. It is worth every penny. Your *mind* will respond. Your *heart* will find new fire. Your *body* will receive a surging of new energy and vitality. Most of all, the Holy Spirit will manifest His presence.

8. Singers Were An Essential Part Of Battles In The Old Testament. Listen to the conduct of Jehoshaphat. "When he had consulted with the people, he appointed singers unto the Lord, and that should praise the beauty of holiness, as they went out before the army, and to say, Praise the Lord; for His mercy endureth for ever" (2 Chronicles 20:21).

9. Singers Were Often The Reason For Victories Against The Enemies Of God. "And when they began to sing and to praise, the Lord set ambushments against the children of Ammon, Moab, and mount Seir, which were come against Judah; and they were smitten" (2 Chronicles 20:22).

▶ Your singing to the Holy Spirit *will create an atmosphere of thanksgiving.*

▶ Your singing will greatly *influence your focus.*

▶ Your singing can dispel *every demonic influence designed to distract you.*

▶ Your singing will arouse the energy and passion of your own body to focus on your Creator.

▶ Your singing is an act of obedience to the Holy Spirit.

10. Your Singing Can Affect Nature Itself. Read again the incredible story of Paul and Silas in prison. Everything was going against them. They had been beaten. They were alone and in incredible pain. But, they understood the *Weapon of Singing.* "And at midnight Paul and Silas prayed, and sang praises unto God: and the prisoners heard them. And suddenly there was a great earthquake, so that the foundations of the prison were shaken: and immediately all the doors were opened, and every one's bands were loosed" (Acts 16:25,26). The foundations were destroyed...*as they began to sing.*

11. Sing To Cause Your Enemy To Become Demoralized, Discouraged And Decide To Move Away From You. Paul watched this happen when he and Silas sang in the prison. "And the keeper of the prison awaking out of his sleep, and seeing the prison doors open, he drew out his sword, and would have killed himself, supposing that the prisoners had been fled" (Acts 16:27).

12. Your Singing May Be The Turning Point In Someone's Personal Salvation. It happened for the jailer when Paul and Silas sang. "Then he called for a light, and sprang in, and came trembling, and fell down before Paul and Silas, And brought them out, and said, Sirs, what must I do to be saved?" (Acts 16:29,30).

Singing Can Change Everything Around Your Life. Everything. So, begin this very moment. Close this book and begin to sing *aloud* to the Holy Spirit. Your words may be simple, but they will become powerful.

"I love You, Holy Spirit!
I love You, Holy Spirit!
You are good, so good to me!"

So, you and I can learn from the champions. Those who have conquered in battle have discerned the hidden and mysterious power of singing. You must do it in your own life today! "Saying, I will declare Thy name unto my brethren, in the midst of the church will I sing praise unto Thee" (Hebrews 2:12).

Always remember, the Holy Spirit is delighted when you sing to Him.

13. Sing Regardless Of What Is Going On Around You. Paul and Silas in prison..."And at midnight Paul and Silas prayed, and sang praises unto God: and the prisoners heard them" (Acts 16:25).

14. Sing Songs Of Remembrance. Moses...Miriam...

15. Sing To Follow The Pattern Of Uncommon Great Men. David said, "I will sing of mercy and judgment: unto Thee, O Lord, will I sing" (Psalm 101:1).

16. Sing To God Because He Is To Be Praised And Feared Above All The Other Gods Of This World. "Sing unto the Lord, bless His name, shew forth His salvation from day to day. Declare His glory among the heathen, His wonders among all people. For the Lord is great, and greatly to be praised: He is to be feared above all gods. For all the gods of the nations are idols: but the Lord made the heavens" (Psalm 96:2-5).

17. Sing To God To Celebrate His Greatness. "Let us come before His presence with thanksgiving, and make a joyful noise unto Him with psalms. For the Lord is a great God, and a great King above all gods" (Psalm 95:2,3).

18. Sing Your Thanksgiving Because Of His Blessings. *David did.* "I will sing unto the Lord, because He hath dealt bountifully with me" (Psalm 13:6).

"Return unto thy rest, O my soul; for the Lord hath dealt bountifully with thee" (Psalm 116:7).

19. Sing Because Of His Delivering Power From The Hand Of Evil Doers. "Sing unto the Lord, praise ye the Lord: for He hath delivered the soul of the poor from the hand of evil doers" (Jeremiah 20:13).

"Hearken my beloved brethren, Hath not God chosen the poor of this world rich in faith, and heirs of the kingdom which He hath promised to them that love Him? But ye have despised the poor. Do not rich men oppress you, and draw you before the judgment seats?" (James 2:5,6).

20. Sing So The Heathen And The Ungodly May Know About Him And His Glory. "Sing unto the Lord, bless His name: shew forth His salvation from day to day.

Declare His glory among the heathen, His wonders among all people. For the Lord is great, and greatly to be praised:" (Psalm 96:2-4).

21. Sing To God To Worship Him And Celebrate Him As My Shepherd And Provider. "O come, let us worship and bow down: let us kneel before the lord our maker. For He is our God; and we are the people of His pasture, and the sheep of His hand" (Psalm 95:6,7).

He is our Shepherd.

I am His sheep.

His provision is worth celebrating. His care for me is worth celebrating. So, I sing and worship Him!

22. Sing Because Your Mouth Is Your Deliverer. It is your weapon!

23. Sing To Celebrate His Benefits, Forgiveness And Healing Power. "Bless the Lord, O my soul: and all that is within me, bless His holy name. Bless the Lord, O my soul, and forget not all His benefits: Who forgiveth all thine iniquities; Who healeth all thy diseases; Who satisfieth thy mouth with good things; so that thy youth is renewed like the eagle's" (Psalm 103:1-3,5).

24. Sing With Victory, Breaking The Focus And Attention Of Demonic Spirits. Paul and Silas...David and Saul...Moses and Miriam...

25. Great Healing Ministries Emphasize Singing. Sometimes, I have sat for two to three hours before the miracles and healings began. Songs that honored the Holy Spirit and the greatness of God seemed to unlock faith into the atmosphere. He always comes when He is celebrated and honored. You see He instructed us how to approach Him—come with singing (see Psalm 100:2).

26. Sing To God Because Everything He Created Was Commanded To Rejoice Before Him.

"O sing unto the Lord a new song: sing unto the Lord, all the earth. Let the heavens rejoice, and let the earth be glad; let the sea roar, and the fulness thereof. Let the field be joyful, and all that is therein: then shall all the trees of the wood rejoice" (Psalm 96:1,11,12).

27. Sing Because It Is Proof Of Your Thankfulness And Gratitude For Him. "Enter into His gates with thanksgiving, and into His courts with praise: be thankful unto Him, and bless His name. For the Lord is good; His mercy is everlasting; and His truth endureth to all generations" (Psalm 100:4,5).

28. Sing As Evidence That You Have Recognized The Victory God Has Given You. "O sing unto the Lord a new song; for He hath done marvellous things: His right hand, and His holy arm, hath gotten Him the victory" (Psalm 98:1).

29. Sing As A Sign Of Victory. *Moses did.*

"Then sang Moses and the children of Israel this song unto the Lord, and spake, saying, I will sing unto the Lord, for He hath triumphed gloriously: the horse and his rider hath He thrown into the sea. The Lord is my strength and song, and He has become my salvation: He is my God, and I will prepare Him an habitation; my Father's God, and I will exalt Him. The Lord is a man of war: the Lord is His name. Pharaoh's chariots and his host hath He cast into the sea: his chosen captains also are drowned in the Red sea...Thy right hand, O Lord, hath dashed in pieces the enemy" (Exodus 15:1-4,6).

Sing when you pray.

Sing in times of trouble.

Sing during times of battle. Moses did.

30. Sing To Celebrate The Mercy That God Has Shown You Throughout Your Lifetime. *I have made mistakes.*

I have missed the will of God.

I have sinned throughout my lifetime.

Yet, the mercies of God have sustained me. My singing to Him is to acknowledge, recognize and show my thankfulness for His times of mercy where He has kept and preserved me.

"I will sing of mercy and judgment: unto Thee, O Lord, will I sing" (Psalm 101:1).

31. Sing To Him Specifically, Not Just To People. I have written over 5,000 songs throughout my lifetime. Yet, the songs I love to sing the most are the Love Songs to the Holy Spirit. I call them, "Songs From The Secret Place." Hundreds of songs have been birthed in my heart since I fell in love with the Holy Spirit on July 13, 1994.

32. Sing From Your Heart, Not Your Mind. He does not need fancy words, unusual philosophy or beautiful sounds. He simply wants you to open your heart and let the "love sounds" flow from you (read 1 Corinthians 13).

33. Sing In Your Prayer Language, Too. The Apostle Paul understood the incredible power of singing. "I will sing with the Spirit, and I will sing with the understanding also" (1 Corinthians 14:15). "And at midnight Paul and Silas prayed, and sang praises unto God:" (Acts 16:25).

34. Sing The Word Of God. "My tongue shall speak of Thy word: for all Thy commandments are righteousness" (Psalm 119:172).

David said in Psalm 119:54, "Thy statutes have been my songs in the house of my pilgrimage."

Our Prayer Together...

"Father, thank You for revealing the Weapon of Singing to my life. I will sing...when things go wrong or right. I will sing regardless of my circumstances. I will sing of the purpose of honoring You and obeying You! I will sing *regardless of my circumstances.* I will sing for the purpose of *honoring You* and obeying You! I will sing *songs of remembrance,* because I remember every blessing You have given me over the years! I will sing *continuously,* knowing that as I sing, angels come and minister to me! I will sing with *victory,* knowing that demonic spirits are becoming fragmented and confused when they hear my words. I will sing, knowing that my mouth is my *Deliverer!* I will teach *my children* to sing to You! I will have songs played in my home, in my car and on my job continuously...to honor Your presence! *Thank You for singing to me* over my life! In Jesus' name. Amen."

RECOMMENDED BOOKS AND TAPES:
CD-01 In Honor Of The Holy Spirit (music CD/$10)
CD-08 Songs From The Secret Place (music CD/$30)

❧ 45 ❧

SPIRITUAL WARFARE

Who Is Your Real Enemy?

Before you enter battle, you must know who your true enemy is.

Believe it or not, your enemy is *not* just people! People are often *tools* of your true enemy. Paul wrote, "For we wrestle not against flesh and blood, but against principalities, against powers, against the rulers of the darkness...against spiritual wickedness in high places" (Ephesians 6:12).

▶ *Your Real Enemy Is The Devil...Satan...Lucifer.* "Because your adversary the devil, as a roaring lion, walketh about, seeking whom he may devour:" (1 Peter 5:8).

▶ *He Is An Ex-Employee Of Heaven—A Fallen Angel.* "I beheld satan as lightning fall from heaven" (Luke 10:18). "The great dragon was cast out, that old serpent, called the devil, and satan, which deceiveth the whole world: he was cast out into the earth, and his angels were cast out with him" (Revelation12:9).

▶ *Satan's Time Is Limited, So His Efforts Are Intensified.* "For the devil is come down unto you, having great wrath, because he knoweth that he hath but a short time" (Revelation 12:12).

▶ *Even His Power To Tempt You Is Limited.* "God is faithful, Who will not suffer you to be tempted above that ye are able; but will...make a way to escape,that ye may be able to bear it" (1 Corinthians 10:13).

The Nature Of Your Enemy

▶ *Satan Despises God.* And he hates anything that receives God's affection.

▶ *Satan Is Quite Aware Of God's Unusual Care And Protection Of You.* Satan reacts with unbridled resentment toward us. His reaction to the blessings upon Job is a prime example (see Job 1:9-12).

▶ *Satan Is Deceptive.* Cunning. Manipulating. The father of all lies. Jesus said, speaking of the devil, "He was a murderer from the beginning...there is no truth in him...for he is a liar, and the father of it" (John 8:44).

Why Does Satan Oppose You?

▶ *Satan Opposes You Because You Are A Potential Source Of Pleasure To God.* "For Thou hast created all things, and for Thy pleasure they are and were created" (Revelation 4:11).

▶ *Satan's Real Enemy Is God.* But because he is powerless against God, he attacks that which is *closest* to the heart of God...you and me.

▶ *Satan's Main Purpose Of Warfare Is To Pin God's Heart, To Insult Him, To Frustrate His Purposes In Your Life.*

▶ *Satan Wants You To Grieve God's Heart By Doubting God's Integrity.* "God is not a man, that He should lie; neither the son of man, that He should repent: hath He said, and shall He not do it? or hath He spoken, and shall He not make it good?" (Numbers 23:19).

The devil wants to prevent the arrival of any miracle that would bring glory to God. Satan's aim is to:

▶ *Paralyze Your Planning.*

▶ *Abort Your Dreams.*

▶ *Destroy Your Hope.*

Satan's 4 Favorite Weapons

1. Delays. Satan tries to thwart or abort the arrival of your desired miracles. He knows that a delay can weaken your desire to keep reaching. Daniel shares this kind of experience in Daniel 10:2-14, which we will discuss further later in this chapter.

2. Deceit. Satan is a master at deception and error. He knows that if he can infiltrate a generation through *erroneous* teaching, he can destroy millions. *One single falsehood* from the mouth of an articulate speaker can derail the dreams of millions.

Only eternity will reveal how many dreams have crashed on the Rocks of Prejudiced Teachings against divine healing, the Holy Spirit or financial prosperity.

3. Distractions. *Broken focus* is the goal of all satanic attacks. "Turn not to the right hand nor to the left:" (Proverbs 4:27). Your energy and time are too precious to waste on unproductive friendships, unworthy criticisms or any other *distracting* interests.

4. Disappointment. With yourself or others. Refuse to replay the guilt of previous mistakes, nor become preoccupied with past losses, nor magnify the weaknesses of others.

Maybe people around you think of you as a failure...and maybe you even agree with them. But the truth of the matter is *God created you to win!*

You are a Champion.

"Choose you this day whom ye will serve;" (Joshua 24:15). Are you going to give in to satan and fail? Or will you trust God and win? The decision is yours.

Be prepared for the enemy's attack. Know where it is most likely to come from, someone you love or trust. "For the son dishonoureth the father, the daughter riseth up against her mother, the daughter-in-law against her mother-in-law; a man's enemies are the men of his own house" (Micah 7:6).

How To Predict Your 6 Seasons Of Satanic Attack

1. When You Become Physically Exhausted. I travel a lot. Sometimes, up to 20,000 miles in a single month. I have noticed that my faith and enthusiasm want through fatigue.

In fact, satan's greatest attacks on your faith-life will probably happen when you get little or no sleep.

2. When You Face A Major Decision Regarding Your Assignment. They may be in your career or even geographical relocation. Remember, you must patiently endure a crisis to receive the promotion. That is why patience is so beneficial. "The Lord is good unto them that wait for Him," (Lamentations 3:25).

3. The Birth Of A Child Destined To Become A Spiritual Leader. It happened after the birth of Moses when Pharaoh commanded the male children to be murdered (see Exodus 1:16).

Also, the birth of Jesus as I mentioned earlier: "For Herod will seek the young child to destroy Him" (Matthew 2:13).

Great people of God often relate childhood adversities that threatened them in their early life.

4. When A Specific Miracle Has Just Left The Hand Of God Toward You. Daniel waited 21 days for his prayer to be answered. When the angel of the Lord finally appeared, he explained the warfare that necessitated the assistance of Michael, the archangel, to help him (see Daniel 10:13).

Your battle is really a signal. It is announcing, "Something is en route to you from God today."

5.   When You Make An Effort To Launch A New Ministry For God. Jesus faced His wilderness experience just prior to His healing ministry (see Matthew 4). I have seen it happen, almost without fail. Each major project...new television effort...new church building program encounters extreme opposition or setbacks.

6.   When You Are Next In Line For A Promotion From God. When Joseph announced the dream that God had given him, his own brothers, in bitterness, sold him into slavery. His reputation of honor was stripped because of one lie from Potiphar's wife.

Each day of adversity in Joseph's life simply ushered him one day closer to the throne.

Your 6 Most Effective Weapons In Battle

You will never win a spiritual battle *through your own strength or Wisdom.* "Not by might, nor by power, but by My Spirit, saith the Lord of hosts" (Zechariah 4:6).

"For the weapons of our warfare are not carnal, but mighty through God to the pulling down of strong holds;" (2 Corinthians 10:4).

"For though we walk in the flesh, we do not war after the flesh:" (2 Corinthians 10:3).

1.   You Must Know And Speak The Word Of God. "For the word of God is quick, and powerful, and sharper than any two-edged sword, piercing even to the dividing asunder of soul and spirit...and is a discerner of the thoughts and intents of the heart" (Hebrews 4:12).

2.   Your Conversations Should Reflect The Mentality Of A Conqueror. "Death and life are in the power of the tongue...they that love it shall eat the fruit thereof" (Proverbs 18:21). The three men said before going into the furnace, "Our God...is able to deliver us from the ...fiery furnace, and He will deliver us out of thine hand, O king" (Daniel 3:17).

3.   You Must Take Your Authority Over Satan In The Name Of Jesus. "The name of the Lord is a strong tower: the righteous runneth into it, and is safe" (Proverbs 18:10). "God also hath highly exalted Him, and given Him a name which is above every name: That at the name of Jesus every knee should bow," (Philippians 2:9,10).

4.   You Must Clothe Yourself In Spiritual Armor Each Morning In Prayer. "Take unto you the whole armour of God, that ye may be able to withstand in the evil day, and having done all, to stand" (Ephesians 6:13).

5. You Must Respect The Power Of Prayer And Fasting. "The effectual fervent prayer of a righteous man availeth much" (James 5:16). "Is not this the fast that I have chosen? to loose the bands of wickedness, to undo the heavy burdens, and to let the oppressed go free...that ye break every yoke?" (Isaiah 58:6).

6. You Must Pursue And Extract The Wisdom Of God From Mentors He Places In Your Life. "A wise man will hear, and will increase learning; and a man of understanding shall attain unto wise counsels:" (Proverbs 1:5). As one minister says, "Your mentor should be your greatest source of stress."

4 Forces That Shorten Your Season Of Struggle

1. Your Speaking: *Words of faith build you up in the Spirit.* Faith-talk is explosive (see Proverbs 18:21). When God wanted the present to end and the future to begin, He spoke.

2. Your Singing: Singing creates a climate satan cannot tolerate. Songs of worship and praise dispel demonic spirits as Saul discovered when David played the harp (see 1 Samuel 16:23).

Someone has well said, "Motion creates emotion."

3. Your Sharing: The prayer of agreement with others is extremely powerful. It is wise for you to initiate the prayer of assistance from intercessors. "Whatsoever ye shall bind on earth shall be bound in heaven:...whatsoever ye shall loose on earth shall be loosed in heaven...if two of you...agree on earth as touching any thing...it shall be done for them of My Father" (Matthew 18:18,19).

4. Your Seed-Sowing: *Sowing creates partnership with God* that involves Him in your adversity. "Bring ye all the tithes into the storehouse, that there may be meat in Mine house, and prove Me now...saith the Lord of hosts, if I will not open...the windows of heaven, and pour you out a blessing, that there shall not be room enough to receive it. And I will rebuke the devourer for your sakes," (Malachi 3:10,11).

I have always observed significant changes in times of stress, battle and struggle when I have boldly unleashed the above Four Forces.

RECOMMENDED BOOKS AND TAPES:

ST-011 How To Get Back Up When Satan Puts You Down (single cassette/$5)
B-07   Battle Techniques For War Weary Saints (32 pages/$5)
B-19   Seeds Of Wisdom On Warfare (32 pages/$3)
B-21   Seeds Of Wisdom On Adversity (32 pages/$3)

Submission Begins
When Agreement Ends.

-MIKE MURDOCK

～ 46 ～

SUBMISSION

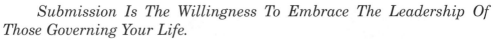

Submission Is The Willingness To Embrace The Leadership Of Those Governing Your Life.

"Obey them that have the rule over you, and submit yourselves: for they watch for your souls, as they that must give account, that they may do it with joy, and not with grief: for that is unprofitable for you" (Hebrews 13:17).

Many assume that leadership is strength. Submission often implies weakness.

True submission is evidence of respect, flexibility, trust and humility.

It is the quality of champions.

31 Facts About Submission

1. Those In Authority Are Commanded To Reward Those Who Submit. "Feed the flock of God which is among you, taking the oversight thereof, not by constraint, but willingly; not for filthy lucre, but of a ready mind; Neither as being lords over God's heritage, but being ensamples to the flock. And when the chief Shepherd shall appear, ye shall receive a crown of glory that fadeth not away. Likewise, ye younger, submit yourselves unto the elder. Yea, all of you be subject one to another, and be clothed with humility: for God resisteth the proud, and giveth grace to the humble. Humble yourselves therefore under the mighty hand of God, that He may exalt you in due time:" (1 Peter 5:2-6).

"When the righteous are in authority, the people rejoice: but when the wicked beareth rule, the people mourn" (Proverbs 29:2).

2. Submission To Qualified Authority Brings Promotion. "The sacrifices of God are a broken spirit: a broken and contrite heart, O God, Thou wilt not despise" (Psalm 51:17).

"For promotion cometh neither from the east, nor from the west, nor from the south. But God is the Judge: He putteth down one, and setteth up another" (Psalm 75:6,7).

3. Uncommon Protégés Submit To Uncommon Mentors. *Elisha submitted to Elijah.* He received a double portion of Elijah's mantle as a reward.

4. Submission Always Results In Inner Joy. "Looking unto Jesus the Author and Finisher of our faith; Who for the joy that was set before Him endured the cross, despising the shame, and is set down at right hand of the throne of God" (Hebrews 12:2).

5. Submission Must Become Your Personal Choice. "God resisteth the proud, but giveth grace unto the humble. Humble yourselves in the sight of the Lord, and He shall lift you up" (James 4:6,10).

6. Jesus Himself Knew The Rewards Of Submission. When He prayed in the garden of Gethsemane, He prayed before Calvary. "Oh My Father, if it be possible, let this cup pass from Me: nevertheless not as I will, but as Thou wilt" (Matthew 26:39).

"But that the world may know that I love the Father, and as the Father gave Me commandment, even so I do. Arise, let us go hence" (John 14:31).

"If ye keep My commandments, ye shall abide in My love; even as I have kept My Father's commandments, and abide in His love" (John 15:10).

"If ye love Me, keep My commandments. And I will pray the Father, and He shall give you another Comforter, that He may abide with you forever;" (John 14:15,16).

7. Those Who Refuse To Submit To Authority Often Experience Seasons Of Tragedy. "But if ye refuse and rebel, ye shall be devoured by the sword: for the mouth of the Lord hath spoken it" (Isaiah 1:20).

Korah refused to submit to the authority of Moses. His entire family was destroyed because of it.

Ananias and Sapphira refused to submit to the standard of integrity expected by the Holy Spirit and Pastor Peter. Both fell dead in the sanctuary.

8. Submission Is Your Personal Gift Of Cooperation To Those Who Govern You. *Every great leader began as a great follower.* They honored the authority established by God.

"Obey them that have the rule over you, and submit yourselves: for they watch for your souls, as they that must give account, that they may do it with joy, and not with grief: for that is unprofitable for you" (Hebrews 13:17).

It was not their weakness that makes them easy to govern. It was their deep understanding of the laws of promotion. "Seest thou a man diligent in his business? He shall stand before kings; he shall not stand before mean men" (Proverbs 22:29).

9. Children Are Commanded To Submit To Their Parents. "Children, obey your parents in the Lord: for this is right. Honour thy father and mother; which is the first commandment with promise; That it may be well with thee, and thou mayest live long on the earth" (Ephesians 6:1-3).

10. The Word Of God Commands Submission To Wise And Qualified Leadership. "Remember them which have the rule over you, who have spoken unto you the word of God: whose faith follow, considering the end of their conversation" (Hebrews 13:7).

11. Submission To True Prophets Always Births Uncommon Prosperity. "Believe in the Lord your God, so shall ye be established; believe His prophets, so shall ye prosper" (2 Chronicles 20:20).

12. Fathers Are Commanded To Submit To The Word Of God In Rearing Their Children. Fathers are instructed, "...provoke not your children to wrath: but bring them up in the nurture and admonition of the Lord" (Ephesians 6:4).

13. Submission To Authority Affects Your Health. Paul emphasizes to children, in submitting to their parents. "Honour thy father and mother; which is the first commandment with promise; That it may be well with thee, and thou mayest live long on the earth" (Ephesians 6:2,3).

14. Submission To Parents Determines The Longevity Of Your Life On Earth. "Honour thy father and mother; which is the first commandment with promise; That it may be well with thee, and thou mayest live long on the earth" (Ephesians 6:2,3).

"Children, obey your parents in all things: for this is well pleasing unto the Lord" (Colossians 3:20).

15. Employees Are Instructed To Have A Submissive Attitude Toward Their Bosses. "Servants, be obedient to them that are your masters according to the flesh, with fear and trembling, in singleness of your heart, as unto Christ; Not with eyeservice, as menpleasers; but as the servants of Christ, doing the will of God from the heart; With good will doing service, as to the Lord, and not to men:" (Ephesians 6:5-7).

"Knowing that whatsoever good thing any man doeth, the same

shall he receive of the Lord, whether he be bond or free" (Ephesians 6:8).

16. Wives Are Instructed In The Word Of God To Submit Themselves To The Spiritual Authority Of Their Husbands. "Wives, submit yourselves unto your own husbands, as unto the Lord. For the husband is the head of the wife, even as Christ is the head of the church: and He is the saviour of the body. Therefore as the church is subject unto Christ so let the wives be to their own husbands in every thing" (Ephesians 5:22-24).

17. The Word Of God Commands Our Submission In Honoring And Respecting One Another. "Submitting yourselves one to another in the fear of God" (Ephesians 5:21).

"Whosoever therefore shall humble himself as this little child, the same is greatest in the kingdom of heaven" (Matthew 18:4).

18. Submission Often Produces Rewards That Agreement Can Never Produce. "Likewise, ye wives, be in subjection to your own husbands; that, if any obey not the word, they also may without the word be won by the conversation of the wives; While they behold your chaste conversation coupled with fear" (1 Peter 3:1,2).

19. Submission To Parental Authority Guarantees Lifetime Blessing. "Honour thy father and thy mother: that thy days may be long upon the land which the Lord thy God giveth thee" (Exodus 20:12).

20. Your Submission To Authority Is Often Reproduced In Those Who Serve You Also. *David honored Saul, king of Israel.* Likewise, his own men proved to be incredibly loyal and steadfast in following him.

What You Are, You Will Create Around You.

When you submit to those over you, it motivates those under your rule to submit to you as well. You become their prototype and example.

21. The Word Of God Documents Those Who Are Rewarded For Submission. Ruth submitted to Naomi. "Whither thou goest, I will go; and where thou lodgest, I will lodge: thy people shall be my people, and thy God my God: Where thou diest, will I die, and there will I be buried: the Lord do so to me, and more also, if ought but death part thee and me" (Ruth 1:16:17).

22. Submission To The Holy Spirit Always Produces Prosperity. "And he sought God in the days of Zechariah, who had understanding of the visions of God: and as long as he sought the Lord, God made him to prosper" (2 Chronicles 26:5).

23. Uncommon Leaders Choose Uncommon Protégés To

Succeed Them. *Joshua was loyal and submissive to Moses.* After the death of Moses, they answered Joshua saying, "All that thou commandest us we will do, and whithersoever thou sendest us, we will go. According as we hearkened unto Moses in all things, so will we hearken unto thee: only the Lord thy God be with thee, as He was with Moses" (Joshua 1:16,17).

24. The Submission Of Parents To Authority Directly Affects The Behavior Of Their Children. When your child sees a radar detector on the dash of your car, it is a monument to your personal rebellion to law. It will become impossible to persuade your children that submission to governmental authority and law brings benefit.

25. Humble Submission Always Guarantees Uncommon Provision. "By humility and the fear of the Lord are riches, and honour, and life" (Proverbs 22:4).

26. Submission To Qualified Authority Offers Protection. *God guaranteed it for Israel.* "And I will rebuke the devourer for your sakes, and He shall not destroy the fruits of your ground; neither shall your vine cast her fruit before the time in the field, saith the Lord of hosts" (Malachi 3:11).

God did not simply instruct you to bring the tithe. He promised to protect everything you created and generated. The covenant rewards everyone involved.

Fathers, in authority, are commanded to protect their families and children.

Ministers protect their flocks.

Counselors even provide protection. "Where no counsel is, the people fall: but in the multitude of counsellors there is safety" (Proverbs 11:14).

27. Those Who Govern You Are Under The Authority Of God As Well. *Husbands are commanded to treat their wives as Christ treated the church.* "Husbands, love your wives, even as Christ also loved the church, and gave Himself for it;...So ought men to love their wives as their own bodies. He that loveth his wife loveth himself. For no man ever yet hated his own flesh; but nourisheth and cherisheth it, even as the Lord the church:" (Ephesians 5:25,28,29).

28. Submission Offers Uncommon Reward.

29. Submission To Qualified Authority Produces Provision. *God offered this.* "And it shall come to pass, if thou shalt hearken diligently unto the voice of the Lord thy God, to observe and to do all His commandments which I command thee this day, that the Lord thy God will set thee on high above all nations of the earth: The Lord shall command the blessing upon thee in thy storehouses, and in all that thou settest thine hand unto; and He shall bless thee in the land which the Lord thy God giveth thee. And the Lord shall make thee plenteous in goods, in the fruit of thy body, and in the fruit of thy cattle, and in the fruit of thy ground, in the land which the Lord sware unto thy fathers to give thee. The Lord shall open unto thee His good treasure, the heaven to give the rain unto thy land in his season, and to bless all the work of thine hand: and thou shalt lend unto many nations, and thou shalt not borrow" (Deuteronomy 28:1,8,11,12).

30. Employers Are Instructed To Submit To The Authority And Standards Of God. "And, ye masters do the same things unto them, forbearing threatening: knowing that your master also is in heaven; neither is there respect of persons with him" (Ephesians 6:9).

31. You Are Commanded To Submit To The Word Of God And The Chain Of Authority It Teaches. The Scriptures are..."able to make thee wise unto salvation through faith which in Christ Jesus...that the man of God may be perfect, thoroughly furnished unto all good works" (2 Timothy 3:15,17).

"But Jesus called them unto Him, and said, Ye know that the princes of the Gentiles exercise dominion over them, and they that are great exercise authority upon them...But it shall not be so among you: but whosoever will be great among you, let him be your minister; And whosoever will be chief among you, let him be your servant:" (Matthew 20:25-27).

RECOMMENDED BOOKS AND TAPES:

B-20 Seeds Of Wisdom On Obedience (32 pages/$3)
TS-08 The Strategy Of Hourly Obedience (6 tapes/$30)

❧ 47 ❧

TALENTS AND SKILLS

The Holy Spirit Planted Greatness Within You.

The Holy Spirit is a Gift. And the Giver of Gifts.

"If ye then, being evil, know how to give good gifts unto your children: how much more shall your heavenly Father give the Holy Spirit to them that ask Him?" (Luke 11:13).

The Holy Spirit put the gifts and talents within you. Natural and spiritual gifts! "Now there are diversities of gifts, but the same Spirit. And there are differences of administration, but the same Lord...For to one is given by the Spirit the word of wisdom; to another the word of knowledge by the same Spirit; To another faith by the same Spirit; to another the gifts of healing by the same Spirit;" (1 Corinthians 12:4,5,8,9).

The Holy Spirit decides if you get one, two or five talents. "But all these worketh that one and the selfsame Spirit, dividing to every man severally as He will" (1 Corinthians 12:11).

Every man receives different amounts of gifts and skills from the Holy Spirit. "And unto one He gave five talents, to another two, and to another one; to every man according to his several ability; and straightway took his journey" (Matthew 25:15).

You were planned by the Holy Spirit before your parents ever saw your face. "Before I formed thee in the belly I knew thee; and before thou camest forth out of the womb I sanctified thee, and I ordained thee a prophet unto the nations" (Jeremiah 1:5).

Destiny is to be discovered, not decided. God has already developed a plan for your life. You must enter His presence to discover it. "I know the thoughts that I think toward you," (Jeremiah 29:11).

Your gift may be music, writing, drawing or administration. Give attention to it. The Holy Spirit expects you to develop and grow your gift.

9 Important Facts Concerning Your Gifts, Talents And Skills

1.   Remember Nobody Else Is Aware Of All The Gifts The

Holy Spirit Has Placed Within You. The teacher of famous opera singer, Enrico Caruso, said Caruso had no voice and could not sing.

Walt Disney was fired by a newspaper for "lacking ideas."

An expert said of famous football coach, Vince Lombardi: "He possesses minimal knowledge. Lacks motivation."

Regarding Fred Astaire—a 1933 memo from the MGM testing director said, "Can't act. Slightly bald. Can dance a little."

Louisa May Alcott, the author of the famous book, *Little Women*, was told by her family that she should find a job as a servant or a seamstress.

The teacher of the famous musician, Beethoven, called him hopeless as a composer.

2. Realize That Your Gifts May Not Surface Immediately But Over A Period Of Time. Eighteen publishers turned down Richard Bach's ten thousand word story about a soaring sea gull before MacMillan finally published it in 1970. By 1975, *Jonathan Livingston Sea Gull* had sold more than seven million copies in the U.S. alone.

3. Be Patient When Your Gifts Take Time And Seasons Of Preparation To Become Strong. Beethoven handled the violin awkwardly and preferred playing his own compositions instead of improving his technique. "Study to shew thyself approved unto God," (2 Timothy 2:15).

4. Do Not Be Discouraged If You Experience A Number Of Failures Before You Reach Your Place Of Destiny. Walt Disney went bankrupt several times before he built Disneyland. Most of your great achievers have collected a number of outstanding failures as well.

Look at the apostle Peter. He was weak, and intimidated by a woman at the home of the high priest. Yet, he became the great preacher on the day of Pentecost. Historians teach that when he died, he was crucified but ask that he be crucified upside down. He felt unworthy to be crucified like Jesus. "And let us not be weary in well doing: for in due season we shall reap, if we faint not" (Galatians 6:9).

"For a just man falleth seven times and riseth up again:" (Proverbs 24:16).

5. Use Your Gifts To Bless Those Closest To You Today. Some spend all their life looking around the earth for a place to land. There is an old saying that few of us have really grasped: "Bloom where you are presently planted." "Withhold not good from them to whom it is due, when it is in the power of thine hand to do it" (Proverbs 3:27).

When you excel in your present situation, somebody "in the

palace" will call for you as Pharaoh called for Joseph (see Genesis 41:14).

6. Expect Your Gifts And Skills To Bring You Before Great Men. "Seest thou a man diligent in his business? he shall stand before kings; he shall not stand before mean men" (Proverbs 22:29). When Joseph interpreted the dream of the butler, it brought him before Pharoah. David came before Saul as a musician and song writer.

7. Accept The Reality That Your Gifts May Not Be Celebrated By Those In Your Own Home. Joseph experienced this. His brothers did not recognize the gift of God within him. But, he knew that his ability to interpret dreams came from God. Jesus was misunderstood by His own family who did not believe (read John 7:5), and even thought He was beside Himself (read Mark 3:21). Never lose hope because, "Thy faith may become effectual by the acknowledging of every good thing which is in you" (Philemon 1:6).

8. Remind Others Of The Gifts Within You, Placed There By The Holy Spirit. It is not wrong to advertise. It is not wrong to tell others that your gifts are resident within you. When the butler left the prison where Joseph was the chief jailer, Joseph told him that he had done nothing to be there. And he asked him to spread the word about him. The butler remembered two years later.

Jesus Himself promoted the gifts He possessed that could bless others. He told the woman at the well that He would give her water—she would never thirst again (see John 4:14). "Know them which labour among you, and are over you" (1 Thessalonians 5:12).

9. Invest In Seminars, Tapes Or Books Or Whatever It Takes To Develop Your Gifts And Skills. Seasons of preparation are in every achiever life. Jesus took thirty years. Moses took eighty years. "Study to shew thyself approved" (2 Timothy 2:15).

Always remember, the Holy Spirit chooses which gifts, talents and skills you receive from the Father.

Our Prayer Together...

"Precious Holy Spirit, thank You for the wonderful gifts You have placed within us. Those gifts are *discerned* by us...by the things we love, hate and grieve us. Thank You for the appetites and passions You planted deep within us. Reveal where our gifts are *most needed* today. *Open* doors. Enable us to recognize the Golden Connections around us and to quickly be obedient to *walk through those doors.* In Jesus' name. Amen."

Tithe Is Not The Payment Of A Debt, It Is The Acknowledgement Of A Debt.

-MIKE MURDOCK

❧ 48 ❧
TITHING

Tithing Is The Golden Door To Financial Favor.

17 Powerful Facts You Should Remember About Tithing

1. Tithing Is The Biblical Practice Of Returning Ten Percent Of Your Income Back To God After You Have Earned It. "And concerning the tithe of the herd, or of the flock, even of whatsoever passeth under the rod, the tenth shall be holy unto the Lord" (Leviticus 27:32). Throughout the Old Testament, Abraham and others tithed. In the New Testament, even the Pharisees, the hypocritical religious crowd, remembered to tithe.

2. The Old Testament Confirms Giving As Honoring The Lord. "Honour the Lord with thy substance, and with the firstfruits of all thine increase: So shall thy barns be filled with plenty, and thy presses shall burst out with new wine" (Proverbs 3:9,10).

3. Tithing Was The Practice Of Abraham. Tithe means "tenth." The great patriarch Abraham, gave back ten percent of his income as proof and evidence that he honored God as his Provider. He was blessed incredibly for it. "And Abram was very rich in cattle, in silver, and in gold" (Genesis 13:2).

4. The Tithing And Obedience Of Abraham, Produced Blessing For His Son, Isaac. "Then Issac sowed in that land, and received in the same year an hundredfold: and the Lord blessed him. And the man waxed great, and went forward, and grew until he became very great: For he had possession of flocks, and possession of herds, and great store of servants: and the Philistines envied him" (Genesis 26:12-14).

5. Tithing Is Holy Unto The Lord. "And all the tithe of the land, whether of the seed of the land, or of the fruit of the tree, is the Lord's: it is holy unto the Lord" (Leviticus 27:30).

6. Tithing Is Your Golden Gate To Your Personal Financial Supply. "Bring ye all the tithes into the storehouse, that there may be meat in Mine house, and prove Me now herewith, saith the Lord of hosts, if I will not open you the windows of heaven, and pour you out a blessing, that there shall not be room enough to receive it" (Malachi 3:10).

7. Tithing Can Create A Financial Flow For Your Children And Generations After You. It happened for the children of Abraham. "And the Lord appeared unto him the same night, and said, I am the God of Abraham thy father: fear not, for I am with thee, and will bless thee, and multiply thy seed *for My servant Abraham's sake*" (Genesis 26:24).

8. Tithing Reveals Humility. Your tithe is proof that you recognize the worthiness and authority of God over your life. The arrogant will not tithe. You see, there are three kinds of atheists: 1) Those who believe that God does not even exist; 2) Those who believe they are capable of doing anything God can do; and 3) Those who believe that they themselves are god in their own life. Non-tithers position themselves like the atheist—they keep the tithe. They feel that they are their own god in their own life. It is the ultimate proof of arrogance and pride.

9. Tithing Can Break Any Financial Curse On Your Life And Family. You see, those who rob God of the tithe and offerings that belong to Him are living under a curse. You can be the member of your family that "breaks the curse." Your Seed is the proof of your faith. Obviously, God always penalizes a thief. But, he always promotes and prospers the tither and those who sow Seed. "Will a man rob God? Yet ye have robbed me. But ye say, Wherein have we robbed thee? In tithes and offerings. Ye are cursed with a curse: for ye have robbed me, even this whole nation" (Malachi 3:8,9).

10. Tithing Is Evidence Of Your Love For God. Your giving is one of the proofs that God lives within you. It is the evidence that the nature of God is flourishing inside your heart. Whether it is money, mercy or love, giving is the first true evidence of love. "For God so loved the world, that He gave" (John 3:16).

11. Tithing Is The Proof You Have Conquered Greed. Satan steals. Satan hoards. God gives. What You Can Walk Away From, You Have Mastered. Tithing Is The Proof That You Have Mastered Greed.

12. Tithing Is The Proof You Have Mastered Fear. "For God hath not given us the spirit of fear; but of power, and of love, and of a sound mind" (2 Timothy 1:7). Fear torments. It makes you hoard instead of release. You become afraid that you cannot replace the money that you are "giving to God." The truth? The tithe is already His. He permits you the privilege of returning it to Him as proof of your confidence in Him.

13. Tithing Is The Proof That You Believe The Word Of God To You. The Word of God is a collection of instructions. God longs to be believed. He promised that those who would tithe and bring offerings to Him would see financial Harvest as a result. "But he shall receive an hundredfold now in this time, houses, and brethren, and sisters, and mothers, and children, and lands, with persecutions; and in the world to come eternal life" (Mark 10:30).

14. Tithing Documents Your Faith In God. When you write out a check for your tithe, it documents your faith in God. *It is proof of your confidence in His Word.* You really do believe that His Word works. You have fully embraced the wonderful truth that "God is not a man, that He should lie; neither the son of man, that He should repent: hath He said, and shall He not do it? or hath He spoken, and shall He not make it good?" (Numbers 23:19)

Yet millions attend church every Sunday and walk out with the holy tithe still in their pockets. Sometimes, they will drop a few dollars in its place in the offering as a substitution. Why? They do not believe His promise of provision.

15. Tithing Creates A Memory Of You In The Mind Of God Forever. He beholds His giving nature in you. "And He saw also a certain poor widow casting in thither two mites. And He said, Of a truth I say unto you that this poor widow hath cast in more than they all:" (Luke 21:2,3). Jesus documented this memory.

16. Tithing Consistently Creates A Consistent Supply. Erratic tithing creates an erratic Harvest. The tithe is an act of faith, a Seed of Obedience that creates momentum. When you tithe consistently, you create a consistent Harvest. You establish a rhythm. Stay in obedience long enough to taste the rewards of momentum.

Consider the four basic seasons each year. Regularity and routine are very important forces in our lives, especially in a Seed-faith lifestyle. So, cooperate with the Law of Sowing and Reaping. Do not become erratic and unpredictable. Nature itself has a pattern, a rhythm and *a routine.* When you honor it, the benefits will far outweigh any cost and risk involved. "While the earth remaineth, seedtime and harvest, and cold and heat, and summer and winter, and day and night shall not cease" (Genesis 8:22).

17. Keeping The Tithe Is Theft. When you keep something that belongs to another, you are a thief. Thieves will not enter Heaven. "But lay up for yourselves treasures in heaven, where neither moth nor rust doth corrupt, and where thieves do not break through nor steal:" (Matthew 6:20).

Picture this scene with me for a few moments. Suppose a businessman flew home from a business transaction. His son meets him at the airport. The father, excited, puts his arm around his son and says, "I really love you son. I'm so proud of you. Here's a $10 bill to buy yourself a little present. I just made an extra $100, on this business deal."

"Thanks, dad!"

"Well, son, go ahead and take several more of these $10 bills. Actually, you can have *nine* of these $10 bills for yourself. I will just keep one with me for a snack later," the father remarks, good naturedly.

Imagine further with me. Both go home. The son goes into his bedroom to sleep that night. The father takes everything out of his pockets, leaving the remaining *tenth* $10 bill inside the dresser drawer. He goes to sleep. During the night, the son cannot sleep. He turns and tosses. Something inside him that he cannot explain makes him keep thinking about that $10 bill in his father's dresser drawer, and then he *stole* the tenth $10 bill. What are your feelings about that? I imagine you would be incensed and infuriated. You would exclaim with anger, "That son is an idiot, a fool and a thief. He was so unthankful of the nine $10 bills his father gave him, he stole the tenth."

Yet, this happens every single day on earth.

Many, unthankful for the 90 percent God permits them to keep, steal the other 10 percent. Instead of gratitude and thankfulness for their health, their energy, favor and friendships—the last $10 bill is stolen from the hand of the very One Who gave the first $90 to them.

Another scene. Suppose I told you that the son substituted a $1 bill in its place in his father's drawer—in place of the $10 bill! He hoped his father would not notice the *difference* between the $1 bill and the $10 bill. (Maybe he feels that his father would not notice the missing zero!) He steals the $10 by replacing it with a $1 bill.

Yes, you are angry again.

Yet this too happens in every church in America every single Sunday morning. People *substitute* a small offering for the tithe God instructed them to give. How tragic!

Do not steal the holy tithe.

RECOMMENDED BOOKS AND TAPES:

B-16   Seeds Of Wisdom On Seed-Faith (32 pages/$3)
B-22   Seeds Of Wisdom On Prosperity (32 pages/$3)
B-82   31 Reasons People Do Not Receive Their Financial Harvest (253 pages/$12)
B-218 The Tither's Topical Bible (400 pages/$10)
TS-38 31 Reasons People Do Not Receive Their Financial Harvest (6 tapes/$30)
VI-17 31 Reasons People Do Not Receive Their Financial Harvest (Video/$25)

⁓ **49** ⁓

UNTHANKFULNESS

Thankfulness Is A Force.

It is more than an attitude. It is a lifestyle, a way of life. It is a way of looking at things. *It is impossible to be too thankful throughout life.*

11 Facts About Thankfulness

1. **Thankfulness Is A Learned Attitude.** It is not necessarily something born inside you. I have watched unthankful people make turnarounds *after a crisis.* Suddenly, their words of appreciation are elusive and many because they have memories of lack, pain and losses. He who God has forgiven much is thankful for much. Read Luke 7:36-50 concerning the waste implication of Jesus regarding Mary Magdalene.

2. **Thankfulness Is Magnetic.** When you work around someone who is thankful, they are happy.

3. **Thankful People Are Always Joyous People.** It does not mean that their life is free from stress, heartache or difficulties. But rather they have chosen to focus on the wonder and the miracle of blessing.

4. **Thankfulness Is Created By Focus.** (See Deuteronomy 8:10-14).

5. **Thankfulness Is Required For Entering The Presence Of God.** "Enter into His gates with thanksgiving, and into His courts with praise: be thankful unto Him, and bless His name" (Psalm 100:4).

6. **Thankfulness Should Occur Because Of The Goodness Of God, Not Because Of Perfect Circumstances.** "Be thankful unto Him, and bless His name. For the Lord is good; His mercy is everlasting; and His truth endureth to all generations" (Psalm 100:4,5).

7. **You Are Commanded To Be Thankful.** "In everything give thanks: for this is the will of God in Christ Jesus concerning you" (1 Thessalonians 5:18).

8. **Thankfulness Occurs When You Begin To Remember**

Good Things God Has Done For You. "We give thanks to God always for you all, Remembering without ceasing your work of faith, and labor of love, and patience and hope in our Lord Jesus Christ" (1 Thessalonians 1:2,3).

9. **Thankfulness Occurs When You Replay The Memories Of God's Blessings In Your Life.** He is a good God. He is a powerful God. He is a loving God.

He has brought you through *the fire*.

He has brought you through *the flood*.

He has preserved you through *false accusations*.

He has walked in *when others walked out*.

You are serving a miracle, loving and powerful God. If nothing else good ever occurred in your life, His presence is enough to inspire gratitude, appreciation and thankfulness.

10. **Sing Your Gratitude And Thankfulness To God.** Compose songs. They do not have to be fancy, articulate and profound words. He just wants to hear you sing praise and worship to Him.

11. **Write Notes Of Thankfulness And Gratitude To God And Those You Love.** Five minutes with a handwritten note will unlock a river within you. Suddenly, you will remember all the wonderful things God has done for you.

14 Facts About Unthankfulness

1. **Unthankful People Are Not Replaying The Right Memories.** "Remember ye not the former things, neither consider the things of old. Behold, I will do a new thing; now it shall spring forth; shall ye not know it? I will even make a way in the wilderness, and rivers in the desert" (Isaiah 43:18,19).

2. **Gratitude Is A Gift To Those You Love.** "Withhold not good from them to whom it is due, when it is in the power of thine hand to do it" (Proverbs 3:27).

3. **What You Are Most Thankful About Will Begin To Multiply In Your Life.** When you are thankful for friends, you will multiply your friendships. When you are thankful for the opportunity your boss gives you, money will begin to increase in your life.

4. **The Proof Of Thankfulness Is Joy And The Willingness To Protect.** You will protect and fight for the things for which you are most thankful. Have you ever seen a mother race across the yard when a dog approached her child? That protectiveness came because of her thankfulness and appreciation for her child. Her baby is her life. *You*

will always fight to keep what you truly love. When an employee is thankful, they will fight to keep their job. You will not find them coming late to work, taking extra time away during the lunch hour. Why? They are grateful. Thankful.

5. Unthankfulness Is A Dangerous Cancer That Can Enter So Quickly. It comes when a contentious loved one or friend fuels a misunderstanding. They feed your anger. Something upsets you. Your focus is broken. A husband and wife can feed each other's agitation. The wife is angry because the boss requested overtime. The husband ponders and meditates and receives the offense as well. Within weeks, they cannot look the boss in the eye. When a fellow employee shares their complaint, they add theirs with it.

6. Unthankfulness Is Contagious. I walked off the plane recently with great joy. My life was going wonderfully. The ministry was touched by God. The finances were up. I simply felt good. Two minister friends of mine were waiting. They suggested a meal, and I agreed. Within moments, they began to share some of the trials they were going through. My heart filled with compassion. I listened. They continued and suddenly almost without warning, I was in a completely different arena. I heard myself discussing things I should never have discussed. I shared my trials, my complaints and those who had failed me. Within two hours from my arrival, my heart was in such turmoil and frustration I could not explain it.

What had happened? I had permitted my focus to be broken. Unthankful people had entered my presence. I permitted it, allowed it and even fed it. My joy left. My enthusiasm waned.

Yet nothing had really changed in my entire life except my attitude.

You see, somebody is speaking into your life continuously.

7. An Unthankful Person Can Wreck The Flow Of Miracles Into Your Life Incredibly.

8. Unthankfulness Blinds You To Every Gift Of God. You become critical, cynical and faultfinding. You refuse to be thankful for your car because you see your neighbor drive up in a new one.

9. Ingratitude Can Be Cured. I have found two major methods whereby God deals with unthankfulness.

His first choice is for you to *enter The Secret Place,* beholding His goodness and becoming thankful in His presence. It is impossible to habitually enter your private place of prayer, praising and worshipping Him, and remain unthankful when you leave.

The second method for dealing with unthankfulness is devastating.

10. Loss Is The Best Cure For Unthankfulness. God simply takes away something you are not thankful for. "Because thou servest not the Lord thy God with joyfulness, and with gladness of heart, for the abundance of all things; Therefore shalt thou serve thine enemies which the Lord shall send against thee, in hunger, and in thirst, and in nakedness, and in want of all things: and he shall put a yoke of iron upon thy neck, until he have destroyed thee" (Deuteronomy 28:47,48).

11. Unthankful People Are Often Militant Influencing Others With Their Ingratitude. They are not satisfied to sit at home alone. They do not want to eat alone in restaurants. They cannot thrive alone. *Their unthankfulness requires fuel.* They pursue others to sow their Seeds of contention, discord and strife. If you do not remove them from your life, you will enter into a covenant with them, thus *destroying every blessing God is trying to place near you.*

12. Unthankful People Create An Atmosphere Of Discouragement. Motivation is drained in their presence. You lose energy. The projects that excited you suddenly look too impossible to achieve. You start looking at hurdles instead of potential blessings. They are burdens not burden-bearers.

13. Unthankful People Demotivate You. They demoralize you and destroy every dream of God within you.

14. You Cannot Afford The Tragedy Of An Unthankful Person In Your Life.

Ingratitude and lack of appreciation for what God has already done is one of the most important reasons people will never taste the one hundredfold return.

8 Keys In Staying Thankful During Crisis

1. Recognize Unthankfulness As A Sin And Grievous To The Holy Spirit. "And grieve not the Holy Spirit of God, whereby ye are sealed until the day of redemption" (Ephesians 4:30).

2. Stop Discussing Anything That Does Not Build Up Another. "Let no corrupt communication proceed out of your mouth, but that which is good to the use of edifying, that it may minister grace unto the hearers" (Ephesians 4:29).

3. Focus On The Wonderful Blessings So Evident And Obvious In Your Life. "Blessed be the Lord, Who daily loadeth us with benefits, even the God of our salvation" (Psalm 68:19).

4. Cry Out To God When You Sense An Unthankful Spirit Growing. "The righteous cry, and the Lord heareth, and delivereth them out of all their troubles" (Psalm 34:17).

    5. Confess Your Sin Of Ingratitude With A Broken And Contrite Heart. "The Lord is nigh unto them that are of a broken heart; and saveth such as be of a contrite spirit" (Psalm 34:18).

    6. Believe Your Trial Will Cease And God Will Give You Full Deliverance. "Many are the afflictions of the righteous: but the Lord delivereth him out of them all. He keepeth all his bones: not one of them is broken" (Psalm 34:19,20).

    7. Keep A Picture Of The Miracle You Are Pursuing In Front Of You At All Times. "Forgetting those things which are behind, and reaching forth unto those things which are before, I press toward the mark for the prize of the high calling of God in Christ Jesus" (Philippians 3:13,14).

    8. Withdraw From Unthankful And Contentious People. "Evil communications corrupt good manners" (1 Corinthians 15:33). "As coals are to burning coals, and wood to fire; so is a contentious man to kindle strife" (Proverbs 26:21).

Our Prayer Together...

"Jesus, forgive my unthankfulness. I see how deadly ingratitude can be. I purpose to remember Your goodness, Your grace and Your miracles. Cleanse me. I will sing a new song of thankfulness and those who come close to me will hear about Your greatness and Your goodness. I shall prosper and experience Your Harvest. In Jesus' name. Amen."

RECOMMENDED BOOKS AND TAPES:
B-58 Mentors Manna On Attitude (32 pages/$5)

The Holy Spirit Is
The Only Person
Capable Of Being
Satisfied With You.

-MIKE MURDOCK

≈ 50 ≈

VOICE OF GOD

The Master Communicator Is The Holy Spirit.

Nobody talks more than the Holy Spirit. He even created the universe by His words. "Through faith we understand that the worlds were framed by the word of God, so that things which are seen were not made of things which do appear" (Hebrews 11:3).

The cry of Jesus was that the church listen to the Spirit. "He that hath an ear, let him hear what the Spirit saith unto the churches;" (Revelation 2:7).

Jesus talks to the *Father* (see John 14:16).

The Father talks to the *Holy Spirit* (see John 16:13).

The Holy Sprit talks to *us* (see Revelation 2:7,11,29).

The Holy Spirit intercedes for you daily. "Likewise the Spirit also helpeth our infirmities: for we know not what we should pray for as we ought: but the Spirit itself [Himself] maketh intercession for us with groanings which cannot be uttered...because He maketh intercession for the saints according to the will of God" (Romans 8:26,27).

8 Rewards For Recognizing The Voice Of The Spirit

1. The Holy Spirit Often Warns Us Of Impending Danger. A choice and valued friend of mine pastored a large church in Texas many years ago. I was stunned when I heard of his tragic death in an airplane crash. It left me baffled, confused and disappointed. One year later, I was eating supper with his widow who related a fascinating insight.

"Mike, the morning of the crash, my husband sat on the edge of the bed at 5:30 a.m. and spoke to me, 'Honey, something tells me I should not fly today."

He made a decision to override *the still small Voice.* Perhaps, his speaking engagement was urgent and the expectations of others weighed heavily on him. Whatever the reason, he chose to ignore The Voice. His death occurred within hours.

2. Recognition Of His Voice Could Stop Thousands Of

Unnecessary Deaths, Tragedies And Difficulties. Many times, I have received reports of those who died untimely and unnecessary deaths. Over and over, it has come back that the person felt uneasy and reluctant to keep their plans, but did so...overriding the small Voice.

3. Recognition Of His Voice Could Avoid Many Broken Marriages And Homes. When I was nineteen years old, I fell in love. One night in the prayer room, I wept for hours over the relationship. The Holy Spirit spoke clearly, "I do not want you in this relationship. End it." After I ended it, some of my college professors confirmed that Voice by saying, "Mike, I think it is a wise decision that you and the young lady move separate directions."

Three weeks later, I overrode The Voice. I *returned* to the relationship.

Thirteen years later, while standing on the courthouse steps of Houston, Texas, after the divorce proceedings, the Holy Spirit reminded me gently, "I gave you the instruction over thirteen years ago."

4. Recognition Of His Voice Can Unlock Waves Of Favor And Blessing. One afternoon my kitchen telephone rang in Houston, Texas. It was a dear friend, Roger McDuff. Roger has been a legend in gospel music for many years.

"Mike, while praying, the Holy Spirit spoke to me to ask you to go with me to California. Paul and Jan Crouch head Channel 40 in Santa Ana, California. Have you heard of them?"

I had not.

"If you can purchase your ticket, I would like to introduce you to them. I believe that there is a connection between you and them."

Within days, Paul Crouch invited me to be a continuous guest on scores and scores of programs. He and Jan sponsored my telecast on their station for over four years. Many miracles occurred. Thousands of people received our ministry. It was astounding.

Roger heard The Voice of the Spirit.

I heard The Voice of the Spirit.

Miracles have been a wave ever since then. I met some of the most wonderful people such as Rosie Greer, Laverne Tripp, Dwight Thompson and many others.

5. The Voice Will Always Connect You With Uncommon People In Your Life. Philip was led by the Spirit to the desert of Gaza. There he met the Ethopian Eunuch (see Acts 8).

6. Recognition Of His Voice Brings Inner Peace. It happened to the disciples during the storm while they were on the ship.

7. Recognition Of His Voice Unlocks Uncommon Prosperity. "And it shall come to pass, if thou shalt hearken diligently unto the voice of the Lord thy God, to observe and to do all His commandments which I command thee this day, that the Lord thy God will set thee on high above all nations of the earth: And all these *blessings shall come* on thee, and overtake thee, if thou shalt hearken unto the voice of the Lord thy God" (Deuteronomy 28:1,2).

8. The Voice Of The Spirit Can Change The Financial Seasons Of Your Life In A Moment. My first year of evangelism was a financial catastrophe. One month my income was $35. Another month, it was $90. The first twelve months of evangelism, my income was $2,263. I owned a 1953 Chevrolet during my second year of evangelism, 1967. During the month of June, as I recall, I was invited to attend the South Texas District Council of the Assemblies of God. The speaker was Charles Greenaway, a beloved and respected missionary. He spoke and mentioned Leviticus 19:9,10. I had not noticed it before. I can almost hear him today...

"How big is your corner? In the Old Testament, the rich were instructed to leave the corners of their barley or wheat fields for the poor. God promised to bless them if they would sow back and make their corners big to God and the people who were hurting." He continued, "Your field is your *income.* Your corners represent your *outgo* to God. If you will increase the size of your corners, God will increase the size of your field, or your income."

I do not recall ever hearing that philosophy before. It was an Assemblies of God missionary evangelist who told me that I could influence my financial income through returning a portion of it back to God.

Charles Greenaway was raising money for the missions department and encouraged us to make twelve month faith promises. I was not familiar with this. But, I got inspired and while sitting there, decided I would "take a leap of faith."

He shouted, *"I dare you to prove God!* The only place God told you to prove His existence was in Malachi 3. He simply said to throw Him something up toward Heaven and if more came back than you threw up...that was the proof of His existence."

Something in me decided to believe.

Shaking, I stood to my feet. I made a $100 faith promise. I did so because they gave me twelve months to come up with $100. That was one-half of a month's income for me.

Driving back to Lake Charles, Louisiana, where I lived, was quite an emotional trip.

Where on earth was I going to find $100?

The house I was living in was purchased by my father for the grand total price of...$150! He had purchased the entire house for $150 and moved it on some land he had. So, I was living in it. My bedroom suite cost $35. I had purchased it from one of my father's deacons, Brother Stanley.

That was Thursday morning as I drove back from Victoria, Texas, to Lake Charles.

Sunday morning, an old pianist for the Stamps Quartet had dropped by our church. His name was Merle Daley. When he finished playing a piano solo for my father's church, he stood.

"Folks, God has been so good to me! Right now, my pockets are full of $100 bills!" I stared wide-eyed.

Suddenly, he looked at me sitting in the far left seat of the building.

Then he said, "In fact, God just spoke to me to give one of these $100 bills to Mike!"

I knew he knew God!

Monday morning, I deposited his gift of $100 in my checking account and promptly wrote a check to the South Texas District Council of the Assemblies of God to pay my faith promise.

Tuesday morning, I drove to Beeville, Texas, to minister at the First Assembly of God church where James Brothers was host pastor. While driving through Beeville, I saw a small trailer with a FOR SALE sign on it of $100. It was precisely the very kind of trailer I had been wanting to bring my clothes, books and belongings around to the meetings. I was sick inside because I had paid my faith promise...and *no longer had the $100 to purchase the little trailer.* It seemed to me that satan whispered to my heart, "See what you could have had if you had not paid your faith promise!" I agreed, of course.

That night, I went early to the church and sat at the old upright piano on the platform. While practicing before service, a couple walked in. In a few minutes, she walked up behind me at the piano and tapped me on the shoulder.

"My husband and I felt impressed to give this to you."

I turned around and looked at one of the most beautiful sights I have ever seen—her check for $150!

"This is God, my sister! I saw a small trailer today while driving through town that I desperately wanted that costs $100. Now I have more than enough to buy it!" I exclaimed with joy.

The next day, Wednesday, I purchased the trailer and had $50 left over. So, I immediately rushed another Seed of $50 to the South Texas District Council Assemblies of God Office in Houston. I had already paid my faith promise, but I felt that anything that works with God that fast...I was determined to work the living daylights out of!

Wednesday night came. While I was practicing the piano again, the couple walked in. Again, she approached me with another beautiful check.

"We could not sleep last night. The Holy Spirit spoke to our hearts and said we were supposed to buy this trailer for you also. Here's another check for $100 to pay for the trailer."

My miracle parade of Harvests had just been birthed.

His still small Voice had activated a collection of miracles that would change my life forever.

When Any Minister Of God Speaks Under The Anointing, You Are Hearing The Voice Of The Holy Spirit. "Believe in the Lord your God, so shall ye be established; believe His prophets, so shall ye prosper" (2 Chronicles 20:20).

When Your Conscience Feels Convicted, You Are Hearing The Voice Of The Spirit. "And when He is come, He will reprove the world of sin, and of righteousness, and of judgment:" (John 16:8).

When You Read The Word Of God, You Are Hearing The Voice Of The Spirit. "All scripture is given by inspiration of God, and is profitable for doctrine, for reproof, for correction, for instruction in righteousness:" (2 Timothy 3:16).

The Most Important Thing In Your Life Is Recognition Of The Voice Of The Holy Spirit.

RECOMMENDED BOOKS AND TAPES:

B-15 Seeds Of Wisdom On Miracles (32 pages/$3)
B-151 The Craziest Instruction God Ever Gave Me (144 pages/$10)
B-197 The Memory Bible On Faith (32 pages/$3)
B-218 The Tither's Topical Bible (400 pages/$10)

When You Let Go
   Of What Is In Your Hand,
God Will Let Go
   Of What Is In His Hand.

-MIKE MURDOCK

51

VOWS

Vows Are Invisible Forces In The Spirit World.

5 Facts About Vows

Vows Are Not Frivolous Things To God.
God is not playful, frivolous nor trivial.

1. God Takes Your Promises To Him Quite Seriously. "When thou vowest a vow unto God, defer not to pay it; for He hath no pleasure in fools: pay that which thou hast vowed. Better is it that thou shouldest not vow, that thou should vow and not pay" (Ecclesiastes 5:4,5).

2. God Describes Promise Breakers As Fools. That is why it is so important not to position yourself as a fool because fools are ultimately destroyed (see Ecclesiastes 5:4,5).

God humiliates fools.

God moves away from fools.

God uses fools as illustrations for destruction.

3. The Wise Always Keep Their Promises. To your family. To your wife or husband. To the Lord Who promised you His best. It is important that you develop impeccable and unwavering integrity when you give your word in a business transaction or to your children.

4. God Is A Covenant God. He remembers every vow you have made before Him and man. Oh, stop and re-examine your life this very moment! Have you made any financial vows to your church or to the man of God in your life? Pay them. Whatever it takes. *Pay your vows.*

It will break "the curse."

5. When You Keep Your Vow, God's Very Best Begins To Come To You. (Read Deuteronomy 28 and Leviticus 26.) God guarantees that incredible blessings always come to those who "observe and do all His commandments" (Deuteronomy 28:1).

After an anointed banquet one evening, an articulate and well-dressed lady approached me.

"I know God has spoken to me tonight to plant a Seed of $1,000 in your ministry. You will receive it in a few days," she said wiping tears of joy from her eyes.

A few days later, her letter arrived. It was an apology. "After I talked to my husband, I felt that I should break my promise to you. I do not believe we can really afford to sow this special Seed at this time," she wrote. Oh, the heartache that broken promises are creating in our lives.

You see, *while she was in the presence of God* and the anointing of the Holy Spirit was hovering over the congregation, *the Seeds of her faith exploded within her heart.*

God spoke.

She heard.

She moved swiftly.

She quickly declared her covenant with God. After she moved *away* from His presence, discussed this gigantic step of faith with *an unbelieving* husband, she *withdrew* from her covenant which she had entered into with God. Oh, only time will reveal the curse that such an attitude of frivolity and light-heartedness will produce in our lives.

Many years ago, I was sitting in my bed watching a religious television program. Suddenly, a famous evangelist looked into the camera and forcibly said, "If you have made a vow to God at any time and not paid it, you have launched a parade of tragedies. Please sit down today and pay your vows."

Conviction smote my heart.

Over two years before, I had promised a missionary in Africa that I would help sponsor some students for scholarships in his Bible college. I had asked him to rush me material about it. When I did not receive the material, I did nothing. I did not telephone him or pursue a reason. I simply used it as an excuse to "escape my vow" that I had made to him.

As I watched the telecast that night, God reminded me of my promise. As I felt my heart pound, I knelt beside my bed and prayed, "Please forgive me. Give me another chance. Do not withhold your Harvest from me." It was midnight, but I called my secretary anyway. "Whatever you do, when you arrive at the office tomorrow morning, please take the checkbook. Write out a check to this Bible school in East Africa. Air-mail it. I cannot live another day without the blessing of God flowing upon me. I cannot afford a curse in my life and ministry."

I have seen hundreds lift their hands and make faith promises, "Yes, I will plant a monthly Seed to help you spread the Wisdom of God." Yet, over 50 percent will never sit down and plant that Seed of Promise they vowed publicly to plant.

"Maybe they cannot afford to do it!" is a common explanation.

I have seen many people make this claim, yet they continue to receive salary raises, new television sets and purchase new automobiles. They take their family out to eat at the nicest restaurants, purchase new clothes and send their children through college.

When You Let Go Of What Is In Your Hand, God Will Let Go Of What Is In His Hand.

Patience Is The Weapon That Forces Deception To Reveal Itself.

-MIKE MURDOCK

❧ 52 ❧

WAITING ON GOD

Waiting On God Is Proof Of Trust.

Waiting also provides God time to address the problems we encounter as Christians in life—miraculously. God is a miracle God. But when you get ahead of Him, you rob Him of an opportunity to prove His power in your life. So learn to wait.

16 Rewards For Waiting On God

1.   Waiting Reveals Patience. Patience is a Seed that always produces a desired Harvest.   Patience is always rewarded. "In your patience possess ye your souls" (Luke 21:19).

"Through faith also Sara herself received strength to conceive seed, and was delivered of a child when she was past age, because she judged Him faithful Who had promised" (Hebrews 11:11).

2.   Waiting Time Is Not Wasted Time. "But let patience have her perfect work, that ye may be perfect and entire, wanting nothing" (James 1:4).

3.   Waiting Guarantees Favorable Results. "The Lord is good unto them that wait for Him, to those that seeketh Him. It is good that a man should both hope and quietly wait for the salvation of the Lord" (Lamentations 3:25,26).

4.   Waiting Is Learning Time.   As long as you are learning, you are not losing. Your Assignment will require warfare. Battles are normal on the field of your Assignment. The integrity of the general demands that he qualify his soldiers for the battle.   God will train and teach you in the waiting time.

"Blessed be the Lord my strength, which teacheth my hands to war and my fingers to fight:" (Psalm 144:1).

Your flesh will react to waiting. It hates waiting. It wants action. It pursues activity. Waiting forces your flesh to die.

5.   Waiting Will Reveal The True Motives And Intentions Of Those Around You. Motives are not always easily discerned. This is why Joseph was willing to wait before revealing his identity to his brothers when they approached him for food during a famine in the land.

Joseph's brothers did not know he was related to them. He knew them. Undoubtedly, the desire to reveal himself was intense. But he knew the limitations of intuition. He remembered the excitement of sharing his dream with his brothers only to be sold into slavery because of it.

Wise men never trust their intuition—they rely on tests.

▶ The young trust.

▶ The wise test.

6. Waiting Reveals That You Trust God, But Are Willing To Test Men. It is biblical:

"Some trust in chariots, and some in horses: but we will remember the name of the Lord our God" (Psalm 20:7).

You see, the wrong people can keep their mistakes covered for long periods of time, but waiting forces the truth to emerge.

7. Waiting Enables You To Gather Accurate And Untainted Information. The quality of your information determines the quality of your decisions. And the quality of your decisions determines the quality of your life.

8. Waiting Brings You Truth.

9. More Waiting Brings You More Truth.

10. Enough Waiting Brings You Enough Truth.

11. You Will Never See The Hand Of God If You Keep Trusting The Hand Of Man In Your Life. Unwillingness to wait for supernatural provision will produce tragedies every time.

If you could have attended a workshop of Abraham, you would have heard him weep and tell you a thousand times, "Do not birth an Ishmael in your life. Wait for the timing of God. He will always fulfill His promise."

Your Father knows you very well. He is not faint. He is not weary. There is no limit to His understanding.

12. Waiting Increases Strength. "He giveth power to the faint; and to them that have not might He increaseth strength. Even the youths shall faint and be weary, and the young men shall utterly fall: But they that wait upon the Lord shall renew their strength; they shall mount up with wings as eagles; they shall run, and not be weary; and they shall walk, and not faint" (Isaiah 40:29-31).

13. Waiting Is A Weapon Satan Dreads For You To Ever Discover. "Lest satan should get an advantage of us: for we are not ignorant of his devices" (2 Corinthians 2:11).

Waiting On God's Timing Will Produce The Desired Results Of Your Assignment.

Time is the hidden and mysterious ingredient in an Uncommon Harvest.

"The Lord is good unto them that wait for Him, to the soul that seeketh Him" (Lamentations 3:25).

14. Waiting Reveals The Weaknesses Of Impatient Enemies.

15. Waiting Provides God Time To Interrupt Any Attack On Your Life With A Miraculous Deliverance.

16. Waiting Gives Time For Others To Become What Wisdom Is Producing Within Them.

Patience is the willingness to assign Time to work on a solution. In *your* life. In the life of *others* to you.

▶ Patience produces exceptional friendships.

▶ Patience produces great marriages.

▶ Patience will produce what money cannot produce.

▶ Patience has turned around weak and unhealthy people through exercise and focus, producing powerful, strong bodies.

36 Facts About Waiting On God

1. Your Waiting Reveals Trust. "It is good that a man should both hope and quietly wait for the salvation of the Lord" (Lamentations 3:26).

2. Your Waiting May Be Painful. But, it is the season between sowing and reaping. That is why the Bible calls it—Seedtime and Harvest. *Time is the season between the Seed and the Harvest.* "Weeping may endure for a night, but joy cometh in the morning" (Psalm 30:5).

3. You May Have Lost Your Harvest Because Of The Pain Of Waiting.

4. Waiting Is Burdensome. It breeds agitation, a critical spirit and can leave you frustrated.

While waiting, words of doubt and unbelief are spoken. This often aborts the *cycle of blessing*. Unthankfulness brings a curse, not a reward.

5. Ingratitude Does Not Inspire God To Hasten The Harvest. *It stops the Harvest. You must be willing to trust God through the seasons of waiting.* He has promised a change.

6. Your Anger Does Not Intimidate God To Speed Up His Schedule.

7. Your Schedule Does Not Obligate God To Change His Timing. He is God.

8. He Will Decide When You Deserve And Qualify For The Harvest. "For My thoughts are not your thoughts, neither are your ways My ways, saith the Lord. For as the heavens are higher than the earth, so are My ways higher than your ways, and My thoughts than your thoughts" (Isaiah 55:8,9).

9. God Has Already Promised Your Harvest In Due Season. "For as the rain cometh down, and the snow from heaven, and returneth not thither, but watereth the earth, and maketh it bring forth and bud, that it may give seed to the sower, and bread to the eater: So shall My word be that goeth forth out of My mouth: it shall not return unto Me void, but it shall accomplish that which I please, and it shall prosper in the thing whereto I sent it" (Isaiah 55:10,11).

10. Keep Your Excitement About Your Harvest. "For ye shall go out with joy, and be led forth with peace: the mountains and the hills shall break forth before you into singing, and all the trees of the field shall clap their hands" (Isaiah 55:12).

11. God Will Replace Every Financial Disaster With A Financial Miracle. "Instead of the thorn shall come up the fir tree, and instead of the brier shall come up the myrtle tree: and it shall be to the Lord for a name, for an everlasting sign that shall not be cut off" (Isaiah 55:13).

12. You Must Refuse To Permit Words Of Discouragement In Your Mouth. "Fear thou not; for I am with thee: be not dismayed; for I am thy God: I will strengthen thee; yea, I will help thee; yea, I will uphold thee with the right hand of My righteousness" (Isaiah 41:10).

13. Those Who Oppose And Battle Against Your Progress, Will Be Confronted By God Himself. "Behold, all they that were incensed against thee shall be ashamed and confounded: they shall be as nothing; and they that strive with thee shall perish" (Isaiah 41:11).

14. Your Enemies Shall Not Succeed Against You. "Thou shalt seek them, and shall not find them, even them that contended with thee: they that war against thee shall be as nothing, and as a thing of nought. For I the Lord thy God will hold thy right hand, saying unto thee, Fear not; I will help thee" (Isaiah 41:12,13).

15. The Holy Spirit Is Involved Against Your Enemy. "When the enemy shall come in like a flood, the Spirit of the Lord shall lift up a standard against him" (Isaiah 59:19).

16. Every Scheme, Strategy And Trap Against You Shall Ultimately Fail If You Are Patient In Waiting. "No weapon that is formed against thee shall prosper; and every tongue that shall rise against thee in judgment thou shalt condemn. This is the heritage of the servants of the Lord, and their righteousness is of Me, saith the Lord" (Isaiah 54:17).

17. Keep Your Eyes Upon The Rewards That Will Follow Your Waiting. Men fight for a reason—to gain something they want. When David faced Goliath, he was fully aware of the benefits offered to the person who could defeat Goliath. He would have the hand of the king's daughter. He would not have to pay any taxes. So, armed with the inner picture of his success and his rewards, he ran to Goliath to conquer him.

Jesus went to Calvary, fully aware of the resurrection— "for the joy that was set before Him."

18. Keep Focused. The spoils of war are worth the battle and the tormenting season called waiting.

19. Refuse To Sin With Your Mouth. Your enemy reacts to your words. If you feed on doubt and unbelief, it will energize and motivate him to rise up against you.

20. Never Speak Words That Encourage Your Enemy. Your enemy will believe anything you are telling him. If you feed faith words into his ear, he will be demoralized, disappointed and discouraged. If you talk like the *victim*, he will be encouraged to attack you again and again and again. "Death and life are in the power of the tongue: and they that love it shall eat the fruit thereof" (Proverbs 18:21).

21. Your Words Of Faith Will Always Influence The Heart Of God. "For by thy words thou shalt be justified, and by thy words thou shalt be condemned" (Matthew 12:37).

22. While You Are Waiting, Create A Climate Of Gratitude And Thanksgiving. "In every thing give thanks: for this is the will of God in Christ Jesus concerning you" (1 Thessalonians 5:18).

23. Continuously Pray In The Spirit Throughout The Day. "Pray without ceasing" (1 Thessalonians 5:17). "But ye, beloved, building up yourselves on your most holy faith, praying in the Holy Ghost," (Jude 20).

24. Avoid The Temptation To Create A Backup Plan. "Neither give place to the devil" (Ephesians 4:27).

When one of the great explorers came to America, he burned the ships behind him and his soldiers. It made escape impossible. It made exploration a necessity and requirement. His men could not go back. *You cannot plan your success and failure at the same time.* Your success will require your total focus and attention.

25. Make No Plans To Go Backwards.

26. Fuel, Energize And Strengthen The Picture Of Your Future. This develops your faith. Discuss with everyone the miracle that is en route to you. Work on your expectation. Obedience is always rewarded. Everything God has promised you will come to pass. "All these blessings shall come on thee, and overtake thee, if thou shalt hearken unto the voice of the Lord thy God" (Deuteronomy 28:2). Your life lived holy produces results. "No good thing will He withhold from them that walk uprightly" (Psalm 84:11).

27. You Are Not Fighting Your Battle Alone. "I will be an enemy unto thine enemies, and an adversary unto thine adversaries" (Exodus 23:22).

28. Refuse To Give Anyone Access To Yourself Who Is Not

In Agreement With The Word Of God. *When Satan Wants To Destroy You He Sends A Person Into Your Life.* "Be not deceived: evil communications corrupt good manners" (1 Corinthians 15:33).

29. Avoid Broken Focus. When wrong people talk to you, you make the wrong decisions.

30. When You Make A Mistake, Consider Yourself That Much Closer To Your Harvest. "The Lord upholdeth all that fall, and raiseth up all those that be bowed down" (Psalm 145:14). Do not be too hard on yourself. The rewards of change are coming. Patience works. Overcoming involves more than one battle. It is the man who refuses to quit that wins. Always.

31. Keep Feeding Your Faith During The Painful Season Of Waiting. "So then faith cometh by hearing and hearing by the word of God" (Romans 10:17).

32. Your Seasons Of Waiting Are Not Seasons Of Inactivity. *Much is going on.* Angels are positioning to minister. Demons are being confronted. Strategies are being developed. God is moving people into your life just like a Boaz was moved into the life of Ruth. Never believe that a season of waiting is a season of doing nothing. *The opposite is true.*

33. Seasons Of Waiting Are The Busiest Seasons Ever In The Spirit World.

34. Remind Yourself That Joy Still Flows In The Heat Of Battle. "And you became followers of us, and of the Lord, having received the word in much affliction, with joy of the Holy Ghost:" (1 Thessalonians 1:6).

35. Do Not Permit Your Ship Of Financial Harvest To Be Dashed On The Rock Of Impatience. Thousands have not received their financial Harvest because they got in a hurry, unwilling to trust the Lord of the Harvest for His timing. "But they that wait upon the Lord shall renew their strength; they shall mount up with wings as eagles; they shall run, and not be weary; and they shall walk, and not faint" (Isaiah 40:31).

36. Never Consider Quitting. Never. Get up and try again. And, again. And, again. Hell fears a fighter. "Blessed is the man that endureth temptation: for when he is tried, he shall receive the crown of life, which the Lord hath promised to them that love Him" (James 1:12).

My greatest blessings have come after my longest waiting.

Several years ago, I was preaching for Rod Parsley, a friend of mine, in Columbus, Ohio. At the end of the service, the Holy Spirit spoke to me to receive an offering for the pastor instead of my own ministry. Well, I desperately needed a miracle. I needed finances badly for a special project I was facing. So, any Seed I planted would be a

Crisis Seed. (Remember that a Crisis Seed increases in its influence with God.) *It is possible that a small Seed sown during a crisis produces a greater Harvest than a generous Seed during good times.*

So, I agreed to give the offering in its entirety to the pastor. Then, the Holy Spirit made an unusual suggestion. I really did not feel that it was a command but rather an *invitation to an investment.* I had just received a royalty check for $8,500. (Actually, it was everything I had to my name.) I do not recall any money in my savings account other than this check I had in my briefcase.

"How would you like to explore and experiment what I could do with your $8,500?" the Holy Spirit spoke.

It brought a moment of torment and torture. Then, I just quietly spoke in my spirit back to Him, "That's all right. I really appreciate this wonderful $8,500! It is enough Harvest for me."

He spoke the second time. Oh, how thankful I am for the *second chances* He gives to use to try again, reach again and plant again.

"How would you like to explore and experiment what I could do with your $8,500?" the Holy Spirit spoke.

Something in me took a careful evaluation. What could I really do with $8,500? It certainly was not enough to pay my house off. What could I do? Buy a small car, or put a down payment on a rent house or fly to Europe and vacation for a month?

I decided to believe His Word.

That decision changed my lifetime income forever.

Six weeks later, God gave me an idea that brought me hundreds of thousands of dollars in return. In fact, every 90 days I receive a royalty check for that idea.

Now, here is the powerful principle about waiting that you must grasp.

It was over two years after I sowed the $8,500 that I received my first nickel of profit from that idea. I went through several battles and difficulties. I thought the idea would never get off the ground. But, it did. My willingness to wait through eight seasons of Harvest was worth every single hour of waiting.

Some want to plant on Sunday morning in church and reap Monday morning on their job. That is not even logical, scriptural or promised by God. "But he that endureth to the end shall be saved" (Matthew 10:22).

Our Prayer Together...

"Father, You do all things well. You understand the Seasons. You give me the ability to wait. Your timing is perfect. Your schedule is better than mine. I will trust You, wait on You and You will reward me abundantly. In Jesus' name. Amen."